ROUTLEDGE LIBRARY EDITIONS: DEMOGRAPHY

Volume 4

ANALYSING POPULATION TRENDS

ANALYSING
POPULATION TRENDS

Differential Fertility in a
Pluralistic Society

LINCOLN H. DAY

Routledge
Taylor & Francis Group

LONDON AND NEW YORK

First published in 1983 by Croom Helm Ltd

This edition first published in 2024
by Routledge
4 Park Square, Milton Park, Abingdon, Oxon OX14 4RN

and by Routledge
605 Third Avenue, New York, NY 10158

Routledge is an imprint of the Taylor & Francis Group, an informa business

British Library Cataloguing in Publication Data
A catalogue record for this book is available from the British Library

ISBN: 978-1-032-53819-8 (Set)
ISBN: 978-1-032-54915-6 (Volume 4) (hbk)
ISBN: 978-1-032-54918-7 (Volume 4) (pbk)
ISBN: 978-1-003-42809-1 (Volume 4) (ebk)

DOI: 10.4324/9781003428091

Publisher's Note
The publisher has gone to great lengths to ensure the quality of this reprint but points out that some imperfections in the original copies may be apparent.

Disclaimer
The publisher has made every effort to trace copyright holders and would welcome correspondence from those they have been unable to trace.

ANALYSING POPULATION TRENDS

Differential Fertility in a Pluralistic Society

LINCOLN H. DAY

CROOM HELM
London & Canberra

© 1983 Lincoln H. Day
Croom Helm Ltd., Provident House, Burrell Row,
Beckenham Kent BR3 1AT

Croom Helm Australia Pty Ltd., 28 Kembla St.,
Fyshwick, ACT 2609, Australia

British Library Cataloguing in Publication Data

Day, Lincoln H.
   Analysing population trends: differential fertility
   in a pluralistic society.
   1. Population
   I. Title
   304.6'2   HB871
   ISBN 0-7099-0847-4

All rights reserved. For information, write:
St. Martin's Press, Inc., 175 Fifth Avenue, New York, NY 10010
Printed in Great Britain
First published in the United States of America in 1984

Library of Congress Cataloging in Publication Data

Day, Lincoln H., 1928-
   Analyzing population trends.

   Includes bibliographical references and index.
   I. Fertility, Human—Australia. I. Title.
II. Differential fertility in a pluralistic society.
HB1085.D39   1984   304.6'32'0994   83-40176
ISBN 0-312-03281-1

Printed and bound in Great Britain

CONTENTS

To the memory of my mother and father
Vera Hills Day
John Armstrong Day
who early acquainted me with the intellectual interest inherent in
ethnic and religious identity in a pluralistic society.
And also
to my teachers and classmates in the mid-1940s at
North High School, Denver, Colorado
who, in their ethnic and religious diversity, gave to that interest
a human dimension.

This work has benefited from discussions I have had with my wife, Alice Taylor Day, and with my colleagues in the Department of Demography at the Australian National University, in particular, Peter F. McDonald and Terence H. Hull.

INTRODUCTION

There are two general approaches to the study of group differences in human fertility. In the one, the groups under consideration are regarded as 'samples drawn from a single universe of phenomena'; in the other, they are regarded as 'discrete universes of fertility phenomena'.[1] The former is the more narrowly demographic, its focus being on the shares of some demographic phenomenon (total births in the population, for example) originating within the various groups under consideration. The latter, by way of contrast, is essentially behavioural, its focus being on how each group's pattern of fertility compares with that of other groups in the population.

Either approach can be useful. For example, the first is essential to certain policy considerations, and also to population forecasting. But the second is essential to any real understanding of fertility behaviour. The present study, with this understanding as its goal, is thus of the second type. It is a study not of fertility levels as such, but of human behaviour, based on a particular outcome of that behaviour, namely, the distribution of different groupings of married women, by the number of children born to the current marriage. What the study seeks is, essentially, an understanding of desired levels of fertility — or at least of the levels of fertility individual married women (presumably collaborating in some measure with their husbands) have been willing to accept. The various sectors of the population are, therefore, considered here as discrete universes. For present purposes, it is of no particular moment whether Catholics or non-Catholics, Italian-born or Greek-born, early school-leavers or late school-leavers account for the greater number of Australian births. What matters is the fertility differences among such groupings within the population, and what these differences can tell us about the forces that underlie fertility behaviour in general. Given the uniquely detailed Australian data available for such an inquiry, any other focus would have been intellectually wasteful.

Understanding fertility as an element of human behaviour — particularly as an *intended* element of human behaviour — requires either eliminating or suitably discounting the influence exerted by

1

both physiology and the ability to control fertility. For the purpose of eliminating the influence of physiological differences, analysis is here confined not just to the fertility of married women, but to the fertility within current marriages of women who commenced these marriages before the age of 26: those women, in short, (1) most likely to have been exposed to intercourse, and (2) least likely to have been affected by involuntary infecundity. If this does not completely eliminate the potential effect of physiological differences on fertility within the study population, it most assuredly minimises it.

With ability to control fertility, the issue is rather different. Certainly some of the observed fertility differences — especially at the highest ages among some of the overseas-born — can be at least partially accounted for in terms of a differential ability to exercise such control, but, for the most part, differences in this ability are unlikely to be very significant. So extensive is control over fertility in Australia that the major proportion of fertility differences — certainly within the particular population studied here — can, in fact, be more reasonably attributed to differences in attitudes: precisely the variable of particular interest to this inquiry.

Why Study Fertility Differences?

Everything affecting the demographic character of a population — its size, rate of increase, geographic distribution, age and sex structure, life expectation and family composition — must work through one of three demographic variables: fertility, mortality and migration. Of these, fertility is the major dynamic element. In most instances, it is the prime determinant of age structure, of family composition and of population growth rates. Rarely do developments in the other two variables — mortality and migration — possess a demographic significance comparable to that attaching to fertility. To understand fertility is, therefore, to understand not only a major portion of all demographic behaviour, but a fundamental element in social structure and the human condition, generally.

A necessary first step to such an understanding is the description of group differences. This holds, of course, for any kind of behaviour, and not merely for fertility. Who manifests this behaviour, and who does not; who carries it further towards its limits, and who stops well short of them? Group differences help point up the range of possibilities and, with specific reference to human behaviour, the ranges of variation respecting what is permissible and, more narrowly, what is desirable.[2] Only after these differences have been reasonably ascertained, can one logically proceed to an assessment of the characteristics of the groups manifesting the various forms of the behaviour in question, and ultimately to the investigation of the pattern of causation underlying it.

The study of group differences may also yield clues to future developments, for there is frequently in these differences an implicitly dynamic element. Even if one's observations pertain to but a single time, behavioural differences among various sectors of a society can presage the direction of future change.

'The lower birth and death rates of the urban middle classes,' Petersen has written, 'have often been seen as a kind of forecast of the levels to which rural or working-class rates would fall some time later. By the rationale of the demographic transition, thus, social sectors are roughly of two types, those that introduce and help disseminate modernizing attitudes and behavior patterns and those that, for whatever reasons, lag behind.'[3]

But group differences in behaviour can also have a more direct, less analytical significance. Particularly respecting fertility, behavioural differences, at the very least, signify inequality: demographic inequality in the form of differential group rates of increase, social inequality in the form of differential group demands on a society's resources and services, and personal inequality with reference, for children, to the differential results of having different numbers of siblings, and, for adults, to the different mixes of the considerable variety of costs and benefits (economic, social, physical, emotional, and those respecting the expenditure of one's time) associated with the bearing and rearing of children.

Group fertility differences may also signify unequal 'life chances' (in the Weberian sense) and unequal participation between groups in the life of society as a whole. However, the causal association is by no means always clear in specific instances. For example, higher fertility may mean a greater number of persons with whom one has close emotional ties, and simultaneously fewer opportunities for forming similar bonds elsewhere in the society. It may mean an expanded network of economic support, and yet a limitation on one's opportunities for the acquisition of additional schooling or capital with which to improve one's economic position.[4] Specifically with reference to the assimilation of immigrants, it may increase the number of one's contacts outside the family by increasing the number of persons in a position to have them, or it may decrease these contacts by rendering the family a more self-contained unit.

Certainly, the study of fertility differences is of more than merely passing significance. This is perhaps especially so in an increasingly heterogeneous society like that of Australia. Long a major immigrant-receiving country, Australia, in terms of its population base, has been the world's major immigrant-receiver since the end of the second world war. The last census taken before that war (that of 30 June 1933), showed almost 14 per cent as overseas-born.[5] The comparable figures for the United States, the world's major immigrant-receiver in terms of sheer numbers, were less than 12 per cent in 1930 and less than 9 per cent in 1940.[6] By 1947, on the eve of its massive post-war immigrant programme, and following (as in the United States) a period of depression-induced re-emigration on the part of many who had earlier immigrated, Australia's overseas-born population was down to 10 per cent of the total. But thereafter, in response to an official policy encouraging immigration policy, the overseas-born proportion rose rapidly. That policy, one careful analysis has concluded, was initiated largely for the purpose of population-building as a defence measure; later defended on economic grounds, primarily as a means of overcoming a perceived deficiency of skilled workers; and later still, maintained in consequence of a varied combination of forces, including political pressures on behalf of family reunions on the part of now-resident immigrants, employers' demands for workers to meet situations that in many cases had been engendered or fostered by earlier immigration (e.g. the failure of Australian employers to inaugurate training programmes for the native-born), and the vested interest of the large federal department established to administer the immigration programme.[7] It reached 14 per cent of the total by 1954, 17 per cent by 1961, 18 per cent by 1966 and 20 per cent by 1971, where it has remained ever since.[8] In addition to that 20 per cent reported as overseas-born in the census of 1971, an almost equal proportion (19.4 per cent) were reported as Australian-born with at least one parent born overseas.[9] For the United States, the comparable figure in 1970 was slightly less than 12 per cent.[10]

Two aspects of this development — both relating to ethnic composition — are of particular interest here: first, the differential distribution of the overseas-born by duration of Australian residence; and second, the composition of the total population with respect to native language.

Because of changes in both Australian immigration policy and overseas conditions and circumstances, the ethnic composition of arriving immigrants (and of foreign-born re-emigrants) varied considerably over the years. The result by 1971 was an overseas-born population distribution as shown in Table I.1 by duration of residence in Australia:

Table I.1: Per Cent Distribution of Foreign-born Population by Selected Country of Birth and Duration of Residence in Australia (1971)

Country of Birth	Years' Duration of Residence in Australia					Not Stated	Total
	<5	5−9	10−16	17−23	24+		
British Isles	28	18	14	15	22	4	101
Italy	14	15	29	23	9	9	99
Greece	23	29	24	7	7	10	100
Netherlands	9	6	39	37	2	5	98
Germany	12	8	30	37	7	6	100
Yugoslavia	44	14	17	11	5	10	101
All Countries	26	16	19	19	14	6	100

Source:
Calculated from data in *1971 Census of Population and Housing*, Bulletin 4, part 9, Canberra: Commonwealth Bureau of Census and Statistics (1972), Table 4, p. 6.

Only British immigration had proceeded at an essentially steady rate (and the rate would be seen to have been even steadier if that higher proportion in the less than five years category were reduced to take account of re-emigration, which not only may have approached 25–30 per cent within most nativity groupings during the 1947–74 period — purely marginal return rates being confined largely to refugees and non-Europeans[11] — but would doubtless have been participated in more by those resident in Australia for shorter periods of time). Non-British immigration has been largely a phenomenon of the post-second world war period; that from the Netherlands and Germany being more concentrated in the 1948–61 period; that from Greece in the periods since 1954; and that from Yugoslavia in the period since 1966. Although steadier and of generally longer duration than the immigration of other non-British categories, Italian-born immigration, like the Dutch- and German-born, was particularly heavy in the 1948–61 period.

Predictably enough, this change in composition by country of birth was paralleled by a similar one in native language. From a country of overwhelmingly English-speaking stock at the end of the second world war (something in excess of 98 per cent[12]), Australia had, by the 1970s, become a country in which some 20–1 per cent had a native language other than English. The corresponding figure in the United States was 16 per cent, while in a third major immigrant-receiving country, Canada, those of non-native language (taking both English and French to be native languages) were some 13 per cent of the total.[13] This heterogeneity in Australia is reinforced by the fact that its non-English portion is distributed over a considerable variety of languages, with none occupying a predominant place. While the situation is much the same in Canada, in the United States there is a marked concentration on Spanish. Moreover, as the immigration forming the basis for the Australian figure is generally of more recent origin than that in either the United States or Canada, the prognosis — at least as far as language groupings are concerned — is for greater future heterogeneity in Australia than in either of these other two countries.

Yet there is more than increasing heterogeneity to warrant a closer look at Australia's fertility differences. In addition to religious and ethnic variety, there is the high degree of control its people exercise over their fertility and, in particular, the unusually comprehensive and detailed nature of the data available for such an inquiry.

While Australia is assuredly toward the lower end of the fertility spectrum, the extent of its group fertility differences is considerable. Take, for example, the women born in 1927–31 and married before age 26 (a limitation on marriage ages intended to standardise for possible differences in both fecundity and the incidence of marital breakdown and remarriage). Had all these wives conformed to the childbearing pattern of those in the *most fertile* category (namely, Australian-born, rural-dwelling Catholics), their median issue would have been 50 per cent higher than it was; the proportion bearing no more than one child, 43 per

Table I.2: The Range of Certain Group Fertility Differences in Australia. Wives 40–4 Years of Age who Commenced Current Marriage before Age 26. Total and Highest and Lowest Fertility Groupings (Australia, 1971)

	Median Issue	% with 0–1 Issue	% with 5+ Issue
Total Population	2.51	10	19
Highest Fertility Grouping (Australian-born, Rural-dwelling Catholics)	3.77	6	46
Lowest Fertility Grouping (German-born, Metropolitan-dwelling non-Catholics)	1.67	28	9
Range	2.10	22	37
As % of figure for total:			
Highest*	150	57	237
Lowest*	67	271	46

* Calculated from figures carried to two decimal places.

cent lower; and the proportion bearing at least five children, 137 per cent higher (see Table I.2). On the other hand, had all of them conformed instead to the childbearing pattern of those in the *least fertile* category (German-born, metropolitan-dwelling non-Catholics), the result would have been a median issue 33 per cent lower, and the proportion with no more than one child 171 per cent higher, and that with five or more children 54 per cent lower. This range of differences is hardly minimal: 2.10 children in the case of the median; 22 and 37 per cent, respectively, in the case of the proportions with no more than one and as many as five children.

The Data

Most studies of fertility differences are significantly limited by their data in one of two ways: either these data pertain to so few persons as to permit little statistical confidence in any but the most general of findings, or they are of a sort that obscures certain demographic attributes of possible significance in accounting for the group differences observed. In the one instance (as with studies based on detailed interviews), much is known, but it is known of too few; in the other (as with the usual study based on census and vital registration data), it is impossible to eliminate or adjust for the effects of such potentially significant demographic variables as age at marriage and rate of remarriage following divorce or widowhood.

The data of the present study are not so limited. They are, in fact, unusually comprehensive and detailed. Far from pertaining to just a few hundreds or thousands, those underlying the major portion of this analysis pertain, instead, to the entire population of currently married women (below age 65) enumerated in the 1971 census; while the supplementary data introduced from the censuses of 1954 and 1961 pertain to random samples of 20 per cent of this population. So large, in fact, are the numbers involved that, in an effort to eliminate distortion from random variation, it was decided that analysis could be restricted to cross-tabulations in which N > 100. But while this doubtless very considerably reduced the likelihood of such distortion, it does not seem to have eliminated it altogether, for there are suggestions in some of the tabulations used here that random variation is capable of introducing material distortion even with N approaching 150−200 — something that should, at the very least, caution one still further against concluding too much from the kind of data underlying most research on fertility differences.

The data relating to individual attributes in this study are the following, provided for each currently married woman:

1. Age in single years
2. Duration of marriage in single years
3. Number of children born to current marriage (to an upper limit of six or more)
4. Age at marriage in single years (derived by combining age in single years with duration of marriage in single years)
5. Residence (metropolitan, other urban, rural)
6. Religion (Catholic, all other)
7. Country of birth (Australia, British Isles (including Ireland), Italy, Netherlands, Greece, Germany and Yugoslavia)
8. Husband's occupational category (professional, technical and related, administrative, executive, managerial, clerical and sales, farmers, graziers, lumbermen and fishermen, workers in transportation and communications; tradesmen, production process workers and labourers; all others (including unemployed) not in the labour force, miners, service workers,

sports and recreation workers, not stated)
9. Years of schooling (< 6, 6–7, 8, 9+ or more)
10. Husband's years of schooling (< 6, 6–7, 8, 9+)
11. Years of residence in Australia (if foreign-born)
12. Labour force status (in labour force, not in labour force).

Items 1–4 provide an unusual amount of demographic detail for a study based on census or survey data. Such detail, especially in combination with the large Ns available, not only permits precise standardisation for such potentially significant attributes as age at marriage, but also obviates the necessity of working only with group measures (such as average number of children born) of a sort that can mask potentially significant group differences.

There are two limitations, however. First, it is only for 1961 that the data on issue are in a form that permits calculation of an average as well as a median. Because of misunderstandings discovered too late to permit corrective action, the 1954 and 1971 tabulations provide no information on numbers of children born to wives of 6+ parity, which means that the analysis of central tendency for those years is restricted to medians. This may be of no particular consequence for comparisons within the Australian population. It can, in fact, be argued that the median, being little affected by extreme cases, is more suited than the average to the analysis of group fertility differences, particularly when (as in the present case) it can be used in conjunction with detailed data on the distribution of the population by individual parities up to 6+. None the less, not having averages does limit the kinds of comparisons that can be made with those other populations for which the more general nature of the available data permits calculation only of group averages.

The other limitation arises from the way in which age at marriage is derived by taking the difference between marriage duration and age. That both these are expressed in single years is certainly an advantage over the more usual five-year intervals, but there is still the possibility of an error of as much as two years. A woman reporting herself (correctly) to the last year as 40 years of age and of 20 years' marriage duration could be anywhere from 40.00 to 40.99 years of age and of a marriage duration anywhere from 20.00 to 20.99 years. Subtracting the extremes of these two ranges shows that she could have married at an age as low as 19 or as high as 21 (actually, 19.01 and 20.99 in this example). However extensive such errors may be, the impossibility of adjusting for them requires that one assume they have no effect on the result. This is probably the case, but that such errors are possible constitutes just one more limitation on the degree of assurance we can have about either the existence or the significance of small differences between groups.

Of the remaining items, the last four (those relating to schooling, years of residence in Australia, and labour force status) are available only in the data from the 1971 census. All the others — with some variations in definition or coverage, to be described later — are available for all three census years.

Each set of data was cross-tabulated to my specifications and supplied to me by the Australian Bureau of Statistics: in the form of a matrix tape in the case of the 1971 data, and in the form of the tabulations themselves in the case of the 1954 and 1961 data.

Aboriginals, numbering 106,000 (0.83 per cent of the total population) in 1971, are excluded. The population studied is thus the other 99.17 per cent, fewer than 1 per cent of whom were reported as being of other than European origin.

The attributes are as reported by (or on behalf of) the persons being enumerated. The one exception is residential classification, which was determined at the processing stage on the basis of the respondent's address.

Any such data are subject to some inaccuracy, particularly concerning those attributes like years of schooling or husband's occupation, to which attach some connotations of prestige and status. But it is impossible in the present circumstances either to determine the nature or extent of such inaccuracy or to assess its significance to the pattern of group fertility differences. The only available course, therefore, is to assume that it is nil.

Probably a more important matter for present purposes is the fact that these personal attributes were those in existence at the time of the census. Yet, apart from country of birth, each of them is subject to change in the course of one's lifetime. This may be of little potential significance with respect to religion and schooling, neither of which is likely to change much during adulthood (at least not to the extent likely to alter one's position in one or another of the broad sub-categories used in the present analysis); but it can be of considerable significance with respect to labour force status, and of only slightly less significance with respect to residence and husband's occupation. The implications of such possible changes will be discussed subsequently where appropriate.

The Prime Indicator of Fertility

For most purposes, the prime indicator of fertility in this inquiry is the number of children born within the current marriage to married women 40 or more years of age at the date of the census. While the deficiencies of such an indicator are probably minimal for present purposes, it is none the less useful to enumerate them here.

By definition, analysis with such data is limited to survivors and their children. One source of bias, therefore, would be any mortality differences among women of different parities — or of different *potential* parities, in the case of those who died before completion of childbearing. Some such differences doubtless exist, particularly by residence and occupation, but it seems highly unlikely that they would be of much consequence to group fertility differences in a low-mortality country like Australia.

A potentially greater source of bias associated with mortality relates to the deaths of offspring, as contrasted with those of mothers. If there is a tendency for underreporting of deceased children — and this may be reasonably presumed on the basis of studies of other populations, although we have no information on this for Australia — any group differences in infant and child mortality could result in a distortion of recorded differences in numbers of children ever born. Nevertheless, bias from this quarter could hardly be more than minimal given Australia's low levels of infant and child mortality, and also (although this could lead to bias in the opposite direction) the tendency for parents of a dead child to compensate for their loss by having an additional one — one who, in the likely event of survival, would not fail to be enumerated.

The general problem of under-enumeration is always of concern in demographic analysis, but an analysis of the present type, confined as it is to adult women, avoids the effects of the most common types of under-enumeration: those involving young adult males and the newborn. To be sure, certain sectors of the population will have been more likely than others to have a newborn child at the time of the census, but the proportions involved are so small as to render any bias from this source hardly worth the effort to remove it, even if the data were in a form to permit such an undertaking (which they are not).

The possibility of bias from group differences in the extent of childbearing at ages 40 and over is more serious, yet the overall frequency of such childbearing is very low and declines markedly with advancing age. Moreover, limiting analysis to women married before age 26 (see below) should considerably reduce the biasing effect of such late childbearing by making it a very small portion of the total, and restricting it primarily to only the highest parities, where it would have no effect on a measure of central tendency like the median, and only a minimal effect on an open-ended measure of dispersion like the proportion of 5 + or 6 + parity.

Whether one or another sector of the population is more susceptible to being under-enumerated, it is difficult to say. One could, for example, expect understatement of births to be more frequent among higher fertility groups in consequence of their having more births to forget about, and that reported group fertility differences would therefore be somewhat less than actual. But even if this were so — and we have no assurance that it is — the bias introduced by such a difference seems hardly likely to be of sufficient magnitude to affect any conclusions in a study like this one.

The possibility of excluding children no longer living with the mother, or of including children born to a previous marriage, seems, in the absence of any data on the matter, to be a potentially more serious source of bias than any mentioned so far. Yet, here again, it hardly seems of sufficient magnitude to have much bearing on the present analysis. If there is, indeed, a group difference in the likelihood of excluding a child no longer residing with his or her mother, it is apt to lie more with the foreign-born and rural-dwelling than with any other sectors of the population, for these are the sectors with the greater experience of migration: their own migration in the case of the foreign-born, and that of their children in the case of rural-dwellers. In the present circumstances, however, it is impossible to determine either the extent of such under-enumeration or whether, in fact, it even exists.

There is the same problem with the possibility of over-enumeration arising from the mistaken inclusion of children born to a previous marriage. It seems reasonable to suppose that a misunderstanding of census instructions on this point would be more frequent among those for whom English was a second language, and that such misreporting would occur, whatever their command of English, among those with whom second marriages were more common. Presumably, second and higher order marriages would be more common among the higher mortality sectors of the population, and particularly among those experiencing a higher incidence of divorce. However because, as already noted, mortality differences among the census groupings used here are probably quite minimal in Australia, there is scant likelihood of much bias from this quarter; while the relatively low incidence of divorce in Australia — at least within the cohorts under consideration here — together with its rather late timing within marriage,[14] suggests that any bias from this source would also be only minimal.

Finally, there is the possibility of age-related differences in the accuracy of reporting on numbers of births. Because an important part of the present analysis relates to fertility changes over time (that is, between successive cohorts), any such differences in accuracy could be an important source of bias. So it is indeed fortunate that whatever their extent, these differences appear unlikely to be of any moment here. The particular nature of the Australian data on numbers of children ever born (being limited to those born to current marriage) does not lend itself to a systematic analysis of this phenomenon, and none has been undertaken. But if American experience can be taken as a guide, age-related inaccuracies in reporting are nearly all to be found in reports on women above the age of 70 — presumably the result either of forgetfulness on the part of older women, or ignorance of the true situation on the part of persons responding on their behalf.[15] As 64 is the oldest age under consideration here, bias from this source would appear to be safely nil.

In sum, it is probably safe to assume that the possible sources of bias in these data — whether from misunderstanding of census instructions, group mortality differences among women or children, ranges in age or duration of marriage, over- or under-enumeration — are of only minimal significance to the present inquiry. They would seem either to cancel one another out, or be of such limited extent as to have no real effect on any conclusions that might be drawn.

The Modified Indicators of Fertility

Given that the interest here is with group differences in fertility behaviour, rather than with either the fertility of the population as a whole or the actual level of reproduction of different groups within the population, I have refined the basic indicator in order to cast these differences in boldest relief. This refinement consisted, as already noted, of restricting analysis to those women who commenced their current marriages before the age of 26. Wives still in the process of childbearing were already largely excluded by the restriction to women aged 40 and over. The further restriction to women whose current marriages began before age 26 excludes those whose childbearing was likely to have been much affected by infecundity, and also those whose marriages ended in divorce or death; and, of course, it retains the exclusion of those who never married at all.

In all this, the effect of temporary separations is an unknown quantity, and one for which no reasonable adjustment seems possible. Those separated at the time of the census should be in the category, 'separated', and, therefore, excluded from the tabulation altogether. But for those separated in the past and living together at the time of the census, the only course open is to assume that separation had no greater effect on fertility in one sector than in another, or, if it did, that the effect was negligible. This may not be an altogether appropriate assumption with certain of the overseas-born, but it is a necessary one to make in the circumstances.

Overall, with this indicator (as refined), the present analysis can focus on fertility differences within a population from which have been essentially excluded all the purely demographic differences (other than temporary separation) to which these fertility differences might otherwise be attributed, namely, differences in proportions marrying (a proxy for exposure to intercourse), age at marriage (a proxy for involuntary infecundity) and duration of marriage.

Selectivity of the Study Population

These efforts on behalf of the clearest portrayal of group differences in fertility behaviour result, of course, in a study population that is necessarily selective — selective, as already noted, with respect to marital status, age and age at marriage; but selective also with respect to reporting: not only concerning these three attributes, but concerning the number of children born to current marriage as well. Failure to report (or to be reported on) with respect to any one of these was enough to exclude a woman from the population to be studied. The situation is summarised in Table I.3.

Table I.3: Ever-Married Women 40–64 Years of Age by Country of Birth and Status Respecting Present Inquiry (Australia, 1971)

Country of Birth		Age, Age at Marriage and Issue Born to Current Marriage				
		Reported				
		Marriage Age under 26	Marriage Age 26+	Not Reported	Other Ever-Married	Total
Australia	N	584 502	298 740	101 304	209 916	1 194 462
	%	49	25	8	18	100
British Isles	N	80 030	40 550	11 850	25 338	157 768
	%	51	26	8	16	101
Italy	N	23 117	11 043	4 640	4 074	42 874
	%	54	26	11	10	101
Netherlands	N	8 299	4 184	1 297	1 538	15 318
	%	54	27	8	10	99
Greece	N	6 384	4 465	2 091	2 179	15 119
	%	42	30	14	14	100
Germany	N	8 462	6 214	1 798	2 778	19 252
	%	44	32	9	14	99
Yugoslavia	N	5 151	3 345	341	1 889	10 726
	%	48	31	3	18	100
Total	N	715 945	368 541	123 321	247 712	1 455 529
	%	49	25	8	17	99

Source:
Calculated from data in the following:
Matrix table specially run for this study
Special Tabulation 051 (unpublished), based on 10 per cent sample of 1971 Census, Australian Bureau of Statistics
1971 Census of Population and Housing, Bulletin 4, Part 9, Canberra: Commonwealth Bureau of Census and Statistics (1972), Table 1

Overall, the analysis relates to about half of ever-married women 40–64 years of age, born in the countries selected for study. Of the remainder, one in six was excluded because she failed to report either age at current marriage or number of children born to current marriage; two in six because, at the time of the census, they were either separated, divorced or widowed; and the remaining three in six because they had married at too high an age.

The extent of this selectivity is predictably different for different sectors of the population. For example, as may be seen in Table I.3, the numbers included in the study extend from 54 per cent of the ever-married among the Italian- and Dutch-born, down to 42 per cent among the Greek-born; and while all the information necessary to the inquiry was reported for all but 3 per cent of the Yugoslav-born, failure to report on one or other of these items extended to 14 per cent of the Greek-born.

In addition to the selectivity summarised in Table I.3, there is a further selectivity associated with age. The higher the age, the higher the proportion who have experienced marital disruption and remarriage. For example, the study included 65 per cent of ever-married, Australian-born women aged 40−4, as against but 37 per cent of their counterparts aged 55−9. Similarly, while only 18 per cent of these 40−4-year-olds had married at age 26 or over, 30 per cent of the 55−9-year-olds had done so; and while only 9 per cent of the 40−4-year-olds were currently separated, divorced or widowed, 23 per cent of the 55−9-year-olds were in this category.

As will be seen later, there is a close association between fertility and marriage age among those marrying before 26. But the point at issue here is whether there is a difference between cohorts: whether, for example, there were changes in the proportions marrying at younger ages of a sort that would result in the study's including a larger proportion of a particular type of person in one category than in another. That is, so far as this study is concerned, do 40−4-year-old women who married at, say, 25 represent a more deviant group than 55−9-year-old women who did? Was marrying at age 25 (or 18, or 21 . . .) somehow different — and therefore selective of a meaningfully different sort of person (so far as the interests of this inquiry are concerned) — for those in the one birth cohort than for those in the other? The fertility analyses I have undertaken by single years of age suggest not; but there is really no possibility of completely answering the question.

Similarly, was becoming divorced, widowed or remarried associated with different types of women among the different birth cohorts? The changes in divorce rates suggest that it may have been to at least some extent, but again, there is no possibility of obtaining a complete answer.

For present purposes, the differences in coverage among the different age groupings would appear to be due mainly to the successively greater exposure to marital disruption and subsequent remarriage that is associated with ageing, whether this arises out of divorce or widowhood. Whatever the effects of these differences in coverage, they must for present purposes be assumed to fall equally upon the different categories of women selected for study.

Notes

1. Robert Gutman, 'Comment' on Clyde V. Kiser, 'Differential fertility in the United States'. In *Demographic and Economic Change in Developed Countries*, National Bureau of Economic Research, Princeton: Princeton University Press (1960), p. 113.

2. Lincoln H. Day, 'Models for the causal analysis of differences in fertility: utility, normative, and drift'. In Lado T. Ruzicka (ed.), *The Economic and Social Supports for High Fertility*, Canberra: Department of Demography, Australian National University (1977).

3. William Petersen, *Population* (1969), 3rd ed, New York: Macmillan, p. 524.

4. For supporting evidence from the United States, see Peter H. Lindert, *Fertility and Scarcity in America*, Princeton: Princeton University Press (1978), chapters 6 and 7.

5. *Official Year Book of the Commonwealth of Australia* (1951), Canberra: Commonwealth Bureau of Census and Statistics, p. 550.

6. *Statistical Abstract of the United States* (1976), Washington: US Bureau of the Census, Table 40, p. 34.

7. Robert Birrell and Tanya Birrell, *An Issue of People*, Melbourne: Longman Cheshire (1981), esp. chapters 2–4, and 9.

8. *Year Book of Australia* (1981), Canberra: Australian Bureau of Statistics, p. 87.

9. Committee on the Teaching of Migrant Languages in Schools, *Report*, Canberra: Australian Government Publishing Service (1976). Cited in Brian M. Bullivant, *The Pluralist Dilemma in Education*, Sydney: George Allen & Unwin (1981), p. 166.

10. Calculated from data in *Statistical Abstract of the United States* (1976), op.cit., Tables 40 and 44, pp. 34, 36.

11. Charles A. Price, 'Australian Immigration: the Whitlam Government 1972–75'. In Charles A. Price and Jean I. Martin (eds), *Australian Immigration: A Bibliography and Digest*, No. 3, part 1, Canberra: Department of Demography, Australian National University (1976), p. A14.

12. Estimated from data on country of birth, in *Year Book of the Commonwealth of Australia* (1951), op.cit., p. 550.

13. Australian figure calculated from Australian Bureau of Statistics Matrix Tape number 38, adjusted for non-English speakers ages 0–4 included in 'not applicable' category. United States figures from US Bureau of the Census, 1970 Census, Subject Reports, final report PO(2)–1A, *National Origin and Language*, Table 19, p. 492. Canadian figure from *Canada Year Book* (1975), Ottawa: Table 4.16, pp. 167–8.

14. Lincoln H. Day, 'Patterns of Divorce in Australia — Another Look'. *Australian Quarterly*, **48** (1976); and Lincoln H. Day, 'Patterns of Divorce in Australia and the United States'. *American Sociological Review*, **29** (1964).

15. Henry S. Shryock, Jacob S. Siegel and Associates, *The Methods and Materials of Demography*, vol. 2, Washington, DC: US Bureau of the Census (1971), pp. 511–12.

1 CHILDREN BORN TO PRESENT MARRIAGE: MAJOR FINDINGS

Introduction

It is probably possible to know more about group fertility differences in Australia than anywhere else in the world. Not only are there unusually comprehensive and detailed data for the analysis of such differences, but the significance of chance and ignorance in the creation of these differences is considerably lessened by the widespread practice of birth control. Certainly the control of fertility in Australia is both extensive and of long duration. When this began cannot be precisely determined, but it was well under way by the mid-1890s, and probably even by the 1860s.[1] Which is not to say that such control is, even now, either universal or particularly convenient in Australia. There is still much to be done to make it so. Obstacles abound — especially for the unmarried. Nevertheless, it seems reasonable to suppose that childbearing reflects the wishes of potential parents about as much in Australia as it is likely to anywhere.

While it need not necessarily lead to low fertility, control over childbearing must of necessity lead to fertility that is lower than it would otherwise be. The most prominent features of the extension of this control in Australia have been a decrease in the proportion of women bearing six or more children, and a corresponding increase in the proportion bearing two or three. Childlessness, by comparison, has fluctuated around 5 per cent, while the proportion bearing one child only, although undergoing a substantial increase and then decrease, seems always to have been comparatively low — seldom exceeding 15 per cent.[2]

The earliest cohort under detailed analysis here (that of 1907−11, whose childbearing took place during the economic difficulties of the 1930s and the wartime disruptions of the early 1940s) is characterised by the lowest, or next to lowest, cumulative fertility in Australian history; the latest such cohort (that of 1927−31, whose childbearing took place during the prolonged 'baby-boom' following the second world war, by the highest fertility this century, and, in fact, the highest since that of the cohort of 1883−7.[3]

18

The initial decline in Australian fertility, which amounted to some 50 per cent overall in a single generation,[4] coincided with a similar decline among western populations generally. But it had pretty well run its course by the completion of childbearing among women born in the first decade of the twentieth century. There are exceptions, to be sure, but in most sectors of the Australian population, the median issue of women born in the first four decades of this century either levelled off, or experienced a modest reversal of the earlier downward trend. Simultaneously, the proportion bearing no more than one child steadily decreased, while the proportion bearing five or more moved in different directions according to age at marriage: that is, declining slightly among those marrying below age 21, remaining about the same among those marrying in their early 20s, and increasing slightly among those marrying in their mid-20s.

But just as control over fertility leads inevitably to a decrease in total fertility, so also does it lead inevitably to an increase in group differences in fertility: to an increase in differences among generations in consequence of the different patterns of diffusion of such control within the population, and to an increase in differences among various sectors of the population in consequence not only of different patterns of diffusion but also of varying group responses to different social and cultural conditions — these latter originating in temporal and sectoral differences in (1) the extent to which birth control is known and resorted to (and skill exercised in its practice); (2) the unequal experience of such social conditions as affect one's decisions about childbearing (whether as to number or timing); (3) the presumed value of children to their parents,[5] itself a function of broader social conditions and also of the perceived availability of alternative sources of those satisfactions presumably associated — positively or negatively — with the bearing and rearing of children;[6] and (4) the play of behavioural 'drift', that is, of behaviour moving (actually or only seemingly so) by small degrees along the continuum of possibilities.[7]

As already noted, to show these differences in boldest relief, discussion will be confined here to women who at the time of the census were 40–64 years of age and living with husbands whom they had married before reaching the age of 26. The restriction to women at least 40 years of age puts the focus on those of essentially completed childbearing age; while the further restriction to those whose current marriages began before age 26 minimises the bias that might arise from possible group differences in either fecundity or patterns of marital dissolution and remarriage. Thus restricted, the analysis — so far as it relates to 1971 census data — extends from half (49 per cent) of the wives in the oldest birth cohort under study (that of 1907–11) to three-quarters (76 per cent) of those in the youngest (that of 1927–31).

Differences among Generations

Median Issue

Fertility differences by generation exist within each sector of the Australian population for which we have any data (see Figure 1.1). Among the Australian-born (that portion of the population for whom — understandably enough — the data go back furthest), there was an almost straight-line decline in median issue from at least as far back as the birth cohort of the early 1870s up to that of the turn of this century; following which there was, first, a period of levelling-off and then, with the cohorts of 1922–6 and 1927–31, a period of increase. Changes among the British-born were less extensive, but they followed the same pattern. However, among those born elsewhere — for whom the data are for a more restricted, and hence more recent, time period — the pattern was a contrasting one of continued fertility declines among the Italian-, Dutch-, Greek- and Yugoslav-born, and of modest fluctuation around an already low level among the German-born.

Given their numerical predominance, it is no surprise that the trend among the Australian- and British-born — namely, a long decline followed by periods of levelling-off and then subsequent increase — should also be that found in each residential category. Nor, for similar reasons, is it any surprise that a similar pattern should obtain within the two groupings by religion. Were appropriate data available, it would probably appear also in each occupation and schooling category, although here the fact that the data go back no further than to the cohorts of 1897–1901 (in the case of husband's occupation) and 1907–11 (in the case of schooling) permits observation only of the later stages of this development, namely, those characterised by levelling-off and subsequent increase.

Distribution by Issue

With distribution by issue, the most prominent development was

Figure 1.1: Median Issue Born to Current Marriage. Wives 40–64 Years of Age who Commenced Current Marriage before Age 26, by Year of Birth and Nativity (Australia, 1971)

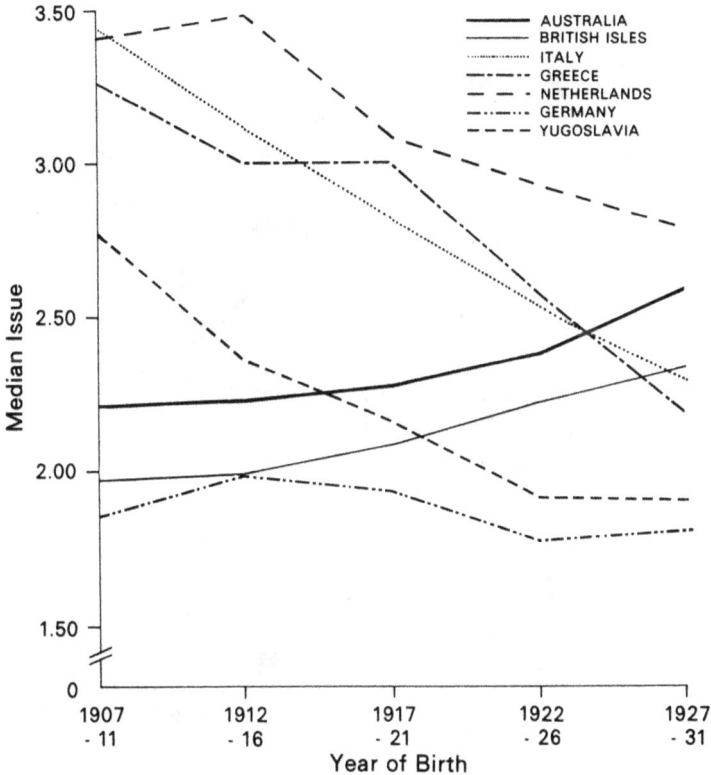

the marked decline in proportions at the highest parities (five or more). This took place within each residential category, both religion groupings and all nativity categories. But while this development continued within the other nativity categories right up to the cohort of 1927–31, it had ceased a generation earlier among the Australian- and British-born. The result was that in those subdivisions of the population where the Australian- and British-born constituted by far the major share of the total (that is, the subdivisions of residence, husband's occupation and years of schooling), the proportions at these highest parities remained

Figure 1.2: Percentage with 5+ Issue Born to Current Marriage.
Wives 40–64 Years of Age who Commenced Current Marriage
before Age 26, by Year of Birth and Nativity (Australia, 1971)

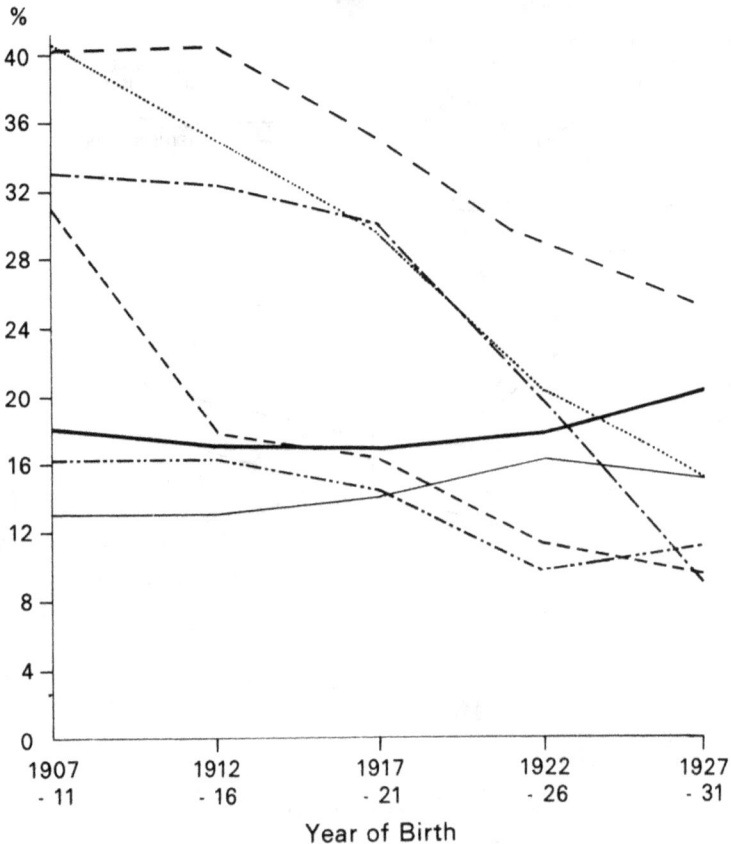

essentially unchanged from the low levels reached by the cohorts of
1907–16.

At the lowest parities (zero to one), developments have been
more varied. Among the Australian- and British-born, for whom
the period of coverage is longest, there was a marked increase up to
the cohorts born at the beginning of this century, and then an
equally marked decline thereafter; and, of course, as with the
proportions at the highest parities, the pattern was essentially the
same in those sectors of the population in which the Australian-and
British-born predominate. But among the other nativity

Figure 1.3: Percentage with 0–1 Issue Born to Current Marriage. Wives 40–64 Years of Age who Commenced Current Marriage before Age 26, by Year of Birth and Nativity (Australia, 1971)

%

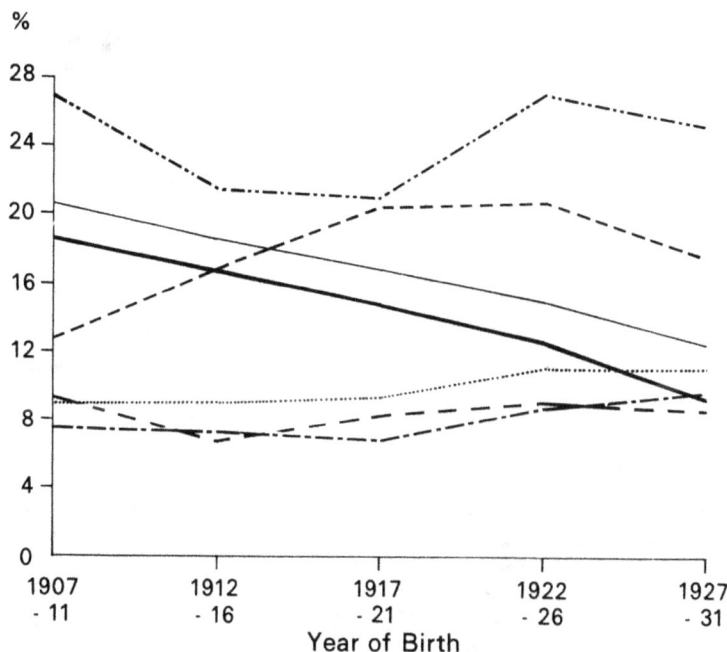

| 1907 | 1912 | 1917 | 1922 | 1927 |
| - 11 | - 16 | - 21 | - 26 | - 31 |

Year of Birth

groupings (for whom, it must be remembered, the data pertain only to cohorts born this century), the proportion with zero or one issue took a contrasting course: either rising or continuing at about the same level throughout.

Discussion

Fertility differences among the earlier cohorts were doubtless associated very largely with the pattern of diffusion of control over childbearing (whatever the reasons giving rise to the exercise of this control); but among more recent cohorts, where these differences were of a more fluctuating, less lineal type — most notably among the Australian- and British-born — they appear to relate more to changing temporal conditions, particularly employment and unemployment, war and demobilisation, wages and prices.

It has been shown that the increases in period fertility in Australia as a whole during the 1950s and 1960s were closely related

Figure 1.4: Relative Levels of Median Issue Born to Current Marriage (1907−11 Median = 100), by Age at Marriage. Australian-born Wives 40−64 Years of Age, by Year of Birth (1971)

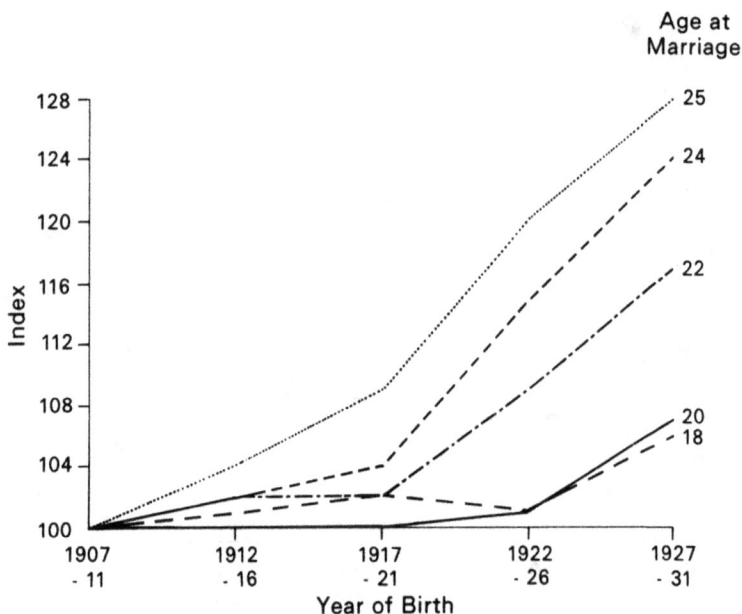

to changing patterns of marriage: to higher proportions marrying and to marriage at generally younger ages.[8] Yet within those sectors of the population experiencing increases in lifetime fertility, the pattern of those increases itself followed a somewhat contrasting course. There is no denying that higher proportions married, and that they did so at generally younger ages. Yet, among those sectors of the population in which fertility increased, it did so among women at all marriage ages, and, moreover, did so to a progressively greater extent at successively higher marriage ages (at least within the range of marriage ages under consideration here, namely, those up to 26 years). Thus, the highest percentage increases in fertility occurred not among women marrying at those younger ages (the teens and early twenties) that most increased their share of all marriages during this period (it is here that the percentage increases were lowest) but, rather, among women marrying at those more advanced ages (23−5) where the share of all marriages underwent its greatest decline. Had the pattern of marriage remained unchanged, and only the pattern of fertility by age at marriage changed in the direction it did, the fertility of these cohorts would have risen even higher; for the tendency to marry younger was in this period unaccompanied by any fully commensurate tendency to conform to the higher fertility patterns of those who had married at these younger ages in previous years. There remained, throughout, a consistently negative association between age at marriage and lifetime fertility (see chapter 7), but the range of this association narrowed considerably during this period, for Australia as a whole, of slightly increasing lifetime fertility.

Differences among Different Sectors of the Population

The broad fertility differences among *cohorts* in Australia have been accompanied by sizable differences, as well, among *sectors within these cohorts*. The latter have, in fact, been a prominent feature of Australian fertility for more than a century. Rural-dwellers have consistently had more children than have city-dwellers; Catholics more than non-Catholics; the Dutch-born more, and the German-born fewer, than those born elsewhere; farmers' wives more, and wives of clerical and sales workers fewer, than the wives of husbands in the other major occupational categories; and, until recently, those with more schooling have tended to have fewer children than have those with less schooling.

However, there have been changes in the nature of these differences: some have diminished, some remained essentially the same, some increased in extent, and still others have changed direction.

Median issue

By the time the cohort of 1927–31 had completed their child-bearing, the negative association between fertility and years of schooling characteristic of earlier cohorts had all but disappeared, while the differences by residence and by husband's occupation had narrowed appreciably. In each instance, the gap closed as fertility rose among the lower fertility sectors while continuing to decline among the higher. However, analysis by single years of age at marriage reveals that, while the narrowing within schooling and occupation categories was pretty general, much of that observed between the residential categories originated in changes in age at marriage, and not in changes in fertility among those marrying at different ages. In fact, within each age at marriage category, the range of fertility differences among the three residential categories declined relatively little, in comparison with the pattern of changes by schooling and husband's occupation.

With religion (Australian-born only) the pattern has been different, for here the differences grew: among earlier cohorts (when fertility was declining) and also among later cohorts (when fertility was rising). Although fertility, in this later period, increased among both Catholics and non-Catholics, it rose more among Catholics.

As might be anticipated, the pattern of differences by nativity is highly mixed. The period saw declines in the fertility of not only the Greek-, Yugoslav- and Italian-born, but also the Dutch-born, at the same time that the Australian- and the British (including Irish)-born were experiencing increases. The result was a considerable narrowing of the range of differences by country of birth. In fact, among the more recent cohorts, it was only the slightly higher fertility of the Dutch-born that kept the Australian-born from having the highest fertility of any nativity grouping. In contrast, among the earlier cohorts the fertility of the Australian-born was exceeded — often substantially so — by that of all but the British- and German-born.

Distribution by issue

The pattern of group differences in the distribution of parities was what could be expected from that of group fertility differences in general: higher parities were more commonly associated with higher fertility, and lower parities with lower fertility. As with fertility differences overall, variations in the ranges of differences within sectors show up in both median issue and distribution by issue, but they do so much more in the latter — particularly at the higher parities, where both the differences themselves and the ranges of these differences within sectors are substantially greater. For example, in the Australian-born cohort of 1927–31, Catholics exceeded non-Catholics by 26 per cent with respect to median issue, but by as much as 97 per cent with respect to the proportion bearing five or more children, and 151 per cent with respect to the proportion bearing six or more (the culmination, incidentally, of an unbroken pattern of increasing differences proceeding from a mere 12 per cent Catholic excess on the part of those bearing five or more children in the cohort of 1880–4).

Group differences in the proportions at the higher parities (five or more) generally increased with successive cohorts born before the turn of the century, but since then these differences have tended to decline. The one real exception is the Catholic:non-Catholic difference (among the Australian-born) already noted. While differences by residence declined only very slightly, those by schooling and husband's occupation declined fairly extensively — mainly in consequence of increases in the proportions at higher parity among the sectors with lower fertility, and stability in these proportions among those with middle and higher fertility.

Among the nativity groupings the gap narrowed appreciably, as the proportion at the upper parities among the Italian-, Dutch-, Greek- and Yugoslav-born underwent extensive declines concurrently with the maintenance of essential stability in this proportion among the Australian-born. With the British-born experiencing much the same pattern of change as the Australian-born (but with a consistently lower proportion in the upper parities), the Australian: British difference remained essentially unchanged. With the German-born, it increased in response to further declines in the already low proportions at these parities. In this development, the direction of the differences among nativity groupings was in several instances reversed: by the cohort of 1927–31, the proportion at this upper parity among the Australian-born was higher than among any nativity grouping other than the Dutch (and, even here, the Dutch figure had been reduced from being 116 per cent higher with the 1907–11 cohort to being but 26 per cent higher with the 1927–31 cohort). In hardly a generation, the proportion with five or more issue had, among the Italian-born, declined from being 119 per cent higher than the Australian-born proportion to being 25 per cent lower; among the Greek-born, from being 78 per cent higher to being 55 per cent lower; and among the Yugoslav-born, from being 68 per cent higher to being 52 per cent lower.

There were general declines in the proportions at the lowest parities (zero to one) among the Australian-born, and also, although to a lesser extent, among the British-born. But among the other nativity groupings, these proportions either remained unchanged (as with the Dutch- and German-born) or increased (Italian-, Greek- and Yugoslav-born). The result was a general narrowing of the gap where the earlier proportion had been lower than the Australian, and an expansion of the gap where it had been higher.

Where the Australian-born predominate (religion, residence, husband's occupation and schooling), there was either a slight diminution of differences (as with husband's occupation) or little change (religion, residence, schooling).

Discussion

As with similar differences in median issue, the increasing group differences among successive cohorts born before the first decade of this century were doubtless associated very largely with the pattern of diffusion of control over childbearing. But unlike the situation with median issue, those relating to the proportions at either the highest or lowest parities were probably particularly related to the distribution of the knowledge of birth control and of access to the means to put this knowledge into practice. In the case of those at the highest parities, ignorance of these means, or lack of access to them, could have led to a higher proportion bearing children in excess of the number they might otherwise have borne; while, in contrast, with those at the lowest parities, this knowledge could have led to postponement of the first or second birth long enough to render it either impossible (because of the onset of infecundity) or personally infeasible or undesirable (because of the development of conflicting tastes or living conditions, or because of the development of alternative sources of satisfaction of the needs children might be presumed to fulfill).

This is not to argue for the absence of other factors in the determination of these differences in patterns of distribution by parity, but only to suggest that when it comes to determining the proportions who will be at one or the other extreme along the continuum of birth parities, these other factors may be less important than the knowledge of birth control itself, and the access one has to the means of effecting such control.

Notes

1. Australia, Bureau of Census and Statistics, *Census of the Commonwealth of Australia* (1911), vol. 1, p. 285.

2. Australia, Bureau of Census and Statistics, *Census of the Commonwealth of Australia* (1947), 'Statistician's Report', p. 319.

3. Calculated from data in ibid., p. 320; and *Year Book Australia 1981*, Canberra: Australian Bureau of Statistics (1981), p. 116.

4. Lincoln H. Day, 'Family size and fertility'. In Solomon Encel and Alan Davies (eds), *Australian Society*, Melbourne: Cheshire (1965); and Lincoln H. Day, 'Differential fertility in Australia'. In Proceedings of General Conference of the

International Union for the Scientific Study of Population, London (1969), D6.3.
5. John C. Caldwell, 'A theory of fertility: from high plateau to destabilization'. *Population and Development Review*, 4 (1978); and John C. Caldwell and Lado T. Ruzicka, 'The Australian fertility transition: an analysis'. *Population and Development Review*, 4 (1978).
6. Lincoln H. Day and Alice Taylor Day, 'Family size in industrialized countries: an inquiry into the socio-cultural determinants of levels of childbearing'. *Journal of Marriage and the Family*, 31 (1969).
7. Lincoln H. Day, 'Models for the causal analysis of differences in fertility: utility, normative, and drift'. In Lado T. Ruzicka (ed.), *The Economic and Social Supports for High Fertility*, Canberra: Department of Demography, Australian National University (1977).
8. W. D. Borrie, L. T. Ruzicka and S. K. Jain, 'The recent and potential demographic dynamics of Australia'. Seminar Paper, Australian National University, Department of Demography (1976).

2 FERTILITY AND URBAN−RURAL RESIDENCE

Introduction

However defined — and for something so widely used in comparative analysis, it is defined in a remarkable variety of ways — the urban−rural dimension of residence is prominently associated with differences in human behaviour. Among these differences, those pertaining to fertility have been particularly consistent: in all types of societies, urban-dwellers have tended to have fewer children than have rural-dwellers.

It is no different in Australia. Fertility differences by urban−rural residence are, in fact, among the most persistent and pervasive of all. By whatever measure, the fertility of rural-dwellers has exceeded that of other urban-dwellers which, in turn, has exceeded that of metropolitan-dwellers. This has been the case for as far back as the data go (that is, to the cohort of 1875−9) in the case of the Australian-born). It has been true of both Catholics and non-Catholics, of each nativity grouping numerous enough to permit such a comparison, of each occupational grouping, and of each category of schooling (whether wife's or husband's). The few exceptions appear in nearly every instance to be explicable in terms of variation among relatively small cell frequencies (although an attempt was made to minimize such variations by restricting analysis to categories in which N was < 100).

Group fertility differences are frequently reported as narrowing with successive generations, but whether or not this is seen to be the case is often a matter of the kinds of observations made, and the extent to which one's focus encompasses phenomena beyond those directly indicative of fertility. In the case of Australia, fertility differences by urban−rural residence may actually be increasing.

The present analysis employs three categories of urban−rural residence: metropolitan, other urban and rural. For the 1971 data, metropolitan refers to all major urban centres with population agglomerations of 100,000 or more, namely:

Agglomeration	1971 Population (000s)	% of Total Population
Sydney	2,808	22.0
Melbourne	2,503	19.6
Brisbane	868	6.8
Adelaide	843	6.6
Perth	703	5.5
Newcastle	352	2.8
Wollongong	199	1.6
Canberra	159	1.2
Hobart	153	1.2
Geelong	122	1.0

'Other urban' refers to urban centres ranging in population from 1,000–75,000 (there was none in the range 75–100,000 in 1971), a third of the population of which was in centres of 25–75,000, although the median point was a population size of 12,100. The remainder is classified as 'rural'.

For the 1961 and 1954 data, the urban definitions are slightly different: metropolitan is restricted to the state capitals and their adjoining municipal areas, together with the national capital, Canberra. This relegates Newcastle, Wollongong and Geelong to the other urban category — a difference, to be sure, but probably not one sufficient to have much effect on the analysis.

The percentage distribution of the population among these three residential categories in the census years under consideration was as follows (excluding the few recorded as of Aboriginal origin — 106,000 in 1971 — and the still fewer recorded as migratory, that is, as persons who, not recorded elsewhere, were, at the census moment, on ships in Australian waters or travelling on long-distance trains, motor-coaches or aircraft: 107,000 in 1971, 25,000 in 1961, 23,000 in 1954):

| Category | % | | |
	1971*	1961	1954
Metropolitan	68	56	54
Other Urban	17	26	25
Rural	14	18	20
Total	99	100	99

*Employing the 1961/1954 definition, these would be:

Metropolitan	63
Other Urban	23
Rural	14
	100

The Pattern of Urban–Rural Fertility Differences

The present analysis of urban–rural fertility differences in Australia is limited with respect to both schooling and nativity. With schooling, comparisons are necessarily confined to cohorts born after 1906 (that is, to wives younger than age 65 in 1971), because it was not until 1971 that a census inquired into this attribute. With nativity, meaningful urban–rural comparisons are altogether impossible among the Greek- and Yugoslav-born because of their almost exclusive concentration in metropolitan areas, and confined to the younger cohorts among the Dutch- and German-born because of their small numbers at the older ages.

Median Issue

Because of small cell frequencies among the other nativity groupings, meaningful consideration of urban–rural fertility differences among cohorts born before the present century is restricted to the Australian-born. The pattern of urban–rural differences in median issue among those of these Australian-born women who were married before age 26 was one of steady increases up to the cohorts of about 1900–9, and then marginal declines with successive cohorts thereafter (see Table 2.1) — a pattern in keeping with what might be expected from the spread of fertility control first to the metropolitan areas, then to the other urban, and last to the rural. Yet if these wives are further sub-divided by religion[1] and narrower age at marriage categories (under 20, 20–1 and 22–5 years, and also single years of age) are employed, the apparent narrowing of the urban–rural differences among cohorts in this century is substantially reduced, giving way to a pattern marked by

Table 2.1: Median Issue Born to Current Marriage, by Residence. Australian-born Wives 40–64 Years of Age who Commenced Current Marriage before Age 26, by Year of Birth (1971)

Year of Birth	Residence		
	Metropolitan	Other Urban	Rural
1907–11	1.95	2.45	2.80
1912–16	1.99	2.48	2.78
1917–21	2.07	2.50	2.82
1922–26	2.21	2.62	2.86
1927–31	2.45	2.75	3.14

Table 2.2: Median Issue Born to Current Marriage, by Residence and Religion: Metropolitan Median and Relative Levels of Other Medians (Metropolitan = 100). Australian-born Wives 40–64 Years of Age who Commenced Current Marriage before Age 26, by Year of Birth and Age at Marriage (1971)

Religion and Year of Birth	Age at Marriage								
	< 20			20–1			22–5		
	Metropolitan Median	Index Other Urban	Rural	Metropolitan Median	Index Other Urban	Rural	Metropolitan Median	Index Other Urban	Rural
Catholic									
1907–11	2.64	129	150	2.34	132	162	2.21	120	132
1912–16	2.72	130	137	2.43	128	133	2.29	121	142
1917–21	2.92	119	134	2.53	119	138	2.40	118	136
1922–26	2.83	119	134	2.59	128	137	2.65	115	135
1927–31	2.92	123	133	2.88	114	128	2.87	112	132
Non-Catholic									
1907–11	2.41	123	144	2.00	126	145	1.72	119	143
1912–16	2.45	129	139	2.08	123	138	1.82	116	136
1917–21	2.52	117	135	2.09	119	135	1.87	115	136
1922–26	2.43	120	140	2.17	118	134	1.99	116	135
1927–31	2.59	119	134	2.31	113	129	2.09	115	133

Table 2.3: Median Issue Born to Current Marriage, by Residence, Nativity and Religion: Metropolitan Median and Relative Levels of Other Medians (Metropolitan = 100). Overseas-born Wives 40–64 Years of Age who Commenced Current Marriage before Age 26, by Year of Birth and Age at Marriage (Australia 1971)

Religion, Age at Marriage and Year of Birth	Country of Birth								
	British Isles			Italy			Netherlands		
	Metropolitan Median	Index Other Urban	Rural	Metropolitan Median	Index Other Urban	Rural	Metropolitan Median	Index Other Urban	Rural
Catholic									
<20									
1907–11	—	—	—	4.11	100	—	—	—	—
1917–21	2.96	—	—	3.14	106	90	—	—	—
1927–31	3.33	—	—	2.49	—	127	3.15	—	—
20–21									
1907–11	2.74	—	—	3.91	—	—	—	—	—
1917–21	2.60	—	—	2.84	—	—	—	—	—
1927–31	2.71	132	—	2.25	114	127	3.03	—	—
22–25									
1907–11	2.21	—	—	2.07	—	—	—	—	—
1917–21	2.63	111	—	2.49	—	124	3.77	—	—
1927–31	2.67	112	—	2.02	121	127	2.86	121	129
Non-Catholic									
<20									
1907–11	2.48	103	130	*	*	*	—	—	—
1917–21	2.41	113	122	*	*	*	2.92	—	—
1927–31	2.55	115	112	*	*	*	3.11	—	—
20–21									
1907–11	2.01	108	115	*	*	*	—	—	—
1917–21	1.95	119	126	*	*	*	2.88	—	—
1927–31	2.22	116	115	*	*	*	2.51	—	—
22–25									
1907–11	1.72	110	125	*	*	*	2.81	—	—
1917–21	1.85	104	110	*	*	*	2.50	109	—
1927–31	2.01	119	118	*	*	*	2.43	108	103

(—) = < 100   * Not Applicable

Table 2.3: — continued

Religion, Age at Marriage and Year of Birth	Greece			Germany			Yugoslavia		
	Metropolitan Median	Other Urban Index	Rural	Metropolitan Median	Other Urban Index	Rural	Metropolitan Median	Other Urban Index	Rural
Catholic									
< 20									
1907–11	*	*	*	—	—	—	—	—	—
1917–21	*	*	*	—	—	—	2.63	—	—
1927–31	*	*	*	1.89	—	—	1.93	—	—
20–21									
1907–11	*	*	*	—	—	—	—	—	—
1917–21	*	*	*	—	—	—	—	—	—
1927–31	*	*	*	1.81	—	—	1.91	—	—
22–25									
1907–11	*	*	*	—	—	—	—	—	—
1917–21	*	*	*	—	—	—	—	—	—
1927–31	*	*	*	1.61	—	—	1.69	—	—
Non-Catholic									
< 20									
1907–11	3.22	—	—	—	—	—	—	—	—
1917–21	3.29	—	—	—	—	—	—	—	—
1927–31	2.54	—	—	1.86	—	—	—	—	—
20–21									
1907–11	3.28	—	—	—	—	—	—	—	—
1917–21	3.09	—	—	1.95	—	—	—	—	—
1927–31	2.20	—	—	1.71	119	—	2.14	—	—
22–25									
1907–11	3.28	—	—	1.47	—	—	—	—	—
1917–21	2.71	—	—	1.68	—	—	1.89	—	—
1927–31	1.96	—	—	1.51	141	—	1.70	—	—

* Not Applicable

(—) = < 100

fluctuations in the extent of these differences, but with no particular trend toward either an increase or a decrease (see Table 2.2).

In fact, what stands out here among the Australian-born is the consistency of the urban—rural fertility difference, rather than any particular tendency for it to disappear. During the period of declining fertility (that involving the childbearing of cohorts born before about 1905—9), the ratio of other urban median issue to metropolitan median issue fluctuated but little around 130:100, and the ratio of rural median issue to metropolitan but little around 155:100; while in the period that followed, when the long-term pattern of declining fertility gave way to movement in the opposite direction (at least up through the childbearing of the 1927—31 cohort), analysis by *single* years of age at marriage shows that within each marriage age category the other urban median quite consistently exceeded the metropolitan by some 15 per cent and, in similar fashion, the rural exceeded the metropolitan by some 35 per cent (see Table 2.2).

It is much the same with the overseas-born. The paucity of such wives residing other than in the metropolitan areas permits few comparisons within older cohorts, but those few that can be made suggest a similar pattern of essential stability. Only the Italian-born have a different pattern: with them the urban—rural difference expanded. Use of more detailed age at marriage categories alters the picture in no discernible way — although the fact that it does not may derive less from the nature of the phenomenon itself than from the relatively small numbers involved despite the fact that, as already noted, in every instance these are at least 100, (see Table 2.3).

Essential stability in urban—rural differences in median issue is also found among wives categorised by schooling, whether their own or their husband's (see Table 2.4). But with husband's occupation, it is somewhat different: while differences in median issue by urban—rural residence among farmers and blue-collar workers have remained essentially unchanged, those among white-collar workers have tended to narrow (see Table 2.5). Nevertheless, here too the dominant pattern overall is one of marked stability.

Distribution by Issue

It is conceivable that the pattern of urban—rural differences by

Table 2.4: Median Issue Born to Current Marriage, by Residence, Schooling and Husband's Schooling: Metropolitan Median and Relative Levels of Other Medians (Metropolitan = 100). Wives 40–64 Years of Age Who Commenced Current Marriage before Age 26, by Year of Birth and Age at Marriage (Australia, 1971)

Age at Marriage and Year of Birth		Wife's Schooling					
		< 6			6–7		
			Index			Index	
		Metropolitan Median	Other Urban	Rural	Metropolitan Median	Other Urban	Rural
< 20	1907–11	2.67	118	138	2.47	114	130
	1917–21	2.81	112	127	2.59	115	129
	1927–31	2.72	122	133	2.62	121	134
20–1	1907–11	2.31	115	133	2.05	127	138
	1917–21	2.32	113	129	2.18	121	134
	1927–31	2.38	118	130	2.35	116	131
22–5	1907–11	1.89	117	138	1.81	119	135
	1917–21	1.98	116	135	1.93	118	135
	1927–31	2.13	120	133	2.15	118	135
		Husband's Schooling					
< 20	1907–11	2.68	118	136	2.45	115	133
	1917–21	2.82	114	125	2.56	117	133
	1927–31	2.73	120	132	2.61	120	132
20–1	1907–11	2.29	116	136	2.02	124	137
	1917–21	2.36	117	127	2.13	122	134
	1927–31	2.41	115	128	2.34	117	130
22–5	1907–11	1.90	117	136	1.77	123	141
	1917–21	2.00	117	135	1.91	120	138
	1927–31	2.13	118	134	2.13	118	138

Age at Marriage and Year of Birth		Wife's Schooling					
		8			9+		
			Index			Index	
		Metropolitan Median	Other Urban	Rural	Metropolitan Median	Other Urban	Rural
< 20	1907–11	2.38	111	123	2.02	120	123
	1917–21	2.44	115	117	2.27	119	120
	1927–31	2.52	117	127	2.39	120	124
20–1	1907–11	2.08	120	137	1.88	110	124
	1917–21	2.09	118	132	2.02	118	121
	1927–31	2.35	113	127	2.33	116	125
22–5	1907–11	1.80	114	133	1.70	116	134
	1917–21	1.94	115	131	1.95	112	127
	1927–31	2.22	114	126	2.31	113	126

Table 2.4 (continued)

Age at Marriage and Year of Birth		Husband's Schooling					
		8			9+		
			Index			Index	
		Metropolitan Median	Other Urban	Rural	Metropolitan Median	Other Urban	Rural
< 20	1907–11	2.33	107	—	2.09	115	139
	1917–21	2.51	110	113	2.32	115	122
	1927–31	2.52	117	126	2.42	117	121
20–1	1907–11	2.06	120	147	1.89	113	122
	1917–21	2.11	119	130	2.07	115	124
	1927–31	2.32	114	128	2.34	114	123
22–5	1907–11	1.80	117	133	1.71	112	126
	1917–21	1.93	115	133	1.96	111	121
	1927–31	2.18	114	131	2.32	114	122

(−) N < 100

specific numbers of children ever born could be at variance with that of median issue, but this has not been the case in Australia. The pattern of differences by parity has differed only marginally from that relating to medians — although it has not displayed the same degree of cohort-to-cohort stability.

As one might expect, the period of declining fertility (that of cohorts born before about 1905–9, for which the nativity data necessarily pertain only to the Australian-born) was marked by declining proportions in the higher parities (five or more, and six or more children) and increasing proportions in the lower (zero to one child). Because the decline at the higher parities was greatest among metropolitan-dwellers (where there was a drop of some 80 per cent) and least among rural-dwellers (where the drop was just over half), the difference by residence increased over this period (that is, up to the cohorts of about 1907–16). Following this there was some apparent narrowing with the onset of relatively stable and later slightly increasing fertility.

But again, analysis by single years of age at marriage tells a somewhat different story. While differences by residence in the proportions at the higher parities did, indeed, increase during the period of declining fertility, the apparent narrowing thereafter resulted not so much from changes in the relative fertility of women marrying at different ages as from changes in the pattern of age at

Table 2.5: Median Issue Born to Current Marriage, by Residence and Husband's Occupation. Metropolitan Median and Relative Levels of Other Medians (Metropolitan = 100). Wives 40–64 Years of Age who Commenced Current Marriage before Age 26, by Year of Birth and Age at Marriage (Australia, 1971)

Age at Marriage and Year of Birth	Husband's Occupation								
	Professional			Administrative			Clerical & Sales		
	Metropolitan Median	Index Other Urban	Rural	Metropolitan Median	Index Other Urban	Rural	Metropolitan Median	Index Other Urban	Rural
< 20									
1907–11	1.91	—	—	2.17	95	—	2.09	116	—
1917–21	2.27	119	—	2.23	118	118	2.28	113	138
1927–31	2.42	124	—	2.42	115	131	2.44	113	116
20–1									
1907–11	2.05	—	—	1.88	130	—	1.79	132	—
1917–21	2.07	115	133	2.03	121	124	2.02	118	121
1927–31	2.44	111	117	2.31	113	118	2.28	111	121
22–5									
1907–11	1.79	113	—	1.77	121	137	1.68	120	126
1917–21	2.13	108	118	1.94	116	118	1.85	117	117
1927–31	2.49	112	113	2.27	110	111	2.20	110	121

(−) N < 100

Table 2.5 — continued

Age at Marriage and Year of Birth	Husband's Occupation											
	Farmers & Graziers			Transport & Communication			Tradesmen, etc.			All Other		
		Index			Index			Index			Index	
	Metropolitan Median	Other Urban	Rural	Metropolitan Median	Other Urban	Rural	Metropolitan Median	Other Urban	Rural	Metropolitan Median	Other Urban	Rural
< 20												
1907–11	2.80	124	126	2.37	—	—	2.63	117	130	2.63	116	136
1917–21	3.05	106	110	2.65	115	131	2.69	114	128	2.81	111	120
1927–31	2.88	119	120	2.74	121	124	2.58	122	140	2.76	118	131
20–1												
1907–11	2.44	113	128	2.27	116	—	2.31	124	134	2.18	116	131
1917–21	2.38	119	126	2.26	124	126	2.24	117	123	2.24	114	125
1927–31	2.61	119	119	2.47	110	120	2.32	117	127	2.45	114	129
22–5												
1907–11	2.24	115	118	1.90	134	122	1.88	118	127	1.81	114	131
1917–21	2.20	111	124	1.98	120	122	1.94	118	131	1.97	113	125
1927–31	2.24	116	132	2.20	119	129	2.11	119	132	2.20	117	129

(—) N < 100

marriage; for among those within each single-year age at marriage category, the cohort-to-cohort fluctuations in urban–rural differences at the higher parities, although rather marked, were none the less essentially pattern-less (see Table 2.6).

Marked but essentially pattern-less fluctuation also characterised cohort-to-cohort differences by residence among Australian-born wives at the lowest parities; except that here this pattern-less fluctuation was a feature of the entire period — the earlier one of fertility decline as well as the later one of fertility increase — and not merely, as with the highest parities, a feature of only the period of increasing fertility. A further difference, at least in the more recent cohorts, was a consistent narrowing of the urban–rural difference among those marrying at the oldest marriage age under consideration, namely, 25.

Overall, the pattern of urban–rural differences by parity is what could be expected from the pattern of such differences with respect to median issue: metropolitan-dwellers were the most and rural-dwellers the least likely to be of low parity; while metropolitan-dwellers were the least and rural-dwellers the most likely to be of high parity. But among rural–urban residential groupings the ratios of differences in distribution — particularly at the highest parities — have generally been more extensive than those pertaining to medians. It is not uncommon, for example, to find that the proportion with six or more issue is twice as high among some categories of rural-dwellers as it is among their metropolitan-dwelling counterparts, while the corresponding rural–metropolitan difference in median issue may be less than a third.

This great range of differences affords, of course, a greater scope for change; and the relative magnitudes of urban–rural change in distribution by issue have, in fact, generally exceeded those of corresponding changes in median issue — even though following no common pattern among the different social groupings as to either extent or direction. Among the Australian-born, the extent of differences by rural–urban residence remained essentially unchanged at the lowest parities (zero to one child), despite the marked decline overall in the proportions at these parities; while at the highest parities (five or more, and six or more) these differences generally lessened, mainly in consequence of an increase in the proportions at these parities among metropolitan-dwellers (see Table 2.6).

Substantial declines in proportions at the lowest parities also

Table 2.6: Percentages with 0–1, 5+ and 6+ Issue Born to Current Marriage, by Residence and Religion. Metropolitan Percentages and Relative Levels of Other Percentages (Metropolitan = 100). Australian-Born Wives 40–64 Years of Age who Commenced Current Marriage before Age 26, by Year of Birth and Age at Marriage (Australia, 1971)

Religion, Age at Marriage and Year of Birth	0–1			Issue 5+			6+		
	Metropolitan %	Index Other Urban	Rural	Metropolitan %	Index Other Urban	Rural	Metropolitan %	Index Other Urban	Rural
Catholic									
17 1907–11	14.5	54	—	30.0	137	—	17.5	181	—
1917–21	10.9	38	—	33.4	136	—	21.7	142	—
1927–31	6.8	78	35	34.4	139	158	20.8	145	194
19 1907–11	14.3	62	83	27.7	140	172	18.0	146	176
1917–21	12.4	73	52	25.4	157	165	16.8	145	170
1927–31	8.9	55	61	28.3	136	167	16.7	154	197
21 1907–11	20.3	67	41	19.4	143	236	11.4	155	325
1917–21	14.5	74	48	22.6	136	174	12.9	153	209
1927–31	8.9	85	73	28.5	124	158	16.2	136	188
23 1907–11	21.1	73	55	18.2	165	173	9.4	216	276
1917–21	15.3	86	52	20.6	145	180	11.2	154	221
1927–31	9.8	100	58	29.3	121	159	16.0	137	205
25 1907–11	25.4	79	76	18.0	135	170	9.8	150	204
1917–21	16.8	90	67	20.4	140	181	11.4	143	218
1927–31	11.4	82	51	25.3	125	171	12.9	142	184

(–) N < 100

Table 2.6 (continued)

Religion, Age at Marriage and Year of Birth	0–1			Issue 5+			6+		
	Metropolitan %	Index Other Urban	Rural	Metropolitan %	Index Other Urban	Rural	Metropolitan %	Index Other Urban	Rural
Non-Catholic									
17 1907–11	13.8	64	36	24.5	170	198	14.9	190	240
1917–21	9.4	86	63	26.9	124	174	16.7	132	190
1927–31	7.2	72	60	27.4	130	158	15.4	150	184
19 1907–11	16.0	83	56	19.3	153	192	11.0	172	234
1917–21	13.0	75	68	18.6	147	180	10.4	141	197
1927–31	8.8	77	58	17.3	157	195	8.5	169	211
21 1907–11	22.1	72	56	11.6	198	247	6.1	218	289
1917–21	16.2	78	67	10.2	179	254	4.3	233	337
1927–31	10.0	84	60	11.1	169	214	4.4	195	259
23 1907–11	25.8	88	69	8.3	200	252	3.7	238	341
1917–21	17.3	93	70	7.5	173	255	3.1	203	303
1927–31	11.6	94	64	8.6	167	230	3.2	194	284
25 1907–11	28.2	81	60	5.5	187	260	2.3	222	339
1917–21	21.6	87	64	6.6	182	248	2.5	204	304
1927–31	16.0	92	58	7.2	164	235	2.6	177	269

(–) N < 100

Table 2.7: Percentages with 0–1, 5+, and 6+ Issue Born to Current Marriage, by Residence, Selected Nativity and Religion: Metropolitan Percentages and Relative Levels of Other Percentages (Metropolitan = 100). Wives 40–64 Years of Age who Commenced Current Marriage before Age 26, by Year of Birth and Age at Marriage (Australia, 1971)

Religion, Age at Marriage and Year of Birth	Australia Metropolitan % 0–1	5+	6+	Australia Index Other Urban 0–1	5+	6+	Rural 0–1	5+	6+	British Isles Metropolitan % 0–1	5+	6+	British Isles Index Other Urban 0–1	5+	6+	Rural 0–1	5+	6+
Catholic																		
< 20 1907–11	13.8	27.8	18.1	62	111	160	57	178	213	—	—	—	—	—	—	—	—	—
1917–21	11.7	29.1	18.8	69	141	143	50	167	189	8.1	33.3	23.9	—	—	—	—	—	—
1927–31	8.2	20.2	18.2	60	208	149	59	239	188	8.7	36.1	17.6	—	—	—	—	—	—
20–1 1907–11	18.7	20.8	12.9	70	152	150	43	227	284	11.7	25.5	14.6	—	—	—	—	—	—
1917–21	13.7	22.7	13.1	71	146	163	57	183	224	11.0	24.7	14.8	—	—	—	—	—	—
1927–31	8.8	28.5	16.4	83	128	140	75	154	182	10.2	25.6	15.3	45	161	162	—	—	—
22–5 1907–11	21.8	18.8	9.8	76	147	172	62	180	235	16.7	19.8	11.3	—	—	—	—	—	—
1917–21	16.2	20.6	11.6	86	141	147	67	179	206	12.7	25.3	13.7	91	103	104	—	—	—
1927–31	10.5	28.0	15.4	89	123	133	56	164	195	11.2	23.3	12.9	74	133	160	—	—	—
Non-Catholic																		
< 20 1907–11	16.4	21.3	13.0	67	160	176	52	195	230	14.6	24.1	14.2	100	114	134	30	143	194
1917–21	11.8	21.7	12.7	76	143	152	64	181	206	12.3	20.1	11.4	63	135	146	60	156	170
1927–31	8.5	20.9	11.0	74	149	161	60	184	210	10.4	21.7	11.4	88	128	132	110	113	153
20–1 1907–11	20.3	13.5	7.4	73	104	189	56	230	273	20.3	13.3	6.8	76	146	144	73	145	168
1917–21	15.8	11.9	5.4	79	174	209	62	229	283	17.6	11.5	5.1	81	157	173	54	170	186
1927–31	7.8	12.3	5.1	105	163	184	74	212	249	12.5	13.2	5.7	76	136	168	87	158	195
22–5 1907–11	26.0	7.6	3.5	80	183	203	58	259	306	24.7	7.6	3.5	91	132	146	74	225	249
1917–21	18.5	7.5	3.0	94	173	213	63	255	310	21.2	8.8	3.8	87	123	137	95	156	153
1927–31	12.2	8.6	3.2	86	166	191	61	237	222	15.8	8.8	2.9	71	159	169	72	156	231

Table 2.7 (continued)

Religion, Age at Marriage and Year of Birth	Italy Metropolitan % 0–1	5+	6+	Italy Index Other Urban 0–1	5+	6+	Italy Index Rural 0–1	5+	6+	Netherlands Metropolitan % 0–1	5+	6+	Netherlands Index Other Urban 0–1	5+	6+	Netherlands Index Rural 0–1	5+	6+
Catholic																		
<20 1907–11	6.0	51.3	39.4	—	—	—	—	—	—	—	—	—	—	—	—	—	—	—
1917–21	7.3	33.1	19.2	99	103	—	116	92	—	—	—	—	—	—	—	—	—	—
1927–31	8.8	19.7	10.4	55	140	172	70	151	186	7.4	28.7	16.7	—	—	—	—	—	—
20–1 1907–11	8.3	48.7	37.9	—	—	—	—	—	—	—	—	—	—	—	—	—	—	—
1917–21	9.6	26.1	14.2	—	—	—	—	—	—	—	—	—	—	—	—	—	—	—
1927–31	12.6	14.6	7.3	65	123	119	65	201	232	9.3	31.0	17.5	—	—	—	—	—	—
22–5 1907–11	9.7	31.8	22.8	—	—	—	—	—	—	5.2	45.8	29.7	—	—	—	—	—	—
1917–21	11.5	22.4	10.8	—	—	—	43	127	155	—	—	—	—	—	—	—	—	—
1927–31	13.8	10.3	4.4	79	149	182	43	151	170	9.8	26.9	15.4	63	136	157	61	162	193
Non-Catholic																		
<20 1907–11	*	*	*	*	*	*	*	*	*	—	—	—	—	—	—	—	—	—
1917–21	*	*	*	*	*	*	*	*	*	12.4	36.2	24.8	—	—	—	—	—	—
1927–31	*	*	*	*	*	*	*	*	*	11.6	32.8	18.4	—	—	—	—	—	—
20–1 1907–11	*	*	*	*	*	*	*	*	*	—	—	—	—	—	—	—	—	—
1917–21	*	*	*	*	*	*	*	*	*	9.4	26.2	16.0	—	—	—	—	—	—
1927–31	*	*	*	*	*	*	*	*	*	8.5	18.1	9.0	—	—	—	—	—	—
22–5 1907–11	*	*	*	*	*	*	*	*	*	13.6	29.4	18.6	—	—	—	—	—	—
1917–21	*	*	*	*	*	*	*	*	*	10.6	24.6	15.5	68	85	77	—	—	—
1927–31	*	*	*	*	*	*	*	*	*	8.9	15.9	7.1	82	108	148	147	139	185

* Not Applicable
(—) N < 100

occurred among the British-born, only with them the difference between metropolitan- and other urban-dwellers increased slightly, while that between metropolitan- and rural-dwellers declined, also slightly. At the highest parities, where there was a marked increase in the proportions with exactly five issue among both metropolitan- and other urban dwellers, the magnitude of the other urban:metropolitan difference remained essentially unchanged, while that of the rural:metropolitan — as among the Australian-born — declined (see Table 2.7).

With the Italian-born there was a particularly marked increase in urban–rural differences at the highest parities — cohort-to-cohort declines in the proportions at these parities among metropolitan-dwellers having continued to exceed those among other urban- and rural-dwellers. At the lower parities there was essentially no change (see Table 2.7).

Of all nativity groupings, the Dutch-born (in either religion category) were the least likely to be of low parity and the most likely to be of high parity, despite a very considerable downward movement in both these proportions with successive cohorts born this century. Changes in residential differences among the Dutch-born were generally in the direction of a reduction at the lowest parities and an expansion at the highest. While the proportion at the lower parities remained largely unchanged among both metropolitan and other urban-dwellers, among rural-dwellers it increased; and while those in all three residential categories experienced a decline in the proportions at the highest parities, the urban-rural difference grew because the greatest decline was among metropolitan-dwellers and the least among rural-dwellers (see Table 2.7).

With the German-born, the differences by residence increased at the lower parities (where the German-born were already distinguished by having the highest concentrations of any nativity group). This was more in response to declines among other urban- and rural-dwellers than to increases among metropolitan-dwellers. But while the other urban:metropolitan difference increased at the higher parities as well, the rural:metropolitan difference at these parities remained essentially unchanged (see Table 2.7).

With schooling (whether wife's or husband's), the pattern of urban–rural differences in distribution by issue was characterised by consistency and cohort-to-cohort stability. While the urban–rural differences at the upper parities tended to exceed those at the lower, they were much the same among the various age at marriage and years of schooling categories: in general, no greater in one marriage age schooling category than in another, and exhibiting no tendency towards either expansion or contraction with successive cohorts.

With husband's occupation the pattern was more mixed, although still largely characterised by consistency and cohort-to-cohort stability. This was particularly the case with the proportions with zero to one child, where the urban–rural differences among the various occupational categories were essentially the same, and the cohort-to-cohort differences — despite marked changes in the respective proportions bearing this number of children — matters only of fluctuation rather than of movement toward either expansion or contraction. The few exceptions to the general pattern of consistency and cohort-to-cohort stability are confined to the higher parities — particularly to the highest (six and over) — where there was a slight tendency towards an expansion of the urban–rural difference among farmers and blue-collar workers (more among those who married at the later ages than among those who married before age 20) in contrast to either a decline or virtual stability among white collar workers.

Summary

What stands out in this more detailed analysis of fertility differences by urban–rural residence is how little change there was during the period of childbearing represented by the cohorts of 1907–11 to 1927–31, a period that saw stability and then a modest increase in fertility among the Australian- and British-born, and a substantial decline in fertility among the Italian-, Greek and Dutch-born. Whether in terms of median issue or the proportions bearing few (zero to one) or many (five or more, or six or more) children, when standardised for age at marriage, differences by residence were not only persistent and pervasive; they were also remarkably stable in extent. To be sure, there were fluctuations, but there was little tendency toward either expansion or contraction. This was the case with both religion groupings, each nativity sector (apart from the marked expansion of the urban–rural difference at the higher parities among the Italian-born) and each schooling category. Although the situation was somewhat different by husband's occupation, the dominant pattern there was none the less one of overall stability along that dimension as well.

Discussion

There are two important limitations on the analysis of any association between human behaviour and urban–rural residence: the necessary arbitrariness in the definition of urban and rural, and the possibility that — so far as human behaviour is concerned — the meaning of these residential categories will change without there being any change in the way they are defined. At the very least, such limitations would seem to counsel caution in reaching conclusions concerning observed differences in urban–rural patterns of behaviour.

The fundamental criteria for distinguishing urban from non-urban relate simultaneously to human numbers and density: below some minimum of both of these attributes, urban or metropolitan or other urban may no longer be said to exist. But the delineation of positions along an urban–rural dimension of residence is unavoidably arbitrary. In any particular instance the points of separation will have no necessary relation to the condition described. In fact, the criteria of sub-division are likely to originate more in considerations of convenience and conformity to past practice than in any specific association they may have with social or economic conditions. Designations like metropolitan or rural represent but narrower ranges of variation along a broader continuum. In any area of human behaviour or social organisation there is bound to be considerable overlap between them. As in the present instance, where the similarities (the overlapping) in parity distributions among the three residential categories far exceed the differences, differences in behaviour and social organisation between various residential categories are primarily of degree rather than kind.

To the limitations associated with arbitrariness must be added those associated with uncertainty about the continuity of meaning. Even if the definition remained unchanged, can one assume that, say, metropolitan or rural will have meant essentially the same thing at one time as at another, the same thing in the experience of one cohort as in that of another? For example, was the meaning of metropolitan and rural much the same when 64 per cent of the population was categorised as the former and 14 per cent as the latter, as when these percentages were, respectively, 47 and 31 instead; or when radio coverage had become nationwide, as when it was confined to the major cities? Or, more to the issue at hand, can these categories be taken to have meant much the same thing over the years at least so far as the causal elements in fertility are concerned: can they be taken to have meant the same thing, for example, with respect to the *relative* differences between them in conditions of life bearing on fertility decision-making, or with respect to the *relative* likelihood of one's having had a metropolitan or non-metropolitan upbringing?

Yet differences in fertility associated with the urban–rural classification used in this study do exist, however arbitrary and uncertain a classification it may be; and these differences are pervasive, consistent, and, for the most part — so far as wives born this century are concerned — notably stable in extent between cohorts. Moreover, because of the possible masking effect of internal geographic mobility, the actual differences may be somewhat greater than those calculated. Certainly those who move can be expected to differ in some respects from those who do not, but whether in ways that would relate to fertility is a moot point. We cannot rule out the possibility of selective movement, either of lower fertility wives to urban areas or of higher fertility wives to rural; nor can we rule out the possibility of a kind of 'anticipatory socialisation' among these wives to the respectively lower or higher fertility norms associated with the areas to which they eventually moved. But if the fertility of wives who changed their categories of residence after completion of childbearing is at all comparable with the fertility of wives who did not — and this seems a reasonable assumption — the full extent of fertility differences associated with patterns of urban–rural residence will have been to some degree obscured.

What is it, then, that the three categories of urban–rural residence employed in this study signify so far as completed fertility is concerned? What does it mean to find that people living in areas defined as metropolitan have generally had fewer children than those living in areas defined as other urban, and that the latter, in turn, have generally had fewer children than those living in areas defined as rural? Is there a causal connection between fertility and the physical or socioeconomic attributes of these different residential categories, between fertility and the physical or social attributes of their respective populations? The observed urban–rural fertility differences originate neither in different patterns of marriage nor in differences in the composition of the population in these residential categories with respect to certain attributes (e.g. religion, nativity, schooling) often found to be themselves independently associated with fertility. The differences in fertility are real. It is not documenting, but accounting for them that is the task at hand here.

For present purposes, the possible explanations can be conveniently categorised in terms of whether they relate to: (1) physiological differences; (2) differences in the ability and willingness to exercise control over childbearing; or (3) differences in desired numbers of children.

Physiological Differences

With the possible exception of coital frequency, physiological factors are unlikely to have played any very significant part in creating the observed urban–rural differences in completed fertility. Certainly, during the period of time under consideration, the ability to conceive and to carry a conception to term can be assumed to have been distributed fairly equally among the three residential categories used here.

However, it may be different with coital frequency. If this is inversely related to stress — and if urban settings are more stressful than rural — then rural-dwellers could be expected to have been both more successful in their efforts to conceive, and also more likely to have experienced unwanted conceptions. While differences in levels of success attending efforts to conceive seem unlikely to have played any very significant part in the origin of the observed differences — given the general location of all three residential fertility distributions at the lower end of the scale of physiological possibilities — one must at least entertain the possibility that there were differences in the rate of unwanted conception, whether originating primarily in different coital frequencies or in differences in the practice of contraception. If the methods of contraception most widely used in Australia during the major part of the period under consideration here were as inefficient as has been claimed,[2] then urban–rural differences in coital frequencies could well have resulted in some urban–rural differences in unwanted pregnancies as well. But whether these then eventuated in differences in fertility depends on the willingness and ability to resort to abortion among those most directly involved, together with the number of children these people wanted, or were at least willing to accept.

Differences in the Ability and Willingness to Exercise Control over Childbearing

An assessment of their relative importance is impossible in the present circumstances, but there can be little doubt that much of the observed urban–rural differences in completed fertility had their origin in corresponding differences in both the ability to control births and the willingness to do so. It has already been suggested that the practice of birth control in Australia probably spread outward from the metropolitan to the other urban areas and finally to the rural, in keeping with the pattern found, or presumed to have existed, elsewhere among European populations at a corresponding stage of demographic development. Some of this difference in timing can doubtless be attributed to urban–rural differences in the three causally interrelated conditions that define one's ability to control fertility: knowledge about birth control, skill in its practice and degree of access to the most effective means (ranging from supplies like condoms, to services like abortions). That such differences may have played an important part in the origin of the observed urban–rural differences in completed fertility is suggested by the growing urban–rural gap in the proportions at the highest parities in the earlier cohorts; for while these proportions declined in all three residential categories, they did so most rapidly among metropolitan- and least rapidly among rural-dwellers.

However, these three conditions must play their respective parts within the larger framework of one's willingness to exercise control over fertility — something that will be influenced by the extent to which both the idea of birth control and the various means to its attainment are socially acceptable. Having knowledge, skill and access to means will be of account in controlling fertility only to the extent that individuals are willing to avail themselves of the opportunities thus afforded. There are undoubtedly a number of differences in behaviour and attitude associated with the urban–rural categorisation of population used here. It would hardly be surprising to find that, for at least most of the period under consideration, there was a similar difference in both attitudes toward birth control and the willingness to practise it.

Yet the history of cultural diffusion would augur an eventual diminution of group differences in such matters as the ability and willingness to control fertility. The changes in Australian fertility patterns — particularly the declining proportions of rural-dwellers at the highest parities — suggest that this did indeed take place so far as the urban–rural differences are concerned. Yet within the more recent cohorts the ratios of these differences remained much the same. Does this mean that the diminution of urban–rural differences in ability and willingness to control fertility eventually came to a halt? Probably not. A more likely explanation would seem to lie in the desired numbers of children, or at least in the numbers of children people were willing to have.

Differences in Desired Numbers of Children

The possible sources of differences in the numbers of children people want, or are willing to have, are numerous and varied. They range from differences in the distribution of personality traits to differences in life-styles, external living conditions and the costs and benefits thought to be associated with childrearing. In fact, almost anything could be thought to be in some measure related to fertility aspirations. The point at issue here is whether there is anything affecting the desired (or tolerated) number of children that can be singled out as likely to be particularly related to the maintenance of a specifically urban–rural fertility difference. There would appear to be several, of which the more important are:

1. The relatively greater difficulty of caring for children in an urban setting where daily access to the out-doors is more likely to depend on the availability of public land, like parks and playgrounds, and private land in the relatively expensive form of one's own garden.

2. The relatively greater costs — whether in terms of money, psychic energy or time — of rearing children in an urban setting; this originating, in part, in the greater fixed costs in urban areas of things like housing, food, transportation and entertainment, and, in part, in the frequently higher levels of aspiration among urban-dwellers with respect to standards of comfort, convenience, self-fulfilment and the care and training of children.

3. The relatively greater economic returns that rural-dwellers, and to a lesser extent other urban-dwellers, can reasonably expect from children — this in consequence not only of the greater possibilities in these areas for children to work or perform chores in the household or family enterprise, but also of the relative absence of parental participation in work-connected retirement schemes.

4. The relatively greater psychic returns from childbearing that rural-dwellers (particularly women) may anticipate because of their greater residential isolation.

5. The relatively greater availability in urban areas of alternatives on which to expend one's money, time, physical and psychic energy: alternative goods and services, and also alternative activities, of a sort likely to conflict with the demands of children and childrearing.

6. The relatively greater availability in urban areas of alternative sources of the satisfactions (e.g. response, intellectual interest, personal fulfilment, creativity, companionship) presumably associated with the bearing and rearing of children — something particularly important with women because of the expectation that mothers will play the major role in childcare and also derive the greatest benefit from association with children.

7. The relatively greater likelihood in rural areas of having higher fertility role models — either one's own parents or one's friends and associates.

The importance of any one of these in determining urban–rural fertility differences is unlikely to have remained the same over successive cohorts. The urban–rural difference in the specifically economic value of children, for example, may have been diminishing — in response to the relative decline in the family farm and small enterprise; while that in the availability of alternative sources of satisfaction may have been increasing — as employment opportunities for women expanded in the metropolitan areas. Moreover, the effect of these on fertility is necessarily through the medium of what people think during the period surrounding conception and early pregnancy (when abortion could be considered a possible alternative). What one thinks at a particular time may bear little resemblance to the facts; nor what one anticipates, to what eventuates. But in the determination of human behaviour this is irrelevant; in this respect it is thinking that makes it so.

Notes

1. There are two reasons for combining nativity with religion at this early stage in the analysis: (1) the close association that exists between the two attributes so far as fertility differences are concerned — an assocation that results in considerable heterogeneity when fertility is analysed by religion/nativity groupings; and (2) the

numerical predominance of the Australian-born within both religions, which is sufficient to render any comparison between total Catholics and total non-Catholics little more than a comparison between Australian-born Catholics and Australian-born non-Catholics.

2. John C. Caldwell and Lado T. Ruzicka, 'The Australian fertility transition: an analysis'. *Population and Development Review*, **4** (1978), p. 91.

3 FERTILITY BY RELIGION AND COUNTRY OF BIRTH

Introduction

Fertility differences by religion and ethnic group are widespread. Either religion and ethnicity are associated with differences in norms relating to contraception and abortion, or they are associated with a population's composition with respect to some attribute — residence or income, for example — that is itself associated with different patterns of fertility. This is particularly true of populations in which fertility is subject to some measure of conscious control, but it is by no means unknown where conscious control over childbearing hardly exists. In a study of Indian villages, for example, Muslim fertility was found invariably to have exceeded Hindu — not because Hindus were restricting their fertility in any conscious way, but because, for religious purposes, they were engaging more in the practices of periodic abstinence and fasting.[1]

Fertility differences by religion extend in Australia over the entire period for which there are any data. These differences have not only persisted, but in some respects increased — and, as it happens, done so in certain directions that would appear to have particular bearing on the question of maintaining harmonious inter-group relations in a pluralistic society. A somewhat similar situation has existed with fertility differences by ethnic group (taking country of birth as the criterion of membership in such groups); only here the duration of the period of analysis is restricted by the fact that there was no non-British immigration to Australia on a large scale until after the second world war.

To be meaningful, at least in the Australian setting, the analysis of fertility differences by either religion or ethnic group needs to be undertaken in terms of both of these attributes simultaneously. Each is too closely associated with the other — religion is too closely associated with national culture and identity — to justify (as long as the form of the data does not require it) aggregating the adherents of one or another into a single entity for comparative purposes. There is a considerable variety of fertility patterns by nativity among both Catholics and non-Catholics in Australia, and, correspondingly, a persistent Catholic:non-Catholic fertility difference within each nativity grouping. Moreover, the Australian-born constitute such a large proportion of the total of both Catholics and non-Catholics (67 and 80 per cent, respectively, among wives 40–64 years of age and married before age 26) that combining nativity groupings within these two religion groupings would inevitably produce aggregates whose fertility differed little from that of their Australian-born components. This would not only lead to a repetition of the findings concerning the Australian-born themselves, but also entail a loss of information on possibly important differences by nativity among groupings of co-religionists.

As already suggested, only two categories of religion are employed in this analysis — Catholic and non-Catholic — each derived from answers to the optional census question on religion. The Catholic category consists of all those who reported themselves as either Catholic or Roman Catholic; the non-Catholic of every-one else, including those who did not reply. The composition of the total population in these two categories in 1971 was as follows:

	Per Cent of Population	
Catholic		27
Non-Catholic Christian		
Church of England		31
Methodist		9
Presbyterian		8
Greek Orthodox		3
Lutheran		2
Baptist		1
Other Protestant		6
Total		60
Other (Jewish, Moslem, other religion)		1
No religion or no reply		13
Non-Catholic Total	74	
Total	101	

With respect to nativity, the analysis relates to wives born in Australia and the six overseas countries whence came the highest proportion of the foreign-born population recorded in the census of 1971: British Isles (including Ireland), Italy, the Netherlands, Greece, Germany and Yugoslavia, representing, all together, 95 per cent of the total population of wives aged 40–64 and married before age 26.

For present purposes, it was assumed that all the Italian-born were Catholic and all the Greek-born non-Catholic: not an unreasonable assumption, given that in both of these groupings over 95 per cent of those answering the question on religion so reported themselves in each of the three censuses of 1966, 1971 and 1976. The distribution of the study population by country of birth and religion (assumed religion in the case of the Italian- and Greek-born) in 1971 was as follows:

Wives 40–64 Years of Age and Married Before Age 26, by Religion and Nativity (Australia, 1971)

Country of Birth	N		Percentage	
	Catholic	Non-Catholic	Catholic	Non-Catholic
Australia	118 962	465 540	20	80
British Isles	8 406	71 624	11	89
Italy	23 117	—	100	—
Netherlands	3 014	5 285	36	64
Greece	—	6 384	—	100
Germany	2 369	6 093	28	72
Yugoslavia	3 139	2 012	61	39
Other	19 866	24 124	45	55
Total	178 873	581 052	24	76

Findings

General

In a single generation of childbearing, that involving the cohorts of 1907 to 1931, there occurred a marked change in the pattern of Australian fertility differences by country of birth. The relative positions of all but the Dutch- and German-born were reversed; and while the Dutch-born still had the most children among those in the youngest cohort under consideration, the differences between them and the Australian-born had markedly narrowed (see Table 3.1). The fertility of the next lower age grouping (those 35–9, and therefore not quite of completed childbearing in 1971) suggests, in fact, that the Australian-born were in process of

Table 3.1: Relative Levels of Median Issue Born to Current Marriage, by Religion and Nativity (Australian-born = 100). Wives 40–64 Years of Age who Commenced Current Marriage before Age 26, by Year of Birth and Age at Marriage (Australia, 1971)

Religion, Age at Marriage and Year of Birth	Country of Birth						
	Australia	British Isles	Italy	Netherlands	Greece	Germany	Yugoslavia
Catholic							
< 20							
1907–11	100	122	124	—	*	—	—
1912–16	100	97	102	—	*	—	81
1917–21	100	100	92	—	*	—	82
1922–26	100	103	84	—	*	—	76
1927–31	100	102	76	99	*	64	64
20–1							
1907–11	100	103	126	—	*	—	—
1912–16	100	100	105	—	*	—	—
1917–21	100	95	96	146	*	—	—
1922–26	100	104	82	139	*	68	64
1927–31	100	93	72	102	*	63	63
22–5							
1907–11	100	99	111	209	*	—	—
1912–16	100	97	104	173	*	—	93
1917–21	100	105	88	160	*	73	68
1922–26	100	97	74	120	*	61	58
1927–31	100	90	65	101	*	56	58
Non-Catholic							
< 20							
1907–11	100	94	*	—	115	—	—
1912–16	100	91	*	—	116	—	—
1917–21	100	90	*	110	109	86	—
1922–26	100	93	*	119	96	80	87
1927–31	100	92	*	110	79	70	77
20–1							
1907–11	100	90	*	—	136	—	—
1912–16	100	94	*	132	135	—	—
1917–21	100	89	*	129	113	90	—
1922–26	100	93	*	125	94	86	92
1927–31	100	92	*	106	78	72	76
22–5							
1907–11	100	94	*	151	152	88	—
1912–16	100	92	*	148	141	88	—
1917–21	100	94	*	128	113	89	—
1922–26	100	91	*	113	92	73	83
1927–31	100	90	*	107	78	70	75

(—) N < 100
* Not Applicable
Note:
Median issue indices calculated on the basis of figures carried out to two decimal places.

displacing the Dutch-born as the highest fertility grouping of the seven considered.

How much of this change in the pattern of group differences emanated from actual changes in fertility behaviour, and how much from changes in the socioeconomic composition of the nativity groupings themselves, must remain something of a moot point for all but the Australian-born. But we can say with some assurance that among the Australian-born these changes proceeded little if at all from the incorporation within them of higher fertility women of foreign parentage. Not only were such women only a small proportion of the Australian-born total, but the fertility patterns of their foreign-born counterparts suggest that, if anything, the effect of adding their fertility to that of the Australian-born as a whole would have been in quite the opposite direction.

Nor can these changes in patterns of fertility be attributed to changes in age at marriage; for much the same pattern of fertility differences found among the total of women who married before age 26 is found as well within more restricted age at marriage categories: below 20, 20–1 and 22–5; and even within single years of marriage age (where cell frequencies are large enough to permit this further comparison).

What occurred is this: median issue among the Australian-born reached its lowest point with those wives born in the first decade of the twentieth century, after which it rose slightly — by about a sixth altogether. Much the same thing, although at a slightly lower overall fertility level, took place among the British-born. But with those born elsewhere it was different: median issue among the German-born fluctuated slightly, but continued at a lower level than that for any other nativity grouping; while among the Italian-, Greek-, Yugoslav- and Dutch-born it continued to decline — by about a fifth in the case of the Dutch-born, and by about a third with each of the other three.

So far as distribution by issue is concerned, the period was characterised by two dominant movements: away from the higher parities and toward the middle range ones. In each of the seven nativity groupings, the proportion childless tended to fluctuate around 5 per cent, while the proportion bearing one child only seems always to have been comparatively low — seldom exceeding 15 per cent overall (except among the German-born). At the other extreme, the proportions bearing five or more children (and particularly six or more) dropped considerably — and did so through-

Table 3.2: Percentages with Specified Issue Born to Current Marriage, by Religion and Nativity. Wives 40–64 Years of Age who Commenced Current Marriage before Age 26, by Year of Birth (Australia, 1971)

Issue	Year of Birth	Catholic						Non-Catholic					
		Australia	British Isles	Italy	Netherlands	Germany	Yugoslavia	Australia	British Isles	Greece	Netherlands	Germany	Yugoslavia
0	1907–11	5	3	3	2	—	4	5	4	3	2	7	2
	1912–16	5	2	3	1	2	4	5	4	2	2	4	6
	1917–21	4	3	2	2	4	8	4	4	1	2	5	4
	1922–26	3	3	3	3	9	6	3	4	3	3	8	6
	1927–31	3	2	3	2	7	5	3	3	2	3	8	5
1	1907–11	12	10	6	2	—	9	14	16	4	9	21	9
	1912–16	11	9	6	2	19	14	12	15	5	6	18	9
	1917–21	10	8	7	4	14	13	11	14	5	7	17	16
	1922–26	8	8	9	5	17	16	10	12	6	8	20	12
	1927–31	6	8	9	6	17	13	7	9	7	6	17	12
5	1907–11	10	10	10	14	—	9	7	6	13	11	6	13
	1912–16	10	10	13	14	3	7	7	6	14	14	7	11
	1917–21	11	11	13	14	8	6	7	7	13	10	7	7
	1922–26	12	12	9	14	4	6	8	8	10	10	5	8
	1927–31	13	12	8	12	6	6	9	8	5	10	5	6
6+	1907–11	17	17	31	51	—	18	8	7	20	18	10	25
	1912–16	16	14	22	43	15	9	8	6	18	19	9	11
	1917–21	17	16	16	37	12	10	8	6	16	17	7	10
	1922–26	18	17	11	29	5	5	8	7	10	15	5	4
	1927–31	20	16	8	19	7	4	8	7	4	11	5	3
N	1907–11	9 557	710	1 923	171	52	203	41 513	8 082	518	390	270	132
	1912–16	15 628	926	2 855	365	106	317	68 965	10 190	761	744	445	189
	1917–21	23 473	1 657	3 127	585	198	326	94 710	14 682	813	1 139	713	237
	1922–26	31 388	2 396	6 612	734	920	908	123 151	19 112	1 537	1 359	2 029	625
	1927–31	38 916	2 717	8 600	1 159	1 093	1 385	137 201	19 558	2 755	1 653	2 636	829

out the period — with one exception, the Australian-born, where the decline gave way to a levelling-off in most sectors and, in the case of Catholics, to an actual increase (see Table 3.2).

Religion

The fertility differences between Catholics and non-Catholics deserve special mention, in part because of the numerical importance of the Catholic minority in the Australian population (27 per cent of the total in 1971), and in part because Australian experience is somewhat at variance with that reported for other countries.

While a Catholic:non-Catholic fertility differential in favour of Catholics appears to have been all but universal within European populations this century,[2] present indications — on the basis of data that, for the most part, lack the comprehensiveness and detail (particularly respecting age at marriage) of those at our disposal here — suggest that this differential may be narrowing and even in some places disappearing.[3] But in Australia, the Catholic:non-Catholic differences, far from disappearing, persisted throughout the period under consideration. Among the various nativity groupings (excluding the Italian- and Greek-born on account of their religious homogeneity) Catholic fertility was consistently higher than non-Catholic (see Table 3.3). In fact, in whatever detail they can be compared (that is, on the basis of cross-tabulation by nativity, urban–rural residence, schooling and husband's occupation — holding age and age at marriage constant) Catholic fertility nearly always exceeded non-Catholic, whether in terms of median issue or in terms of the proportions at the highest parities. The only exception was with the Yugoslav-born, among whom the fertility of the mostly Croatian Catholics was essentially the same as (or slightly lower than) that of the mostly Serbian and Macedonian non-Catholics. (In terms of literacy, infant mortality and employment in agriculture, for example, Croatia was the more 'developed' area.[4]) Yet even here, disaggregation reveals a consistent Catholic excess at the highest parities and a reduced difference — and in some instances a reversal of direction — at the median.

Not only did this Catholic:non-Catholic difference persist, but it did so at a generally consistent level. Only among the Dutch-born was there any notable diminution with successive cohorts. Among the Australian-born, the difference actually increased at the highest parities.

However measured, whether in terms of central tendency or

Table 3.3: Catholic:Non-Catholic Ratio (Non-Catholic = 100) for Median Issue and Percentage with 5+ Issue Born to Current Marriage, by Nativity. Wives 40–64 Years of Age who Commenced Current Marriage Before Age 26, by Year of Birth (Australia, 1971)

Year of Birth	Country of Birth						
	Australia	British Isles	Italy	Netherlands	Greece	Germany	Yugoslavia
				Median Issue Ratio			
1907–11	122	137	*	178	*	—	79
1912–16	123	132	*	150	*	117	100
1917–21	124	130	*	150	*	99	96
1922–26	121	134	*	134	*	105	89
1927–31	126	126	*	119	*	107	99
				Per Cent with 5+ Issue Ratio			
1907–11	159	208	*	224	*	—	71
1912–16	171	196	*	176	*	112	74
1917–21	181	211	*	190	*	145	96
1922–26	193	206	*	170	*	88	101
1927–31	197	198	*	148	*	82	113

(–) N < 20

* Not Applicable

Note:
Median issue and per cent with 5+ issue ratios calculated on the basis of figures carried out to two decimal places and one decimal place, respectively.

distribution, the extent of this Catholic:non-Catholic difference tended to be least among the German-born and greatest among the British-born — except in the earliest cohorts where it was greatest among the Dutch-born. The change in the relative position of the Dutch-born can be attributed to the marked decline among them in the Catholic:non-Catholic fertility difference overall. But the continuation of a relatively greater difference among the British-born probably derives largely from the fact that the great majority of British-born Catholics are Irish — either Irish-born themselves or English-, Scottish- or Welsh-born of Irish parentage — and for that reason possibly separated from the non-Catholics in their nativity grouping by somewhat greater social and cultural differences than those characterising Catholics born elsewhere.

Residence

Small cell frequencies preclude any very extensive comparisons among nativity/religion groupings along the urban–rural dimension of residence — so few of the overseas-born having resided outside the metropolitan areas. But to the extent that such comparisons are possible (among the British- and Italian-born, and very partially among the Dutch- and German-born), they show a continuation of approximately the same degree of other urban: metropolitan and rural:metropolitan fertility differences throughout the period. In this the overseas-born are but repeating the pattern of the Australian-born. Just as fertility differences based on religion continued relatively undiminished in Australia, so also did those based on urban:rural residence — among both the Australian-born and the overseas-born, whether Catholic or non-Catholic (see Table 3.4).

Husband's Occupation

Small cell frequencies also restrict comparison among nativity groupings on the basis of husband's occupation, the overseas-born being so heavily concentrated in the two very general categories of (1) tradesmen, labourers and production process workers, and (2) all others. However, to the extent such comparisons can be made, they reveal a pattern similar to that already observed.

Among Catholics, in terms of both median issue and proportions at the higher parities, the fertility of the Australian-born in the various occupational groupings was exceeded only by that of the Dutch- and Italian-born; and in the case of the latter, only in the earlier cohorts and in the two categories (1) tradesmen, labourers, and production process workers and (2) all others. Elsewhere, where cell frequencies are high enough to permit comparison (that is, in the administrative, clerical and sales, farmers, and transport and communications categories), the fertility of the Italian-born was consistently lower. Moreover, while the excess among the Dutch-born had all but disappeared by the end of the period, that among the Italian-born in those two categories in which their fertility was higher than the Australian-born at the beginning of the period (namely, tradesmen, etc. and all others) had not only disappeared by the middle of the period but been replaced by successively lower fertility thereafter. Between the Australian-born and the other nativity groupings, the fertility differences increased

Table 3.4: Median Issue and Percentage with 5+ Issue Born to Current Marriage, by Religion and Activity: Metropolitan Values and Relative Levels of Other Values (Metropolitan = 100). Wives 40–64 Years of Age who Commenced Current Marriage Before Age 26, by Year of Birth and Residence (Australia, 1971)

Country and Year of Birth	Median Issue						Per Cent with 5+ Issue					
	Catholic			Non-Catholic			Catholic			Non-Catholic		
	Metropolitan Median	Index Other Urban	Index Rural	Metropolitan Median	Index Other Urban	Index Rural	Metropolitan Per Cent	Index Other Urban	Index Rural	Metropolitan Per Cent	Index Other Urban	Index Rural
Australia												
1907–11	2.33	125	145	1.88	126	145	21	150	193	12	183	234
1912–16	2.39	124	139	1.93	123	140	21	160	187	11	191	238
1917–21	2.51	119	136	1.98	121	139	22	146	180	11	179	240
1922–26	2.67	119	135	2.11	118	136	26	138	170	11	178	229
1927–31	2.85	115	131	2.29	114	130	29	129	160	12	166	216
British Isles												
1907–11	2.54	117	–	1.87	110	125	25	137	–	10	161	209
1912–16	2.55	99	–	1.90	109	124	23	118	–	11	142	172
1917–21	2.68	112	112	1.96	112	120	27	115	123	12	142	165
1922–26	2.85	105	108	2.07	116	123	28	122	125	13	150	173
1927–31	2.80	113	125	2.21	116	115	27	133	162	14	138	139
Italy												
1907–11	3.57	75	93	*	*	*	43	69	88	*	*	*
1912–16	3.14	89	104	*	*	*	35	85	105	*	*	*
1917–21	2.80	100	107	*	*	*	27	108	118	*	*	*
1922–26	2.41	114	122	*	*	*	19	134	146	*	*	*
1927–31	2.18	119	128	*	*	*	14	136	169	*	*	*

Table 3.4 (continued)

Country and Year of Birth	Median Issue — Catholic			Median Issue — Non-Catholic			Per Cent with 5+ Issue — Catholic			Per Cent with 5+ Issue — Non-Catholic		
	Metropolitan Median	Index Other Urban	Index Rural	Metropolitan Median	Index Other Urban	Index Rural	Metropolitan Per Cent	Index Other Urban	Index Rural	Metropolitan Per Cent	Index Other Urban	Index Rural
Netherlands												
1907–11	4.74	—	—	2.80	—	—	62	—	—	30	—	—
1912–16	4.31	—	—	2.98	97	—	55	—	—	32	92	—
1917–21	3.67	129	—	2.66	109	105	44	143	—	27	97	104
1922–26	3.37	122	—	2.52	118	127	39	131	—	22	146	168
1927–31	2.93	117	128	2.54	109	113	28	131	160	20	109	157
Greece												
1907–11	*	*	*	3.26	—	—	*	*	*	33	—	—
1912–16	*	*	*	2.97	—	—	*	*	*	32	—	—
1917–21	*	*	*	2.97	—	—	*	*	*	29	—	—
1922–26	*	*	*	2.52	—	—	*	*	*	18	—	—
1927–31	*	*	*	2.15	117	132	*	*	*	8	227	199
Germany												
1907–11	—	—	—	1.68	—	—	—	—	—	14	—	—
1912–16	—	—	—	1.82	—	—	—	—	—	15	—	—
1917–21	1.85	119	—	1.86	117	—	17	144	—	12	104	—
1922–26	1.73	145	—	1.64	135	135	9	251	—	8	206	240
1927–31	1.77			1.67	137	125	10			9	185	193
Yugoslavia												
1907–11	2.56	—	—	3.40	—	—	28	—	—	41	—	—
1912–16	2.25	—	—	2.45	—	—	16	—	—	24	—	—
1917–21	1.99	—	—	2.27	—	—	15	—	—	17	—	—
1922–26	1.73	—	—	1.98	—	—	9	—	—	10	—	—
1927–31	1.82	—	133	1.89	—	—	9	—	123	9	—	—

(—) N< 100   * Not Applicable

Note: Median issue and per cent with 5+ issue indices calculated on the basis of figures carried to two decimal places and one decimal place respectively.

Table 3.5: Median Issue and Percentage with 5+ Issue Born to Current Marriage, by Religion, Nativity and Husband's Occupation. Values for Australian-born and Relative Values for Overseas-born (Australian-born = 100). Wives 40–64 Years of Age who Commenced Current Marriage Before Age 26, By Year of Birth (Australia, 1971).

Husband's Occupation and Year of Birth	Catholic Index							Non-Catholic Index						
	Australia	British Isles	Italy	Netherlands	Greece	Germany	Yugoslavia	Australia	British Isles	Italy	Netherlands	Greece	Germany	Yugoslavia
Professional														
1907–11	2.52	—	—	—	•	—	—	1.87	96	•	—	—	—	—
1912–16	2.72	—	—	—	•	—	—	2.05	92	•	—	—	—	—
1917–21	3.05	—	—	—	•	—	—	2.11	94	•	—	—	—	—
1922–26	3.25	98	84	—	•	—	—	2.28	92	•	92	—	73	—
1927–31	3.62	87	79	—	•	—	—	2.48	92	•	—	—	67	—
Administrative														
1907–11	2.46	—	—	—	•	—	—	1.91	95	•	—	—	—	—
1912–16	2.39	—	—	—	•	—	—	1.95	91	•	—	—	—	—
1917–21	2.61	111	—	—	•	—	—	2.02	92	•	—	—	—	—
1922–26	2.86	98	88	—	•	—	—	2.16	93	•	123	120	75	—
1927–31	3.06	88	76	104	•	—	—	2.33	90	•	106	101	80	—
Clerical/Sales														
1907–11	2.27	—	—	—	•	—	—	1.77	95	•	—	—	—	—
1912–16	2.50	92	—	—	•	—	—	1.86	93	•	—	—	—	—
1917–21	2.47	94	—	—	•	—	—	1.91	97	•	—	—	—	—
1922–26	2.75	96	88	—	•	—	—	2.03	97	•	121	—	68	—
1927–31	2.97	90	76	—	•	—	—	2.20	97	•	102	100	73	—
Farmers														
1907–11	3.26	—	94	—	•	—	—	2.72	90	•	—	—	—	—
1912–16	3.41	—	93	—	•	—	—	2.69	93	•	—	—	—	—
1917–21	3.49	—	86	—	•	—	—	2.72	93	•	—	—	—	—
1922–26	3.57	—	83	—	•	—	—	2.83	99	•	—	—	—	—
1927–31	3.83	—	72	—	•	—	—	2.97	92	•	—	91	—	—

Table 3.5 (continued)

Husband's Occupation and Year of Birth	Catholic — Index: Australia (Median Issue)	British Isles	Italy	Netherlands	Greece	Germany	Yugoslavia	Non-Catholic — Index: Australia (Median Issue)	British Isles	Italy	Netherlands	Greece	Germany	Yugoslavia
Transport/Communication														
1907–11	2.54	—	—	—	•	—	—	2.13	96	•	—	—	—	—
1912–16	2.67	—	—	—	•	—	—	2.16	93	•	—	—	—	—
1917–21	2.66	—	—	—	•	—	—	2.27	88	•	—	—	—	—
1922–26	2.78	113	85	—	•	—	—	2.38	90	•	—	—	—	—
1927–31	2.97	96	75	—	•	66	—	2.55	94	•	—	—	66	—
Tradesmen, labourers, prod. proc. workers														
1907–11	2.49	101	143	—	•	—	—	2.11	92	•	129	—	—	—
1912–16	2.55	102	126	160	•	—	100	2.13	92	•	132	141	104	—
1917–21	2.61	105	108	151	•	86	82	2.15	95	•	129	141	98	104
1922–26	2.75	103	88	132	•	67	65	2.29	96	•	115	115	79	93
1927–31	2.92	97	75	107	•	66	62	2.43	94	•	112	88	72	80
Others														
1907–11	2.63	105	133	—	•	—	98	2.14	91	•	140	155	81	—
1912–16	2.64	101	116	—	•	—	88	2.19	94	•	151	141	—	—
1917–21	2.72	99	103	148	•	—	—	2.26	93	•	117	133	93	—
1922–26	2.87	107	88	127	•	63	67	2.38	94	•	120	109	76	88
1927–31	3.06	102	78	101	•	68	73	2.55	94	•	108	85	80	71
Percentage with 5+ Issue														
Professional														
1907–11	27	—	—	—	•	—	—	7	135	•	—	—	—	—
1912–16	29	—	—	—	•	—	—	9	99	•	—	—	—	—
1917–21	34	—	—	—	•	—	—	9	97	•	—	—	—	—
1922–26	36	89	—	—	•	—	—	11	106	•	148	—	46	—
1927–31	42	74	—	—	•	—	—	11	96	•	—	—	43	—

Table 3.5 (continued)

Percentage with 5+ Issue

Husband's Occupation and Year of Birth	Catholic Index							Non-Catholic Index						
	Australia	British Isles	Italy	Netherlands	Greece	Germany	Yugoslavia	Australia	British Isles	Italy	Netherlands	Greece	Germany	Yugoslavia
Administrative														
1907–11	24	—	—	—	•	—	—	9	86	•	—	—	—	—
1912–16	24	—	—	—	•	—	—	8	74	•	—	—	—	—
1917–21	29	130	—	—	•	—	—	8	96	•	—	—	—	—
1922–26	28	90	62	—	•	—	—	9	98	•	246	211	61	—
1927–31	31	85	50	114	•	—	—	11	96	•	139	101	64	—
Clerical/Sales														
1907–11	19	—	—	—	•	—	—	8	86	•	—	—	—	—
1912–16	22	89	—	—	•	—	—	8	100	•	—	—	—	—
1917–21	23	93	—	—	•	—	—	8	116	•	—	—	—	—
1922–26	27	93	54	—	•	—	—	9	123	•	211	—	48	—
1927–31	30	80	52	—	•	—	—	11	94	•	188	68	66	—
Farmers														
1907–11	38	—	90	—	•	—	—	25	81	•	—	—	—	—
1912–16	40	—	90	—	•	—	—	23	82	•	—	—	—	—
1917–21	41	—	85	—	•	—	—	23	97	•	—	—	—	—
1922–26	43	—	63	—	•	—	—	24	115	•	—	—	—	—
1927–31	47	—	46	—	•	—	—	25	83	•	—	63	—	—
Transport/ Communication														
1907–11	24	—	—	—	•	—	—	17	73	•	—	—	—	—
1912–16	26	—	—	—	•	—	—	15	71	•	—	—	—	—
1917–21	26	—	—	—	•	—	—	17	84	•	—	—	—	—
1922–26	29	102	54	—	•	—	—	18	88	•	—	—	—	—
1927–31	31	96	37	—	•	—	—	20	86	•	—	—	56	—

Table 3.5 (continued)

Percentage with 5+ Issue

Husband's Occupation and Year of Birth	Catholic Index							Non-Catholic Index						
	Australia	British Isles	Italy	Netherlands	Greece	Germany	Yugoslavia	Australia	British Isles	Italy	Netherlands	Greece	Germany	Yugoslavia
Tradesmen, labourers, prod. proc. workers														
1907–11	24	98	174	—	*	—	—	16	82	*	150	—	—	—
1912–16	24	110	151	215	*	—	97	15	82	*	202	211	124	—
1917–21	25	109	109	198	*	93	55	15	90	*	174	199	103	110
1922–26	28	104	68	155	*	37	39	16	96	*	162	138	77	72
1927–31	30	95	47	103	*	46	29	18	92	*	127	47	66	52
Others														
1907–11	28	108	154	—	*	—	110	18	78	*	184	185	110	—
1912–16	27	81	125	—	*	—	44	18	83	*	192	189	—	—
1917–21	29	92	102	177	*	—	—	18	103	*	163	170	84	—
1922–26	31	110	70	141	*	31	44	20	83	*	137	195	69	55
1927–31	33	102	54	94	*	52	42	21	82	*	105	53	62	32

(—) < 100

* Not Applicable

Note: Median issue and per cent with 5+ issue indices calculated on the basis of figures carried out to two decimal places and one decimal place, respectively.

— as the fertility of the Australian-born rose with successive cohorts, and that of the others either continued to decline or rose to a lesser extent. Particularly interesting in this respect is the growing gap within the professional and administrative categories between the Australian- and British-born (the only two groupings with large enough Ns to permit much assurance concerning such a comparison): the result of a marked increase in the fertility of the Australian-born.

Among non-Catholics there was no such expansion of the Australian:British-born difference, whether in these two occupational categories or any other, for each experienced about the same increase as did the other. But in other respects, the pattern of changes among non-Catholics was much the same as that among Catholics: only the Dutch- and Greek-born had higher fertility than the Australian-born, and, as among Catholics, the Dutch-born excess had all but disappeared by the end of the period, while the fertility of the Greek-born (like that of the Italian-born among the Catholics) had dropped to a point below that of the Australian-born. Similarly, with the other nativity groupings, the Australian: non-Australian-born difference either remained unchanged or else expanded as the fertility of the Australian-born rose while that of the others remained about the same or rose less far (see Table 3.5).

With respect to Catholic:non-Catholic differences within these occupational categories, there was a notable degree of stability. Only among the Dutch-born, and to a lesser extent certain occupational groupings among the British-born, was there any narrowing of the difference — whether the measure of fertility is the median or the proportion with five or more issue.

However, analysis in terms of the proportion with six or more (rather than five or more) reveals a somewhat different association, at least so far as the Australian-born are concerned. Here there was a growing, rather than a stable, Catholic:non-Catholic difference, particularly among wives who married at age 20 or above and whose husbands were in either the white-collar occupations or farming. However, with those born elsewhere there was no such change. A comparison as detailed as this is impossible with most of the overseas-born, but among those for whom it can be undertaken, the result is a pattern little different from that already noted on the basis of the proportion with five or more issue among wives married at the sum of ages below 26.

Here again, then, it is the fertility pattern of the Australian-born that is 'deviant'; its deviancy in this instance lying not only in higher fertility overall, but in the particular increase in fertility among Catholic wives with husbands in white-collar occupations. In fact, by the end of this period, among those marrying before age 26, both median issue and the proportion in the highest parities tended to vary *directly* with age at marriage among Australian-born Catholics whose husbands were in the professions — and to come very close to doing so among their counterparts with husbands in the other white-collar occupations; all of which is in sharp contrast to the pattern of association between fertility and age at marriage within every other category of the population, Catholic or non-Catholic. Moreover while, by the end of the period, the highest median fertility (3.86) was to be found among Australian-born Catholic farmers' wives who had married either before age 20 or at ages 22–5, a close second to these women (median: 3.74) was run by their Australian-born Catholic counterparts among wives married at ages 22–5 whose husbands were in the professions (see Table 3.6). The latter also ran these farmers' wives a close second with respect to the proportion who had borne six or more children (27 per cent *vs.* 33 per cent).

Turning to comparisons within the various nativity categories, we find that fertility differences between occupational groupings generally tended to narrow, in consequence of the fertility of wives of white-collar workers rising rather markedly, and that of wives of husbands in the non-white-collar categories either rising less or remaining about the same. But a more detailed analysis on this point is hampered by the small cell frequencies and the occupational concentration of the overseas-born in the tradesmen, etc. and all others categories. A decline in fertility differences between occupations can be discerned among the Australian-born (although more among non-Catholics than Catholics), and also to some extent among the British-born. But beyond this it is possible to note little more than the fact that whatever the differences at the end of the period, they tended to be slight. This probably represents a change with the past, but whether it does is not something that can be documented by the data available here.

In sum, what stands out in the pattern of fertility differences by husband's occupation among nativity/religion groupings is: (1) the marked increase in fertility among the Australian-born in all occupational categories, but particularly in the white-collar occupations; (2) the persistence over the period of Catholic:non-

Table 3.6: Median Issue and Percentage with 5+ Issue Born to Current Marriage, by Religion and Husband's Occupation, together with Catholic:Non-Catholic Ratio (Non-Catholic = 100). Australian-born Wives 40–64 Years of Age who Commenced Current Marriage Before Age 26, by Year of Birth and Age at Marriage (Australia, 1971)

Age at Marriage, Husband's Occupation, and Year of Birth	Median Issue			Per Cent with 5+ Issue		
	Catholic	Non-Catholic	Ratio	Catholic	Non-Catholic	Ratio
< 20						
Professional						
1907–11	—	—	—	—	—	—
1912–16	—	2.29	—	—	13	—
1917–21	—	2.32	—	—	15	—
1922–26	2.81	2.37	119	30	14	215
1927–31	2.85	2.66	107	32	18	174
Administrative						
1907–11	—	2.17	—	—	16	—
1912–16	2.44	2.39	102	24	21	116
1917–21	2.58	2.33	111	25	17	141
1922–26	2.97	2.39	124	31	14	221
1927–31	3.00	2.56	117	31	18	175
Clerical/Sales						
1907–11	2.12	2.26	94	24	18	134
1912–16	2.71	2.27	119	28	16	179
1917–21	2.69	2.34	115	26	18	148
1922–26	2.75	2.31	119	28	17	170
1927–31	2.96	2.46	120	30	16	187
Farmers						
1907–11	3.64	3.50	104	45	42	107
1912–16	3.87	3.33	116	48	38	127
1917–21	3.82	3.19	120	47	34	135
1922–26	3.53	3.27	108	43	36	121
1927–31	3.86	3.38	114	48	37	131
Transport/Communication						
1907–11	—	2.39	—	—	21	—
1912–16	2.99	2.71	110	34	29	118
1917–21	2.94	2.82	104	33	31	109
1922–26	3.05	2.82	108	35	28	124
1927–31	3.18	2.96	107	36	29	124

Table 3.6 (continued)

Age at Marriage, Husband's Occupation, and Year of Birth	Median Issue			Per Cent with 5+ Issue		
	Catholic	Non-Catholic	Ratio	Catholic	Non-Catholic	Ratio
< 20						
Tradesmen, labourers, prod. proc. workers						
1907–11	2.86	2.66	108	28	26	107
1912–16	2.97	2.81	106	32	28	114
1917–21	3.16	2.77	114	33	27	121
1922–26	2.96	2.69	110	33	24	136
1927–31	3.23	2.84	114	36	27	131
Others						
1907–11	3.10	2.76	112	36	30	122
1912–16	3.14	2.84	111	37	31	120
1917–21	3.30	2.97	111	37	32	116
1922–26	3.38	2.83	119	39	30	133
1927–31	3.31	3.01	110	38	32	119
20–1						
Professional						
1907–11	—	2.14	—	—	9	—
1912–16	—	2.16	—	—	13	—
1917–21	3.00	2.10	143	34	10	331
1922–26	2.99	2.27	132	36	11	318
1927–31	3.54	2.47	143	40	12	348
Administrative						
1907–11	—	2.07	—	—	14	—
1912–16	2.39	2.02	118	21	10	199
1917–21	2.68	2.11	127	24	10	247
1922–26	2.76	2.22	124	27	11	242
1927–31	3.07	2.37	130	30	11	269
Clerical Sales						
1907–11	2.40	1.86	129	21	10	205
1912–16	2.58	2.00	129	22	13	172
1917–21	2.59	2.04	127	24	11	228
1922–26	2.66	2.08	128	25	9	275
1927–31	2.94	2.27	130	30	12	252
Farmers						
1907–11	3.25	2.88	113	39	31	126
1912–16	3.24	2.89	112	38	28	136
1917–21	3.60	2.87	125	43	26	163
1922–26	3.50	2.89	121	41	26	158
1927–31	3.76	3.00	125	45	25	180

Table 3.6 (continued)

Age at Marriage, Husband's Occupation, and Year of Birth	Median Issue			Per Cent with 5+ Issue		
	Catholic	Non-Catholic	Ratio	Catholic	Non-Catholic	Ratio
20−1						
Transport/Communication						
1907−11	—	2.38	—	—	21	—
1912−16	2.97	2.41	123	34	17	204
1917−21	2.80	2.38	118	28	19	149
1922−26	2.74	2.44	112	27	18	153
1927−31	2.99	2.55	117	31	19	165
Tradesmen, labourers, prod. proc. workers						
1907−11	2.71	2.37	114	27	20	140
1912−16	2.65	2.33	114	27	19	141
1917−21	2.61	2.28	114	26	17	155
1922−26	2.79	2.35	119	29	17	170
1927−31	2.91	2.43	120	30	17	181
Others						
1907−11	2.71	2.27	119	28	20	140
1912−16	2.68	2.34	115	29	20	140
1917−21	2.75	2.34	118	28	19	144
1922−26	2.87	2.44	118	32	20	154
1927−31	3.07	2.55	120	34	20	172
22−5						
Professional						
1907−11	2.62	1.80	146	27	6	489
1912−16	2.73	2.01	136	29	8	376
1917−21	2.98	2.09	143	33	9	388.
1922−26	3.40	2.27	150	37	10	370
1927−31	3.74	2.46	152	44	10	453
Administrative						
1907−11	2.47	1.84	134	22	7	307
1912−16	2.38	1.90	125	20	6	313
1917−21	2.59	1.96	132	24	7	352
1922−26	2.89	2.09	138	28	8	376
1927−31	3.06	2.25	136	30	8	390
Clerical/Sales						
1907−11	2.26	1.68	135	18	6	285
1912−16	2.45	1.78	138	20	6	344
1917−21	2.40	1.83	131	21	6	346
1922−26	2.79	1.95	143	27	8	355
1927−31	3.00	2.07	145	30	8	387

Table 3.6 (continued)

Age at Marriage, Husband's Occupation, and Year of Birth	Median Issue			Per Cent with 5+ Issue		
	Catholic	Non-Catholic	Ratio	Catholic	Non-Catholic	Ratio
22–5						
Farmers						
1907–11	3.14	2.53	124	36	19	185
1912–16	3.38	2.51	135	39	18	214
1917–21	3.34	2.55	131	37	18	205
1922–26	3.62	2.69	135	43	20	220
1927–31	3.86	2.78	139	48	19	247
Transport/Communication						
1907–11	2.39	1.96	122	22	14	165
1912–16	2.43	1.92	127	19	10	187
1917–21	2.50	2.01	124	22	12	189
1922–26	2.70	2.16	125	27	14	201
1927–31	2.82	2.29	123	28	14	199
Tradesmen, labourers, prod. proc. workers						
1907–11	2.27	1.88	121	21	11	193
1912–16	2.38	1.90	125	20	10	197
1917–21	2.44	1.92	127	21	11	203
1922–26	2.63	2.08	126	26	12	215
1927–31	2.78	2.21	126	26	12	216
Others						
1907–11	2.36	1.84	128	23	12	197
1912–16	2.43	1.92	127	23	12	185
1917–21	2.51	1.97	127	25	12	202
1922–26	2.68	2.12	126	27	15	180
1927–31	2.93	2.30	127	30	15	203

(−) N < 100

Note:
Median issue and per cent with 5+ indices calculated on the basis of figures carried out to two decimal places and one decimal place, respectively.

Catholic differences at an essentially stable level within each nativity/occupational grouping, except for an expanding difference at the highest parities (six and over) among the Australian-born (particularly those in the white-collar occupations); (3) the persistence of differences by nativity, but with the pattern of these differences undergoing considerable change both in direction and

Table 3.7: Median Issue and Percentage with 5+ Issue Born to Current Marriage, by Religion, Nativity, and Years of Schooling. Values for Australian-born and Relative Values for Overseas-born (Australian-born = 100). Wives 40–64 Years of Age who Commenced Current Marriage Before Age 26, by Year of Birth (Australia, 1971)

Religion, Years of Schooling and Year of Birth	Median Issue							Percent with 5+ Issue						
		Index							Index					
	Australia	British Isles	Italy	Netherlands	Greece	Germany	Yugoslavia	Australia	British Isles	Italy	Netherlands	Greece	Germany	Yugoslavia
Catholic														
<6														
1907–11	2.66	100	123	—	•	—	99	28	96	136	—	•	—	98
1912–16	2.63	96	115	175	•	—	96	27	98	118	211	•	—	66
1917–21	2.66	103	106	145	•	—	82	27	100	103	180	•	—	69
1922–26	2.80	107	89	126	•	60	66	30	110	67	138	•	28	38
1927–31	3.02	102	77	103	•	62	64	32	105	47	97	•	32	32
6–7														
1907–11	2.58	103	—	—	•	—	—	28	91	—	—	•	—	—
1912–16	2.68	104	101	—	•	—	—	27	103	109	—	•	—	—
1917–21	2.70	106	90	164	•	—	—	27	102	66	212	•	—	—
1922–26	2.79	104	83	144	•	69	67	29	106	53	176	•	37	24
1927–31	2.93	100	73	108	•	70	59	30	105	43	114	•	52	33
8														
1907–11	2.61	—	—	—	•	—	—	26	—	—	—	•	—	—
1912–16	2.66	94	—	—	•	—	—	25	76	—	—	•	—	—
1917–21	2.71	108	84	—	•	—	—	27	126	77	—	•	—	—
1922–26	2.86	102	76	—	•	65	—	30	96	49	—	•	34	—
1927–31	3.07	95	61	96	•	55	61	32	91	28	86	•	39	24
9+														
1907–11	2.40	108	—	—	•	—	—	22	132	—	—	•	—	—
1912–16	2.60	98	—	—	•	—	—	24	88	—	—	•	—	—
1917–21	2.87	91	75	139	•	—	—	30	82	63	166	•	—	—
1922–26	3.23	86	58	96	•	55	47	36	79	30	106	•	26	21
1927–31	3.59	77	54	88	•	52	48	42	61	24	74	•	27	23

Table 3.7 (continued)

Religion, Years of Schooling and Year of Birth	Median Issue							Percent with 5+ Issue						
	Australia	Index						Australia	Index					
		British Isles	Italy	Netherlands	Greece	Germany	Yugoslavia		British Isles	Italy	Netherlands	Greece	Germany	Yugoslavia
Non-Catholic														
< 6														
1907–11	2.04	102	*	146	162	—	—	21	78	*	154	148	—	—
1912–16	2.33	88	*	134	127	—	—	20	73	*	176	147	—	—
1917–21	2.39	90	*	122	127	—	100	20	80	*	145	138	—	78
1922–26	2.54	88	*	116	104	65	87	22	79	*	143	93	51	66
1927–31	2.71	88	*	100	82	67	73	25	73	*	110	38	59	39
6–7														
1907–11	2.06	95	*	—	—	—	—	15	89	*	—	—	—	—
1912–16	2.08	96	*	158	—	114	—	14	92	*	256	—	144	—
1917–21	2.17	98	*	129	—	103	—	14	102	*	216	—	110	—
1922–26	2.29	100	*	122	94	86	—	15	107	*	171	83	92	—
1927–31	2.49	98	*	111	83	75	—	18	100	*	126	37	65	—
8														
1907–11	1.98	91	*	—	—	—	—	11	95	*	—	—	—	—
1912–16	2.01	98	—	—	—	—	—	12	102	—	—	—	—	—
1917–21	2.03	99	*	135	—	92	—	10	121	*	244	—	169	—
1922–26	2.17	102	*	127	—	85	—	11	127	*	218	—	95	—
1927–31	2.34	101	*	116	—	80	—	13	120	*	189	—	83	—
9+														
1907–11	1.86	96	*	—	—	—	—	9	102	*	—	—	—	—
1912–16	2.00	93	*	133	—	80	—	9	100	*	275	—	126	—
1917–21	2.08	93	*	114	—	85	—	10	109	*	194	—	100	—
1922–26	2.28	89	*	105	—	69	68	11	110	*	183	—	65	32
1927–31	2.46	88	*	98	76	68	63	12	102	*	125	41	67	45

(–) N < 100
* Not Applicable

Note:
Median issue and per cent with 5+ issue indices calculated on the basis of figures carried out to two decimal places and one decimal place, respectively.

magnitude; and (4) a general decline in fertility differences by occupation within each of the various nativity/religion categories — certainly among the Australian- and (to a lesser extent) British-born, and probably among the others as well, although the data that would document it with respect to these latter groupings are not available.

Schooling

There is much the same pattern with years of schooling (whether wife's or husband's). At each level, there was a virtual disappearance of the excess fertility among the Dutch-born on the one hand and the Italian- and Greek-born on the other, and an increasing difference between the Australian-born and the other nativity groupings as the fertility of the Australian-born rose and that of the others either continued to fall or else rose less. The differences were more pronounced at the upper parities than at the medians, with the Australian-born being the most likely to have large families among Catholics — particularly at the highest schooling level — and the Dutch-born the most likely to have large families among non-Catholics (see Table 3.7).

Overall, what stands out in the pattern of differences by schooling is (1) the marked increase in fertility among Australian-born Catholics at the highest schooling level, to the point where, by the end of the period, it was this sector that had the highest fertility of all; (2) the persistence of Catholic:non-Catholic differences; (3) the persistence of differences by nativity, but with the pattern of these differences undergoing considerable change; and (4) the marked decline in fertility differences among the different levels of schooling.

Duration of Residence in Australia

As already noted, marked changes have taken place in the pattern of fertility differences by nativity (whether or not standardised for religion). While the fertility of the Australian-born rose, that of their age peers fell among those born in Italy, the Netherlands, Greece and Yugoslavia, continued at a low level among those born in Germany, and rose among those born in the British Isles.

To be sure, many of these women bore all, or most, of their children before emigrating to Australia, and could for that reason be presumed to have been responding primarily to conditions in their native lands. The considerable parallel between the fertility of

Table 3.8: Cohort Total Fertility Rates (Total Births per Woman, Assuming No Mortality During Period of Childbearing) (Selected Countries)

Cohort Year of Birth	Australia	England & Wales	Italy	Netherlands	Germany	Yugoslavia
1907−11	2.32	1.82	2.75	2.85	1.99	3.81
1912−16	2.47	1.91	2.59	3.11	1.97	3.53
1917−21	2.68	2.05	2.41	3.08	1.90	3.29
1922−26	2.81	2.13	2.26	2.85	1.92	3.18
1927−31	3.00	2.32	2.25	2.68	2.13	2.72

Sources:
Data for calculations for Australia, Italy and the Netherlands from United Nations, *Demographic Yearbook 1954*, Table 11; *Demographic Yearbook 1959*, Table 12; *Demographic Yearbook 1965*, Tables 14 and 17; and *Demographic Yearbook 1975*, Table 24. In addition, birth rates at ages 15−19 and 20−4 for the cohort of 1907−11, and at ages 15−19 for the cohort of 1912−16, in Australia from: L. T. Ruzicka, *Reflections on Zero Growth of the Australian Population*, Research Report no. 7, National Population Inquiry, Canberra: Australian Government Printing Service (1977), Tables 5−7, p. 58. Rates for the same cohorts at these ages in Italy are my estimates.
  Total fertility rates for England and Wales, Germany and Yugoslavia from: Chantal Blayo and Patrick Festy, 'La fécondité à l'est et à l'ouest de l'Europe'. *Population*, **30** (1975), pp. 855−88.

the overseas-born in Australia and that of their age peers in their respective countries of origin would certainly suggest this (see Table 3.8). Yet among those overseas-born wives who had been longest in Australia there was still no particular tendency to conform more closely to the levels of fertility reached by their Australian-born peers. Even among those who would have borne all, or nearly all, of their children in Australia, the pattern followed seems more often to have been ethnic than Australian, even when that ethnic pattern was undergoing substantial change (see Table 3.9).

Discussion

The association of religious identification with group fertility differences would appear to be unusually direct. Certainly fertility differences among the members of different entities avowing divergent views on contraception, abortion, sexual morality or appropriate roles for women could be readily anticipated.

Table 3.9: Ratio of Median Issue of Selected Overseas-born to Median Issue of Australian-born. Wives married before Age 26, by Country of Birth and Religion, by Duration of Residence (Australia, 1971) (Australian-born = 100)

Religion	Duration of Res. (yrs)	Year of Arrival	Year of Birth	Country of Birth					
				British Isles	Netherlands	Germany	Yugoslavia	Greece	Italy
Catholic	< 5	after 1966	1907–11*	—	—	—	—	—	166
			1917–21*	102	—	—	—	—	143
			1927–31†	89	—	—	73	—	90
	5–9	1962–66	1907–11*	—	—	—	—	—	183
			1917–21*	104	—	—	—	—	125
			1927–31	92	—	—	57	—	81
	10–16	1955–61	1907–11*	—	—	—	—	—	148
			1917–21†	103	156	—	—	—	101
			1927–31	89	98	55	52	—	65
	17–23	1948–54	1907–11†	93	—	—	—	—	115
			1917–21	90	118	—	—	—	97
			1927–31	92	88	56	55	—	70
	24 +	before 1948	1907–11†	100	—	—	—	—	103
			1917–21	100	—	—	—	—	96
			1927–31	85	—	—	—	—	79

Table 3.9 (continued)

Religion	Duration of Res. (yrs)	Year of Arrival	Year of Birth	British Isles	Netherlands	Germany	Yugoslavia	Greece	Italy
					Country of Birth				
Non-Catholic	< 5	after 1966	1907–11*	82	—	—	—	—	—
			1917–21*	88	—	—	—	158	—
			1927–31†	91	—	87	77	86	—
	5–9	1962–66	1907–11*	92	—	—	—	—	—
			1917–21*	100	—	—	—	157	—
			1927–31	91	—	71	79	88	—
	10–16	1955–61	1907–11*	96	—	—	—	—	—
			1917–21†	95	147	104	—	136	—
			1927–31	86	104	67	74	84	—
	17–23	1948–54	1907–11†	85	134	—	—	118	—
			1917–21	82	106	78	—	91	—
			1927–31	87	98	64	—		—
	24 +	before 1948	1907–11†	89	—	—	—	127	—
			1917–21	88	—	—	—	123	—
			1927–31	89	—	74	—	92	—

(−) N < 100
* Reached age 40 before arriving in Australia
† Reached mid-30s before arriving in Australia

Yet one's religious identity, at least theoretically, is always susceptible of change, as is also the strength of this identification and the degree of commitment to the values and teachings associated with it also. Any shift in religious identities between groupings associated with different levels of fertility can be expected to reduce the fertility differences between them on the assumption of some carry-over of the fertility-related behaviour associated with their previous identities. Persons of generally lower fertility background will have been introduced into the higher fertility grouping, and persons of higher fertility background into the lower fertility grouping. But while one can only guess at the importance of such shifts in identity so far as the pattern of fertility differences in Australia is concerned, the persistence of Catholic:non-Catholic differences suggests that it has not been very great. On the other hand, the situation may have been quite different respecting the actual strength of religious identification and the degree of personal commitment to the values and teachings associated with it.

Fertility differences may well be more directly associated with religion than with most other personal attributes. One would certainly expect this to be the case in European populations, given the fertility-related teachings associated in particular with Roman Catholicism; for, despite a number of recent changes, Roman Catholic doctrine concerning the regulation of birth remains essentially pro-natalist, whatever the intentions of its promulgators. The most effective and reliable means of controlling births are rejected, as is also, with respect to the means allowed, the essential reason for resort to birth control in the first place — namely, the enjoyment of coitus without risk of unwanted pregnancy. Moreover, this official position has been buttressed by a substantial literature, both lay and clerical, in direct support of high fertility, and also by an apparent ready availability of Catholic platforms to the advocates of large families.

But whether pro-natalist doctrine or the pro-natalist activity of official, or officially endorsed, spokesmen necessarily leads to higher fertility is another matter. In actual cases, the association seems less than straightforward. In Australia, as elsewhere, one finds not only marked changes over time, but considerable overlap between Catholics and non-Catholics and much within-group variation, none of which would support the claim of causal priority for religious identification as such.

Quite obviously, there is much more than doctrine at work in the relation between religion and group differences in behaviour of any sort. Identification by religion can take on a variety of meanings. Like other personal attributes, religion can indicate the presence or absence of certain characteristics or conditions of life that are themselves in some way related to the behaviour in question; and the extent to which it does so can, of course, be expected to vary over time and between different populations.

In the present study, religion would appear to be less a causal element in its own right than an indicator of the likely existence of a set of conditions that are themselves of some causal significance to fertility: values, life-styles, levels of aspiration, life chances, tradition, position in the social class system, or the likelihood of interaction with pro- or anti-natalist relatives, friends and acquaintances, for example.

When assessing the particular role of religion in the determination of fertility — as with any factor in social causation — one must remember, first, that it need not lead to the same result in every set of circumstances and, secondly, that it does not operate in isolation — that is, that its effect in any particular instance will be enhanced or softened, reinforced or modified, in consequence of the myriad other factors simultaneously operating with it. Two such other factors in the Australian setting are those associated with country of birth and social status.

Unlike religion, one's country of birth admits of no change (although boundary changes may make it appear so in subsequent documents). None the less, so far as behaviour is concerned, there can be quite as much diversity within a population grouped according to nativity as within one grouped according to religion. Categorisation simultaneously by religion and nativity may significantly reduce this diversity in particular instances — as might the introduction of further differentiation in terms of, say, occupation, residence or schooling — but a substantial amount of diversity will inevitably remain. Part of this derives from the diversity inherent in any large population, but some of it will have originated in the selectivity of immigration itself. The characteristics of migrants — even those from the same country — will, predictably, be different at different times: different with respect, for example, to social or economic conditions, expectations about the future, levels of aspiration and degrees of attachment to native land and heritage. No more than with the adherents of different religions can one blandly assume that a particular national origin will have the same implications for behaviour in every circumstance; nor even that it will have the same *relative* implications in comparison with other national origins: that, for example, other things being equal, the natives of country A will invariably have a lower average fertility than the natives of country B.

Nevertheless, group differences by national origin are a significant part of the fertility differences under study here; and they are found within every sub-division by religion, residence, occupation and schooling for which the cell frequencies are large enough to permit comparison. But while fertility differences by nativity exist within each cohort, the pattern of these differences evinces very substantial changes over time, and is thus in marked contrast to the relative stability of the patterns of group fertility differences associated with other attributes. Such changes suggest not only a pattern of causal relations between fertility and nativity of a sort different from those between fertility and these other attributes, but also a pattern that has been different at different times.

Given that group fertility differences along the lines of religion and nativity are real — that, as has been noted, they hinge on differences in neither patterns of marriage nor composition according to such attributes as urban−rural residence, husband's occupation, or schooling — what, then, does being a Catholic or non-Catholic, a native of one country rather than another, imply so far as completed fertility is concerned? Is there a causal connection between fertility and the physical or socioeconomic attributes of Catholics as contrasted with non-Catholics? Or between fertility and the physical or socioeconomic attributes of, say, the Australian-born contrasted with the Italian-born, or British-born Catholics contrasted with German-born non-Catholics? As with the discussion of differences by urban−rural residence, the possible explanations can be conveniently categorised in terms of whether they relate to (1) physiological differences, (2) differences in the ability and willingness to exercise control over childbearing, or (3) differences in desired numbers of children.

Physiological Differences

The possible role of physiological differences in producing group fertility differences has already been discussed with reference to urban−rural residence. As with that attribute, it seems unlikely that such differences could have played more than a very minor role in the origin of the observed fertility differences by religion and nativity; and also that, whatever the role physiological differences may have played, this was likely to have been through differences in the incidence of unwanted conception arising out of differences in coital frequency, which in turn resulted from differences in exposure to stress. Some physiological response to the stress associated with leaving one's native land and adjusting to life in a new one could be anticipated,[5] but that this should have had any very great effect on lifetime fertility in the present situation seems highly unlikely. As with fertility differences by urban–rural residence, the explanation of fertility differences by religion and nativity is to be sought essentially in values, attitudes and knowledge — not physiology.

Differences in the Ability and Willingness to Excercise Control over Childbearing

The rapid decline in fertility among the Italian-, Dutch-, Greek- and Yugoslav-born suggests a marked increase in the ability and willingness to control births, while the persistence of relatively low fertility among the other nativity groupings suggests a continuation of this ability and willingness to an already high degree.

But controlled fertility need not be low fertility. It seems unlikely that where fertility increased during this period — primarily among the Australian-born, and particularly among Australian-born Catholics with husbands in professional and clerical occupations — it did so in consequence of either a growing ignorance of birth control on the part of successive cohorts or a growing failure to exercise that control effectively. In fact, the evidence points in the opposite direction — to a general expansion of effective control at the individual level during this period.[6] The increases in fertility would seem, therefore, to have originated at the least in an increase in the numbers of children these people were willing to allow themselves, and, just possibly, in an increase in desired numbers of children.

However, there is another possibility deserving of mention — one related to the general expansion of the white-collar sector during this period. Among Australian-born wives married before age 26, the proportion with husbands in the professional category in 1971 was 5 per cent among those aged 55–9 as against 8 per cent among those fifteen years younger; for those with husbands in the administrative category, it was 10 as against 14 per cent. If those in the all others category are excluded from the denominator to avoid biasing the comparison through inclusion of a number of retired persons, these proportions become, respectively, 7 *vs.* 10 per cent, and 14 *vs.* 17 per cent. In the clerical and sales category, there was an increase of 2 percentage points (from 10–12 per cent) if the denominator includes those in the all other category, and a decline of 1 percentage point (from 15–14 per cent) if it does not. Overall, the period saw a modest net movement (11 percentage points among Catholics and 9 percentage points among non-Catholics; if the all others category is excluded, 7 percentage points among Catholics, 4 percentage points among non-Catholics) out of occupational groupings characterised at the beginning of the period by markedly higher fertility and into ones characterised at the same time by markedly lower fertility.

If the wives of men who participated in this shift did, indeed, retain the levels of both ability and willingness to exercise control over childbearing once associated with their husbands' prior occupational classifications, this shift in distribution by occupation could have accounted for some of the increased fertility among those in the upper white-collar occupations. But it could not have accounted for much. There appears to be no reason why wives whose husbands moved to a different occupational category should necessarily have retained the fertility pattern characteristic — and at an earlier period, at that — of the category these husbands had left. Nor is there any assurance that the net movement was actually out of the higher fertility categories; there is quite as much likelihood that it was out of the already low fertility clerical and sales category instead. And finally, even if all the net movement did, indeed, originate in the highest fertility occupational groupings and, moreover, the fertility pattern of these groupings was adhered to completely, the net change would still not have been great enough to account more than very partially for the change in fertility that actually occurred.

The very marked fertility increases among Australian-born Catholics with husbands in upper white-collar occupations would appear to have been exceptional. Attributable to neither physiology, increased ignorance of birth control, nor (except very marginally) changes in the composition of this sector of the population as a consequence of occupational mobility, these increases in fertility would initially appear — by subtraction — to have arisen out of quite remarkable increases in desired numbers of children. Yet there is no support for this contention in the few 1971 Melbourne survey data that might shed light on the subject. The number of children a random sample of Australian-born wives of all marriage ages said they would want to have under ideal circumstances ('If you were able to start married life all over again, and if it were somehow possible to prevent pregnancy when you wished, and to become pregnant just when you wanted to . . .') was invariably higher for Catholics than for non-Catholics; but within neither religious grouping was there any difference between the older and younger cohorts (sub-divided along status lines), either in ideal median issue or in the proportion who said they would want five children or more.

And why, anyway, might one expect an increase in desired numbers of children to have taken place at this time specifically among higher-status Australian-born Catholic women? — an increase so much above any that occurred at the same time among either their non-Catholic counterparts or their co-religionists elsewhere in the population? Whatever may have been involved, it seems unlikely that such an increase could have accounted for all, or even most, of a fertility change of the magnitude observed. A more important role would seem to have been played by a decline in the willingness — not in the *ability*, but in the *willingness* — of these women or their husbands to exercise control over childbearing, and particularly by a decline in their willingness to employ the most effective means to that end. That this is a factor of major causal significance is suggested by two things: first the somewhat anomalous position that higher-status Catholics may be presumed to occupy in Australian society, and secondly, the likelihood that these Catholics are generally less limited financially than their co-religionists elsewhere in society.

Catholics are a significant minority in Australia. They also have a history of being somewhat socially disadvantaged, with higher proportions in the lower classes (however defined) and lower proportions in the higher.[7] While these differences dimished considerably after the second world war[8] — in so far as rather crude indicators of social position can be used to assess them — there continued to be a relatively small proportion of Catholics in the upper strata of Australian society, particularly, it would appear, in the uppermost reaches of those strata, namely among top business executives,[9] within the higher echelons of the public service,[10] and on the academic staffs of the universities,[11] for example.

Contacts outside one's ethnic or religious grouping are predictably more frequent for upper status persons than for lower; all the more so if these upper status persons are also members of a large minority. From such contacts can come a greater awareness of being different, of being an outsider, one consequence of which could be that the persons affected become more receptive to the values and attitudes associated with membership in their group.[12] As has been written with reference to entire populations,

> Where Catholics are a majority there is no need to feel threatened or at bay *as a Catholic*, and hence, no particular incentive either to seek out co-religionists for support and example, or to attach oneself more closely to the Church and its teachings on account of the slights (or worse) one feels oneself to have suffered on its behalf.[13]

But this is more probably the case with men than with women because of the greater mobility men have had outside the confines of home and family. Specifically among Catholic women in Australia, higher status may well have led instead, to less, rather than more, contact with persons of backgrounds different from their own. The role of Catholic schooling in effecting this is particularly significant, for it is those children — boys as well as girls — from higher status families who would be the ones most likely to have attended none but Catholic schools and, moreover, to have attended them at later ages: ages of particular significance in the development of self-awareness and the acquisition of adult roles.

But while, with higher status Catholic men, a greater participation in activities outside the home and family could be expected to have enhanced receptivity to Catholic values — through producing a heightened awareness of their Catholic identity and position as an outsider — the situation among higher status Catholic women is more likely to have been one in which a greater confinement to the society of their co-religionists led, more often than not, to a situation in which, quite simply, Catholic values were seldom ever questioned.[14] From the standpoint of fertility the results would be much the same, but the path to those results was presumably different for the two sexes: higher status Catholic men being brought, as it were, to *embrace* Catholic values; their female counterparts to *accept* them, essentially unaware of any genuine alternative.

It may well be that in the period of the 1950s to late 1960s when the cohorts that experienced the major increases in fertility would have been having those fourth and higher-order births that produced this rise in fertility, upper status Australian Catholics were developing a greater feeling of separateness because, as a group, they were moving into positions of greater social equality and power.

To this must be added the fact that during this period when the more recent cohorts were bearing their children — especially those of higher parity — Catholic teaching on contraception and abortion, and perhaps also on women's roles, was being accorded an unusual amount of publicity in response both to various papal decrees and to a growing concern about world population increase and the possible role played by dogma and the institutional power of organised religion (particularly Catholicism) in maintaining it. Moreover, it was a period of particularly vigorous Catholic teaching concerning the family: the period of the family rosary movement ('The family that prays together stays together'), and of a renewed emphasis on Mary and the Holy Family. It was also the heyday in Australia of the Catholic Youth Organisation with its well-developed programmes and facilities intended, in part, to reduce the likelihood of mixed marriages by keeping Catholics separated from non-Catholics outside of school in much the way Church schools kept them separated inside. As perhaps never before, Catholics were being made aware of their Church's teaching concerning the family, and of the fact that that teaching was essentially pro-natalist.

It seems reasonable to suppose that the force of this pro-natalist teaching would have fallen more heavily on those who were most conscious of their Catholic identities and who, at the same time, were favourably enough situated financially to be able, first, to forgo a wife's potential earnings so that she could devote herself more exclusively to home and childcare, and secondly, to accept more readily both the risk of an unplanned pregnancy (in consequence of adherence to the Church's proscription of the more reliable means of contraception) and — to the extent that anyone conditioned to this value-system could think of any child as being unwanted — the birth of an unwanted child (in consequence of adherence to the Church's proscription of abortion). Among Australian-born Catholics, it is in the upper white-collar occupational categories that the highest concentration of such persons would appear to be.

Moreover, those who did avail themselves of the more reliable means of bith control — particularly those of them who were upper level Catholics — seem frequently to have done so with a degree of ambivalence about the practice that one could expect to lead to lower efficiency and, consequently, higher rates of unintentional conception. The Melbourne survey found, predictably enough, that Catholics were less likely than non-Catholics to be using the contraceptive pill. But it also found that those Catholics who did use the pill were much more likely to claim that this use was solely for medical rather than contraceptive purposes and — of particular significance here — that while the proportion claiming a medical reason for its use declined with level of schooling among non-Catholic users, it rose with level of schooling among Catholic users. Among Australian-born Catholic pill users with 13 or more years of schooling, for example, 24 per cent claimed to have used the pill for purely medical reasons, as against but 1 per cent making such a claim among non-Catholic counterparts.[15]

If this assessment is reasonably close to what was actually the state of affairs at the time, the marked increase in fertility among these women over the period under consideration would be seen to have arisen — not entirely, but certainly to an important extent — from a growing unwillingness to undertake the behaviour necessary to prevent childbirth, or at least from a growing acquiescence in accepting what might eventuate from practising birth control less than fully effectively. These women did not eschew birth control altogether — the general outline of their fertility was well below anything approaching 'natural' fertility.[16] But in comparison with previous generations, or with their non-Catholic peers or even with Catholics in their own generations but in other strata of society, the fertility of these higher strata Australian-born Catholic wives seems likely to have included a rather higher proportion of births that were unintended, and possibly even unwanted.

Differences in Desired Numbers of Children

It is entirely to differences in desired numbers of children that the authors of the reports on the *National Fertility Surveys* attribute their finding of higher Catholic fertility (or fertility *expectations*, for more recent cohorts) among white women in the United States.[17] But this conclusion rests on construction — a very careful, logical construction, as it happens — of a simple dichotomy between 'wanted' and 'unwanted':

In the course of the interview with each of our respondents, we obtained a record of their pregnancies, and then inquired into the circumstances of the interval preceding each pregnancy. Whether the couple was or was not using contraception during the interval in question was determined first. Users were then asked, 'Did that pregnancy occur because you deliberately *stopped* using a method in order to have a child, or did it happen even though you did *not want* to get pregnant at that time?' Pregnancies reported to have resulted from interrupting a method in order to have a child were classified as wanted. Those reporting that they had not wanted to get pregnant at that time were asked the following pair of questions: 'Just before you got pregnant that time, did your husband want a child but not until *later*, or did he really want *no more* children?' Non-users of contraception in the interval were asked, 'Was the *only* reason you did not use any method in that interval because you and your husband wanted a baby as soon as possible?' Those who answered in the negative were also routed through the pair of questions about husband and wife wanting a child later or wanting no more children.[18]

The authors recognise that their essentially conservative coding procedure probably yields an under-count of the extent of unwanted fertility,[19] but they do not comment on whether there might be group differences by religion in the extent of this under-counting. They also take the precaution of comparing the women who gave 'noncommittal responses' ('didn't care', 'don't know') with those who gave 'unambiguous' ones when asked the two questions about whether they or their husbands wanted a particular child later or wanted no more children. But while they report on their comparisons respecting race and schooling (they found no differences), they make no mention of having made a similar comparison on the potentially more interesting attribute: religion.[20] Moreover, despite the fact that a third of the respondents who were asked these questions gave noncommittal responses, the authors' interpretation admits of no analytically grey area — no area, that is, based on recognition that there may be varying degrees of 'wantedness' or 'unwantedness', or that there may be group differences in the extent to which people merely acquiesce in accepting what comes. Every birth is thus either 'wanted or 'unwanted'; each, for analytical purposes, the purported equal (at time of conception) of its nominal equivalent.

While not an actually researchable phenomenon in the circumstances, it would still have been good to see more recognition here of the fact of behavioural 'drift',[21] of the fact that much behaviour commences almost by accident at one or another point within the range of possible and socially permissible behaviours and then, 'guided gently by underlying influences',[22] moves (but not necessarily inexorably) towards its conclusion in a manner largely imperceptible to the person doing it. Not all behaviour is like this, but a very high proportion doubtless is — even of behaviour likely to have profound long-run consequences, such as those acts (or failures to act) that result in different fertility levels. 'Choices' are certainly made; and in contracepting societies like the United States and Australia, most births are doubtless 'wanted'. But the 'choices' one makes are very much constrained by the normative setting. Moreover, one's adherence to norms is largely unconscious, and 'selection' among available alternatives ordinarily in terms of behaviours actually, or at least seemingly, but slightly differentiated from one another.[23] Especially where there are apt to be conflicts in values, as in the present instance of religious differentials, explanation in terms of a simple dichotomy resting, essentially, on the presumption of conscious choice would appear to be attributing rather too much to human rationality.

But at least the *National Fertility Survey* made the attempt. The data available here on Australia, being census data, not only afford no firm indication of desired numbers of children, they do not even represent an attempt to gain one. As with the preceding discussion of the respective roles of differences in physiology and in the ability and willingness to exercise control over childbearing, what is said here about desired numbers of children must, therefore, be largely hypothetical in nature.

As already noted, the possible sources of differences in the numbers of children people want (or are willing to have) are numerous and varied. They can range from differences in personality traits to differences in life-styles, external living conditions, and the costs and benefits thought to be associated with the bearing and rearing of children. The question is whether any such differences affecting the desired (or tolerated) number of children can, in the absence of direct evidence, be used in explanation of any part of the pattern of fertility differences by religion and ethnicity observed in Australia. There appear to be several that can.

Group norms as to what constitutes an 'appropriate' number of children, 'too many' or 'too few'. That Catholics are likely to have a higher fertility norm than non-Catholics is suggested by the essentially pro-natalist character of Catholic teaching on the family, and also by the fact that a higher proportion of Catholics would have been reared in large families, Catholic fertility having been so long in excess of non-Catholic. The cell frequencies are not very large, but when asked how many children they 'would want to have altogether' if they were 'able to start married life all over again', and able 'to prevent pregnancy when [they] wished, and to become pregnant just when [they] wanted to', the averages — at all ages and all levels of schooling and husband's occupation — reported by the Australian-born Catholic wives interviewed in the Melbourne survey were invariably higher than those reported by their non-Catholic counterparts. And the Catholic excess was particularly marked with respect to the proportions reporting five or more.[24]

Perceiving a course of behaviour as 'usual' or 'normal' can be a strong incentive to perceiving it as also being 'desirable', or at the least 'acceptable'. A higher fertility norm among Catholics would doubtless receive some reinforcement from the interaction of individual Catholics with their higher fertility relatives and co-religionists, especially if this interaction were in ways that caused larger families to be thought of as normal, and smaller families (possibly) as abnormal.

It could be the same with any social grouping in possession of a more or less identifiable 'sub-culture'; but in the Australian setting, the only groupings that have an association with fertility anywhere approximating that of religion are those based on country of birth. This is perhaps best documented among the Irish who, quite apart from their Catholicism, would appear to be particularly attached (for a European population) to the large family ideal.[25] But there is also evidence of other fertility norms associated with national groupings that may be of significance to the pattern of Australian fertility — in particular, a high fertility norm among the Dutch[26] and a low fertility norm among the Germans.[27]

The possible existence and persistence of different fertility norms among the various nativity groupings deserves a closer look, in particular because of what it might imply about the important processes of immigrant adaptation and absorption. Australia is especially well-suited to inquiry on this topic: first, because the data are unusually good; secondly, because it has been a nation of immigrants since the beginning of its European settlement in 1788 — with post second world war immigrants and their children (a slight majority of whom, incidentally, were non-British in origin) constituting over a quarter of its population by the 1970s;[28] thirdly, because it has been widely assumed in Australia — both officially and unofficially — that immigrants would become not only permanent settlers but assimilated Australians, even though settler losses since the war have approached 25–30 per cent within most nativity groupings (purely marginal return rates being confined largely to refugees and non-Europeans)[29] and successive governments have done little to help immigrants adjust[30] to what for most must have been remarkably different living conditions; and finally, because Catholics, although always a significant minority, have been a prominent and widely-diffused element of the Australian population (both geographically and socially) throughout its European history, continuing to be so with each immigration wave.

Allusion has already been made to the fact that the patterns of fertility among the overseas-born were more in keeping with those in their respective countries of birth than with those among the Australian-born. While the pattern among the German-born persisted at a markedly lower level than that among the Australian-born, those among the Italian-, Greek-, Dutch- and Yugoslav-born moved in a direction quite opposite to it. Even among the Dutch-born, whose fertility moved more into line with that of the Australian-born, and the British-born, whose fertility remained in close approximation to it, the direction and magnitude of the changes in fertility seem still to have conformed more closely to what happened overseas.

While demographers have reported a general narrowing of fertility differences along ethnic and religious lines, at least in western countries,[31] political scientists and sociologists have claimed to see not only a persistence of self-identification by religion and ethnicity but a new, more vigorous individual insistence upon it.[32] Of course, there need be no necessary connection between group fertility differences and the phenomenon of group self-identification, but it seems reasonable to expect a decline or expansion in the one to be associated with a similar change in the other. If that is the case, the detailed data available for Australia would lend some support to the claims of the political scientists and sociologists, and simultaneously cast some doubt on those of the demographers.

If group self-identification by religion or ethnicity has, indeed, increased, or at least persisted — and this is a moot point so far as this particular study is concerned — and if there is, moreover, a positive association between such self-identification and adherence to group fertility norms — with group fertility differences a likely consequence — the failure of other studies to show this difference can probably be attributed to some combination of the following: (a) the fact that in most demographic studies of group fertility differences more refined cross-tabulation is much restricted by either the nature of the data or the relatively small numbers involved;

(b) the fact that most such studies rely almost exclusively on measures of central tendency, particularly averages, thereby obscuring much of any difference there may be at the extremes (particularly the upper extremes), which is precisely where such differences are most likely to exist in any population exercising substantial control over fertility; and

(c) the fact that the focus of most demographic studies of fertility has not been altogether clear. If the goal is to understand fertility behaviour, and not merely to document group differences in numbers of children ever born (however important this latter endeavour may be), it is necessary to exclude structural elements, such as age distribution and patterns of marriage, in order to focus as much as possible on the results of fertility behaviour itself. Making an explanatory variable out of age structure or marriage patterns is logically fallacious in a study of differences in fertility behaviour. It is like studying patterns of household expenditure without first standardising for income or household composition.

But whatever the reason, so far as may be indicated by patterns of fertility — particularly as these pertain to group differences by nativity and religion — Australia appears to have been more of a 'pluralist' than an 'assimilationist' type of society. On at least this one indicator, cultural pluralism would appear to have been alive and flourishing there.

Group differences in status striving. The likely diversity among immigrants has already been remarked on, but it does not seem out of line to suppose that immigrants, as a whole, are likely to be personally more ambitious than the native born, whatever their reasons for migrating. Among some this may be occasioned by a loss — or threatened loss — of status[33] in consequence of their removal to a country where their language skills may be inferior, or their training and experience not formally recognised. But, for most migrants, the Australian setting has probably appeared to offer greater opportunities for personal advancement than were to be found in their country of origin. A related element, one likely to reinforce the incentive to strive for more strictly material (and purchasable) goals, is the fact that things like a car, a pretentious house, a stereo-set — perhaps precisely because of their tangibility — can be particularly effective supports of an immigrant's decision to migrate. They can mitigate the doubts harboured by the immigrant him- or herself about the wisdom of the decision to emigrate, and answer sceptics in the old country who advised against emigration all along.

But whatever the origin of this status striving, there are (in addition to migration itself) two demographic means to the attainment of the goals associated with it: (a) limitation of the number of one's progeny, either to lessen the demands upon the sum of one's resources or to permit greater allocation of these resources to individual family members, and (b) postponement of childbearing until the attainment of a particular status (e.g. steady employment) or the accumulation of a particular resource base (e.g. home-ownership). While postponed births can in most instances be readily made up, any period of postponement will afford just that much more opportunity for infecundity to set in, or for the development of interests and goals of a sort likely to compete with childbearing. By any reckoning, a postponed birth is less likely to occur than one that has already taken place.

That status striving may have played a significant part in reducing fertility among immigrants to Australia is at least suggested by the greater labour force participation rates among immigrant wives; but perhaps its strongest indication is in the higher school retention rates among immigrant children, in particular those from non-English-speaking backgrounds.[34]

Group differences in the extent to which it is thought necessary or desirable for a wife to enter the labour force. Just what causal relation there is between marital fertility and the labour force participation of wives is not altogether clear. As Ware has put it,

Census-type data can show that wives who work outside their

homes have fewer children than their house-bound peers, but they cannot show whether wives have fewer children in order to work, or whether wives who have fewer children for other reasons nevertheless find it easier to remain in the work-force.[35]

Nevertheless, certain immigrant groups, especially those that, like the Italian-, Greek- and Yugoslav-born, combine non-English-speaking origin with possession of a relatively narrower range of marketable skills and experience,[36] could be expected to have to work harder and husband their resources more carefully, just to survive at something approaching an acceptable standard, irrespective of their views on appropriate family size or their interest in achieving higher status. Even those with relatives and friends in Australia — and not all immigrants have such networks — could be presumed, because of their lack of skills, their fewer material resources, and especially their limited ability in English, to be in a generally more vulnerable economic position — one obvious avenue of escape from which would be the employment of additional family members.[37]

Many of the economically more vulnerable, of whatever nativity, have doubtless undertaken just such an approach to their situation; but it is impossible with the data available here to sort out different degrees of causation in a situation in which several factors are surely at work simultaneously and, moreover, often at cross-purposes with one another. A numerous progeny may keep one mother out of the workforce because of the demands her children can be presumed to make upon her time and energy; and yet press another into it because of the additional economic burden these children entail. Underlying such pressures in either case will be the family's interest in achieving higher status and its group's norms about appropriate family size. But also operative will be the group's norms relating to appropriate behaviour for wives and mothers: the non-economic incentives for wives to undertake employment and the extent to which employment is considered a 'normal', or at least 'acceptable', part of the wife's role.

Respecting norms about the wife/mother role and women's employment, the *1970 National Fertility Survey* sought a test of the significance of these to fertility in the United States by asking a series of closed-end questions: whether a mother's having a job was deemed harmful to pre-school children; the age a child should be before a mother took up employment; whether it was 'better' if the

Table 3.10: Percentage in the Labour Force. Metropolitan-dwelling Wives who Commenced Current Marriage before Age 26, by Nativity, Year of Birth and Specified Numbers of Children born to Current Marriage (Australia, 1971)

Religion and Children Born to Current Marriage	Year of Birth	Country of Birth						
		Australia	British Isles	Italy	Netherlands	Greece	Germany	Yugoslavia
Catholic								
0	1907–11	13	—	—	—	*	—	—
	1917–21	36	—	—	—	*	—	—
	1927–31	57	—	64	—	*	—	—
1	1907–11	12	—	—	—	*	—	—
	1917–21	36	45	40	—	*	69	74
	1927–31	49	68	65	—	*	—	—
4	1907–11	10	—	6	—	*	—	—
	1917–21	31	43	29	—	*	—	—
	1927–31	40	57	41	34	*	57	62
Non-Catholic								
0	1907–11	11	14	*	—	—	—	—
	1917–21	32	45	*	—	—	—	—
	1927–31	53	68	*	—	—	64	—
1	1907–11	10	13	*	—	—	51	—
	1917–21	31	47	*	—	76	63	—
	1927–31	47	66	*	—	—	—	—
4	1907–11	9	13	*	—	—	—	—
	1917–21	29	40	*	36	29	—	—
	1927–31	39	51	*	40	56	41	62

* Not Applicable
(—) N < 100

Table 3.11: Percentage in the Labour Force. Metropolitan-dwelling Wives 40–64 Years of Age who Commenced Current Marriage before Age 26, by Nativity, Age at Marriage, Religion and Specified Numbers of Children born to Current Marriage (Australia, 1971)

Religion and Children Born to Current Marriage	Age at Marriage	Country of Birth						
		Australia	British Isles	Italy	Netherlands	Greece	Germany	Yugoslavia
Catholic								
0	< 20	57	—	—	—	*	—	—
	20–1	53	—	—	—	*	—	—
	22–5	58	—	63	—	*	—	—
1	< 20	56	—	64	—	*	—	—
	20–1	50	—	66	—	*	—	—
	22–5	45	—	65	—	*	—	—
4	< 20	40	—	40	—	*	—	—
	20–1	39	66	41	—	*	—	—
	22–5	41	52	41	30	*	—	—
Non-Catholic								
0	< 20	47	—	*	—	—	—	—
	20–1	55	68	*	—	—	—	—
	22–5	53	68	*	—	—	64	—
1	< 20	51	68	*	—	—	—	—
	20–1	49	65	*	—	—	67	—
	22–5	45	67	*	—	78	58	—
4	< 20	42	55	*	—	53	—	—
	20–1	40	51	*	—	51	—	—
	22–5	37	50	*	31	62	—	—

* Not Applicable
(—) N < 100

Table 3.12: Percentages in the Labour Force. Married Women in Specified Countries by Age(1971)

Age	Australia	England & Wales	Italy*	Netherlands	Greece	West Germany	Yugoslavia†
15–19	36	42ᵃ	28ᵇ	24	23	57	
20–24	44	46	54	29	22	56	
25–29 }	33	36	51	18	25	47	
30–34 }		41		16	28	41	
35–39 }	41	51		17 }	29	41	
40–44 }		58	36	17 }		43	
45–49 }	36	59		17 }	27	43	
50–54 }		55		15 }		39	
55–59	23	45		11 }	20	31	
60–64	12	25	—	6 }		18	

* All women, 1978
ᵃAge 16–19
ᵇAge 14–19
† No information.

Sources:
Organisation for Economic Cooperation and Development, *High Level Conference on the Employment of Women, 1980*. National Reports, Paris: OECD (1980) mimeo: Australia: Table 2, p. 5; Italy: Table 3, p. 4; Netherlands: Appendix C, p. 34; West Germany: Table 2, p. 28.

Great Britain, *Census of 1971*. 'Economic Activity', Part 1, London: HMSO (1973), Table 1, p. 1.

Statistical Yearbook of Greece 1976, Athens (1976), Table II–14, p. 28, Table III–7, p. 93.

husband was the 'achiever' and the wife stayed home. Among white wives (net of age at marriage, schooling, current work status and reasons for working or not working), the less 'traditional' answers were associated with lower *expected* fertility: an average of 40 per cent of a child lower — this among both Catholics and non-Catholics. Somewhat surprisingly, given the presumed strength of Catholic support (both lay and clerical) for the more traditional women's role of wife/mother, there was no difference either between Catholics and non-Catholics in the proportions giving the 'traditional' answers: about three-quarters for both.[38] The Australian data afford no direct evidence about norms, but like those from the *National Fertility Survey*, they contain no suggestion of a Catholic:non-Catholic difference in adherence to the more 'traditional' view that a wife's place is in the home — or at the least that it is not in the work force (see Table 3.10). If there is such a difference operating between Catholics and non-Catholics, its effects are counterbalanced sufficiently by the operation of other pressures (e.g. perceived economic necessity, or the desire for higher status) to bring the labour force participation rates of Catholic wives into virtual equality with those of non-Catholic wives of the same age and parity.

Labour force participation is discussed in more detail in chapter 6; but for present purposes it is worth noting that, when standardised for parity and age at marriage, labour force participation rates are generally higher among immigrant wives than among the Australian-born (see Table 3.11 for example), thus suggesting the operation of either greater economic pressure, more ambition, or both; and moreover, that the patterns of these differences in wives' labour force participation in Australia follow quite closely the general patterns of women's labour force participation in the countries of immigrant origin (Table 3.12), thus suggesting the operation, as well, of different norms concerning the wife/mother role. Whatever the mix of motivations — economic necessity, status striving, or normative considerations concerning family roles — immigrants appear in this regard to be, once again, adhering more closely to overseas patterns of behaviour than to Australian.

Notes

1. K. Balasubramanian, *Differential Fertility in India: Evidence from a Survey in Karnataka State*. PhD thesis (Demography), Australian National University (1980).
2. For references, see Lincoln H. Day, 'Natality and ethnocentrism: Some relationships suggested by an analysis of Catholic-Protestant differentials'. *Population Studies*, 22 (1968), fn. 9, p. 29; and Rudolf Andorka, *Determinants of Fertility in Advanced Societies*, London: Methuen (1978), esp. chapters 4.3, 4.4, 5.9.
3. See e.g. H. Peters, 'Die Geburtenhäufigkeit nach der Religionszugehörigkeit'. *Wirtschaft und Statistik*, 10 (1958), pp. 24–5; D. V. Glass, 'Fertility trends in Europe since the second world war'. *Population Studies*, 22 (1968), esp. Table 17, pp. 125–6; Karol Krotki and Evelyne Lapierre, 'La fécondité au Canada selon la religion, l'origine ethnique et l'état matrimonial'. *Population*, 23 (1968); Larry H. Long, 'Fertility patterns among religious groups in Canada'. *Demography*, 7 (1970). Léon Tabah, 'Rapport sur les relations entre la fécondité et la condition sociale et économique de la famille en Europe: leurs répercussions sur la politique sociale'. Strasbourg: Council of Europe, 1971 (cited in Rudolf Andorka, op. cit., p. 312); Charles F. Westoff, 'The blending of Catholic reproductive behaviour'. In Robert Wuthnow (ed.), *The Religious Dimension: New Directions in Quantitative Research*, New York: Academic Press (1979); Charles F. Westoff and Elise F. Jones, 'The end of "Catholic" fertility'. *Demography*, 16 (1979).
4. *Statistical Pocket-book of Yugoslavia, 1965*, 2nd edn., Beograd: Federal Institute for Statistics (1965), pp. 22–3, 29.

5. Aleksandar D. Milojković, Serćo F. Šimić, and Mehmed S. Džumhur, 'Migration and place of work as a cause of male sterility'. In William Petersen (ed.), *Readings in Population*, New York: Macmillan (1972).

6. John C. Caldwell *et al.*, 'Australia: knowledge, attitudes, and practice of family planning in Melbourne, 1971'. *Studies in Family Planning*, 4 (1973); and Donald R. Lavis, *Oral Contraception in Melbourne*, 1961–1971, Australian Family Formation Project Monograph 3, Department of Demography, Australian National University, Canberra (1975).

7. Hans Mol, *Religion in Australia*, Melbourne: Nelson (1971), pp. 77–80.

8. Ibid., pp. 81–6, 118–19.

9. Richard N. Spann, 'The Catholic vote in Australia'. In Henry Mayer (ed.), *Catholics and the Free Society*, Melbourne: Cheshire (1961), p. 123; and Sol Encel, 'The old school tie in business'. *Nation*, 10 October 1959 (both cited in Mol, op. cit., p. 78).

10. Alan F. Davies and Sol Encel, 'Politics'. In Alan F. Davies and Sol Encel (eds), *Australian Society*, Melbourne: Cheshire (1965), p. 103; and Leicester Webb, 'Churches and the Australian Commonwealth'. In E. L. French (ed.), *Melbourne Studies in Education 1958–1959*, Melbourne University Press (1960), p. 101 (cited in Mol, op. cit., p. 78).

11. H. Y. Tien, *Social Mobility and Controlled Fertility*, New Haven, Conn.: College and University Press (1965), p. 65 (cited in Mol, op. cit., p. 78).

12. In this connection, see the suggestive finding relating to the association between Catholic identification and fertility expectations in David Goldberg, Harry Sharp and Ronald Freedman, 'The stability and reliability of expected family size data'. *Milbank Memorial Fund Quarterly*, 37 (1959), esp. pp. 382–4.

13. Lincoln H. Day, 'Natality and ethnocentrism: some relationships suggested by an analysis of Catholic–Protestant differentials'. *Population Studies*, 22 (1968), p. 46.

14. Amusing — yet insightful — support for this may be found in the following account based on interviews with 'scores of ex-collegians and convent girls' from the period of the 1950s to 1970s in Australia: Louise Zaetta, *For Christ's Sake!*, East Melbourne: Unicorn Books (1980).

15. Caldwell *et al.*, op. cit., p. 56.

16. Louis Henry, 'Some data on natural fertility'. *Eugenics Quarterly*, 8 (1961).

17. Charles F. Westoff and Norman B. Ryder, *The Contraceptive Revolution*, Princeton: Princeton University Press (1977), p. 280.

18. Ibid., p. 249.

19. Ibid., p. 253.

20. Ibid., p. 252.

21. See e.g. David Matza, *Delinquency and Drift*, New York: Wiley (1964).

22. The phrase is Matza's, ibid., p. 29.

23. This is discussed in more detail in Lincoln H. Day, 'Models for the causal analysis of differences in fertility: utility, normative, and drift'. In Lado T. Ruzicka (ed.), *The Economic and Social Supports for High Fertility: Proceedings of the Conference Held in Canberra 16–18 November 1976*, Canberra: Department of Demography and Development Studies Centre, Australian National University (1977).

24. Caldwell, *et al.*, op. cit., p. 56.

25. K. Wilson-Davis, 'Ideal family size in the Irish. Republic'. *Journal of Biosocial Science*, 12 (1980).

26. Hein G. Moors, *Child Spacing and Family Size in the Netherlands*, Leiden: Stenfert Kroese (1974), esp. chapters 3, 4 and 5.

27. P. A. Van Keep, 'Ideal family size in five European countries'. *Journal of Biosocial Science*, 3 (1971), esp. Tables 3–7, pp. 263–4.

28. Charles A. Price, 'Australian immigration: the Whitlam Government 1972–75'. In Charles A. Price and Jean I. Martin (eds), *Australian Immigration: A Bibliography and Digest*, no. 3, Part 1, Canberra: Department of Demography, Australian National University (1976), p. A14.

29. Ibid.

30. Jean I. Martin, *The Migrant Presence*, Sydney: George Allen & Unwin (1978), esp. chapter 2.

31. See references cited in note 2 above.

32. See e.g. Nathan Glazer and Daniel P. Moynihan (eds), *Ethnicity: Theory and Experience*, Cambridge: Harvard University Press (1975).

33. David Cox, 'The role of ethnic groups in migrant welfare'. Research report for Commission of Inquiry into Poverty, *Welfare of Migrants*, Canberra: Australian Government Publishing Service (1975), pp. 9, 27.

34. Andrew Sturman, 'From school to work: a review of major research in Australia'. *Australian Education Review*, 13 (1979); and Trevor Williams *et al.*, *School, Work, and Career: 17-Year-Olds in Australia*, Melbourne: Australian Council for Educational Research, Research Monograph no. 6 (1980), p. 66.

35. Helen Ware, 'Fertility and work-force participation: the experience of Melbourne wives'. *Population Studies*, 30 (1976), p. 413.

36. Cox, op cit., pp. 26–7, 42–3, 61.

37. Jean I. Martin, 'The economic condition of migrants'. Research report for Commission of Inquiry into Poverty, *Welfare of Migrants*, Canberra: Australian Government Publishing Service (1974), esp. pp. 157–63, 172–6.

38. Larry L. Bumpass, 'Fertility differences by employment patterns and role attitudes'. In Charles F. Westoff and Norman B. Ryder, *The Contraceptive Revolution*, Princeton: Princeton University Press (1977), pp. 327–30.

4

FERTILITY AND HUSBAND'S OCCUPATION

Introduction

Fertility differences by occupational grouping have a long history, especially in industrialised societies.[1] Some of the differences are, of course, rural–urban, ethnic or religious differences in another guise: perhaps most notably those between farmers and industrial workers (although it is by no means clear whether causation in this instance resides more in the attributes associated with residence or in those associated with occupation). Nevertheless, occupation would appear to have a bearing on fertility independent of that arising from its association with other personal attributes, for fertility differences associated with occupational groupings are to be found not simply between the various categories of the population, but also within them.

In Australia, the major fertility differences by husband's occupation have been those between the generality of clerical workers (professional, administrative, clerical and sales) and all the rest — with farmers and graziers having the highest fertility of all. While the general direction of these differences continued throughout the period under consideration here, their magnitude declined: the result of general increases in fertility among those with the lowest levels, and of stability or lesser increases among those with the highest (see table 4.1).

The present analysis employs seven occupational categories, as follows:

(1) professional, technical and related, (2) administrative, executive and managerial, (3) clerical and sales, (4) farmers, graziers, fishermen and forestry workers, (5) transport and communication workers, (6) tradesmen, production process workers and labourers, and (7) Others (including miners, service workers, sports and recreation workers, unemployed, not in the labour force, and not stated).

In 1971, the respective occupational distributions of the total male working population and the more restricted sector of that

Table 4.1: Median Issue Born to Current Marriage, by Husband's Occupation. Median for Clerical and Sales Workers and Relative Levels of Other Medians (Clerical and Sales = 100). Wives 40–64 Years of Age who Commenced Current Marriage before Age 26, by Year of Birth (Australia, 1971)

Year of Birth	Clerical and Sales Median	Index					
		Professional	Administrative	Farmers	Transport/Communication	Tradesmen, Labourers, Prod. Proc. Workers	Others
1907–11	1.82	103	106	152	121	121	123
1912–16	1.92	107	102	145	117	116	120
1917–21	1.98	110	105	142	118	114	119
1922–26	2.13	108	104	136	114	109	114
1927–31	2.32	109	103	131	112	105	112

population consisting of the husbands of wives in the population under study (i.e. of wives below age 65 and married before age 26) were as follows:

	Total Male Work Force		Husbands of Wives in Population under Study	
	N	%	N	%
Professional, etc.	309 329	9	68 443	7
Administrative, etc.	306 842	9	117 684	12
Clerical & Sales	518 703	14	108 653	11
Farmers & Graziers, etc.	341 128	9	91 662	9
Transport & Communications	251 033	7	66 211	7
Tradesmen, Production Process Workers & Labourers	1 456 850	40	338 087	34
Others	421 947	12	206 881	21
Total	3 605 832	100	997 621	101

Source:
Australia, *Census of Population and Housing, 1971*, vol. 5, Part 9, Tables 1, 3, Canberra (1972).

Findings

General

Despite their heterogeneous composition, these occupational categories have, at the national level, been quite consistently associated with group differences in Australian fertility for at least two generations. Farmers and graziers have had by far the highest fertility overall, and clerical and sales workers the lowest. But the fertility of the latter has remained only marginally lower than that among the other two white-collar groupings (professional and technical; administrative and managerial), and the fertility of the other categories of workers (transport and communications; tradesmen, labourers and production process workers; all others) has never reached the heights attained by farmers and graziers. In fact, if farmers and graziers are excluded, the range of fertility differences along occupational lines had become, with completion of the childbearing of the 1927–31 cohort, less than that associated with either urban–rural residence, religion or country of birth — less, that is, than the difference associated with any attribute save schooling; and the apparent narrowness of the differences by schooling may be spurious (see chapter 5).

Over the period under consideration, each occupational category experienced at the national level an increase in median fertility, a decrease in the proportion at the lowest parities (zero to one child), and either an increase or (as in the farmers and graziers, and tradesmen, etc. categories) virtual stability in the proportion at the highest parities (five or more children). Although this led to a decline in the differences between the various occupational categories, there remained throughout the period a greater degree of heterogeneity in distribution by parity among the wives of non-white-collar workers in industry and commerce than among either the wives of white-collar workers (whose fertility was generally the lowest) or the wives of farmers and graziers (whose fertility was generally the highest).

The most notable differences — and also the most important socially and demographically — were those at the highest parities. Although these declined considerably over the period under consideration, the proportion with five or more issue at the end of the period was, for example, still a full 90 per cent higher among the wives of farmers and graziers (down from 156 per cent at the beginning of the period), and that among the wives of husbands in the all others category still 51 per cent higher (down from 95 per cent at the beginning of the period), than the comparable figure among the wives of clerical and sales workers. The corresponding differences in median issue were a relatively more modest 31 per cent (down from 52 per cent) and 12 per cent (down from 23 per cent). With the proportions having no more than one child — a category involving not only far fewer children, but also a much smaller proportion of wives — the differences by occupation tended to persist at about the same levels throughout the period, with the proportion among farmers and graziers, for example, continuing at a level about half, and the proportion in the all others category at a level about two-thirds, of that among clerical and sales workers.

Nor does the introduction of greater detail by age at marriage have much effect on the pattern of these differences. By and large, the tendency toward a narrowing of group differences in both median issue and distribution by issue found among the total of wives married before age 26 is found also among those married before age 20, and at ages 20–1 and 22–5. Moreover, as with the

Table 4.2: Median Issue and Percentage with 5 + Issue Born to Current Marriage, by Husband's Occupation and Residence. Values for Metropolitan-Dwellers and Relative Values for Other Urban- and Rural-Dwellers (Metropolitan = 100). Wives 40–64 Years of Age who Commenced Current Marriage Before Age 26, by Year of Birth and Age at Marriage (Australia, 1971)

Median Issue

Age at Marriage and Year of Birth	Professional Metropolitan Median	Professional Other Urban (Index)	Professional Rural (Index)	Administrative Metropolitan Median	Administrative Other Urban (Index)	Administrative Rural (Index)	Clerical/Sales Metropolitan Median	Clerical/Sales Other Urban (Index)	Clerical/Sales Rural (Index)	Farmers Metropolitan Median	Farmers Other Urban (Index)	Farmers Rural (Index)
< 20												
1907–11	1.91	—	—	2.17	95	—	2.09	116	—	2.80	124	126
1917–21	2.27	119	—	2.23	118	118	2.28	113	138	3.05	106	110
1927–31	2.42	124	—	2.42	115	131	2.44	113	116	2.88	119	120
20–1												
1907–11	2.05	—	—	1.88	130	—	1.79	132	—	2.44	113	128
1917–21	2.07	115	133	2.03	121	124	2.02	113	121	2.38	119	126
1927–31	2.44	111	117	2.31	113	118	2.28	111	121	2.61	119	119
22–5												
1907–11	1.79	113	—	1.77	121	137	1.68	120	126	2.24	115	118
1917–21	2.13	108	118	1.94	116	118	1.85	117	117	2.20	111	124
1927–31	2.49	112	113	2.27	110	111	2.20	110	121	2.24	116	132

Per Cent with 5 + Issue

Age at Marriage and Year of Birth	Professional Metropolitan Median	Professional Other Urban (Index)	Professional Rural (Index)	Administrative Metropolitan Median	Administrative Other Urban (Index)	Administrative Rural (Index)	Clerical/Sales Metropolitan Median	Clerical/Sales Other Urban (Index)	Clerical/Sales Rural (Index)	Farmers Metropolitan Median	Farmers Other Urban (Index)	Farmers Rural (Index)
< 20												
1907–11	15	—	—	19	114	—	18	144	—	28	146	151
1917–21	16	148	—	15	169	168	17	153	142	31	101	122
1927–31	19	147	—	17	149	175	15	137	125	27	146	140
20–1												
1907–11	8	—	—	11	159	—	10	200	—	18	154	190
1917–21	12	145	235	10	178	207	12	148	174	18	146	172
1927–31	14	139	174	12	155	185	14	136	180	18	167	157
22–5												
1907–11	8	122	—	8	157	248	8	148	151	14	155	171
1917–21	12	129	157	8	156	177	9	139	160	14	153	160
1927–31	14	.134	152	11	138	156	12	143	178	15	146	163

Table 4.2 (continued)

Median Issue

Age at Marriage and Year of Birth	Transport/Communications			Tradesmen/Labourers Prod. Proc. Workers			Others		
		Index			Index			Index	
	Metropolitan Median	Other Urban	Rural	Metropolitan Median	Other Urban	Rural	Metropolitan Median	Other Urban	Rural
< 20									
1907–11	2.37	–	–	2.63	117	130	2.63	116	136
1917–21	2.65	115	131	2.69	114	128	2.81	111	129
1927–31	2.74	121	124	2.58	122	140	2.76	118	131
20–1									
1907–11	2.27	116	–	2.31	124	134	2.18	116	131
1917–21	2.26	124	126	2.24	117	123	2.24	114	125
1927–31	2.47	110	120	2.32	117	127	2.43	114	129
22–5									
1907–11	1.90	134	122	1.88	118	127	1.81	114	131
1917–21	1.98	120	122	1.94	118	131	1.97	123	125
1927–31	2.20	119	129	2.11	119	132	2.20	117	129
Per Cent with 5 + Issue									
< 20									
1907–11	19	–	–	27	126	144	27	131	160
1917–21	26	133	161	26	129	159	29	121	152
1927–31	25	145	154	23	145	187	27	133	162
20–1									
1907–11	18	126	–	20	134	153	19	137	165
1917–21	17	161	169	16	150	168	18	137	177
1927–31	18	134	148	16	150	187	18	156	183
22–5									
1907–11	11	239	182	13	129	150	12	159	182
1917–21	12	158	163	12	140	193	13	143	181
1927–31	16	141	166	12	153	202	14	149	187

(−) N < 100

Note: Median Issue and per cent with 5 + issue indices calculated on the basis of figures carried to two decimal places and one decimal place respectively.

total married before age 26, so also with those in narrower age at marriage categories: the relative differences in distribution among the various occupational groupings continued to be well in excess of those relating to median issue, especially at the highest parities.

While there was some tendency — if the farmers and graziers category is excluded — for the range of differences to be narrower at the more advanced marriage ages, the dominant pattern of these differences by husband's occupation — as to both central tendency and distribution — was none the less one of essentially similar ranges within each age at marriage category.

Urban—rural residence

The analysis of fertility differences by occupation and rural—urban residence involves analysing both the differences across residential categories within each occupational grouping, and the differences between occupations within each residential category.

So far as the differences across residential categories are concerned, the pattern within each occupational grouping is much like that for the country as a whole, whatever the measure used — that is, the highest fertility is found among rural-dwellers and the lowest among metropolitan-dwellers. Moreover, the pattern of these differences by residence is marked more by similarities than by differences. There was no particular tendency for urban—rural differences to be greater in one occupational grouping than another, nor greater at one marriage age than another. While the urban— rural differences were far greater at the higher parities than at the medians, the relative magnitudes of these differences were much the same across all occupational groupings.

The pattern of change in these differences was also similar to that for the population as a whole, characterised, as it was, more by stability than change. What deviations there were seem more in the nature of random fluctuations than of variations in actual patterns of association. Within no husband's occupation category was there any particular tendency toward either a contraction or an expansion of the fertility differences associated with residence (see Table 4.2).

With differences in the other direction — that is, between occupational groupings within each residential category — the general pattern is also like that in the population as a whole, again irrespective of the measure used. Whatever their residence, and whatever their age at marriage, the wives of white-collar workers had the lowest fertility (that is, the lowest median issue, the lowest proportions with five or more children, the highest proportions with only one child), and the wives of farmers and graziers nearly always the highest.

Moreover, the range of relative variation in fertility levels among the different occupation categories (for each age at marriage) was much the same in one residential category as another, with or without inclusion of farmers and graziers in the comparison. This was so whatever the measure of fertility. One could hardly expect the ratios to be identical, but what differences there were followed no particular pattern: the relative differences between highest and lowest fertility levels were much the same within each residential category. This means, of course, that because fertility was generally highest in rural areas and lowest in metropolitan, the absolute differences were greatest in the one and least in the other; but so far as the *relative* differences by occupation are concerned, there was little to choose between them (Table 4.3).

The pattern of fertility *changes* within occupational groupings in the three residential categories also clearly followed that for the country as a whole: increases in median fertility, decreases in the proportions with no more than one child, and either increases or virtual stability in the proportions with five or more. However, here sub-division by residence does reveal some differences.

While median issue increased among the wives of white-collar workers in each residential category, it did not always do so among the wives of non-white-collar workers. In fact, among these latter the pattern within residential categories was often marked more by stability than change. This was particularly so among those urban-dwellers who married at an early age (under 20). Yet stability in median issue also characterised two categories of urban-dwellers who had married at later ages (22–5): those whose husbands were farmers or graziers and those whose husbands were workers in transport or communications. What other exceptions by residence there were to the general pattern of increasing medians (those associated with rural-dwellers who had married before age 20 and whose husbands were workers in either clerical and sales, or transport and communications) can probably be attributed to small cell frequencies (N = 110 and 115, respectively).

The two exceptions among residential/occupational groupings to the general pattern of declining proportions with no more than one child (wives of farmers and graziers married before age 20 and

Table 4.3: Median Issue and Percentage with 5+ Issue Born to Current Marriage, by Husband's Occupation and Residence. Values for Clerical and Sales Workers and Relative Levels for Other Occupations (Clerical and Sales = 100). Wives 40–64 Years of Age who Commenced Current Marriage Before Age 26, by Year of Birth and Age at Marriage (Australia, 1971)

Age at Marriage and Year of Birth	Metropolitan						
	Index					Index	
	Professional	Administrative	Clerical and Sales Median	Farmers	Transport/Communication	Tradesmen, Labourers, Prod. Proc. Workers	Others
< 20							
1907–11	91	104	2.09	134	113	126	126
1917–21	100	98	2.28	134	116	118	123
1927–31	99	99	2.44	118	112	106	113
20–1							
1907–11	115	105	1.79	136	127	129	122
1917–21	102	100	2.02	118	112	111	111
1927–31	107	101	2.28	114	108	102	107
22–5							
1907–11	107	105	1.68	133	113	112	108
1917–21	115	105	1.85	119	107	105	106
1927–31	113	103	2.20	102	100	96	100
			Per Cent with 5+ Issue				
< 20							
1907–11	87	105	18	159	105	154	154
1917–21	93	88	17	183	151	149	169
1927–31	104	93	18	154	139	129	149
20–1							
1907–11	79	113	10	188	186	208	192
1917–21	98	80	12	145	139	132	143
1927–31	102	112	14	133	133	118	132
22–5							
1907–11	105	100	8	177	136	165	155
1917–21	131	95	9	159	140	136	147
1927–31	120	92	12	128	130	104	119

Table 4.3 (continued)

		Index				Other Urban	Index		
Age at Marriage and Year of Birth	Professional	Administrative	Clerical and Sales		Farmers	Transport/Communication	Tradesmen, Labourers, Prod. Proc. Workers	Others
			Median						
< 20									
1907–11	—	85	2.43		142	—	127	125
1917–21	105	102	2.58		125	118	119	121
1927–31	109	101	2.75		124	121	115	119
20–1									
1907–11	—	103	2.36		117	112	121	107
1917–21	100	103	2.39		118	118	109	107
1927–31	108	104	2.52		123	108	108	111
22–5									
1907–11	100	106	2.02		127	126	110	102
1917–21	106	104	2.16		113	110	106	103
1927–31	116	103	2.42		107	108	104	106
			Per Cent with 5 + Issue						
< 20									
1907–11	—	83	25		162	—	135	140
1917–21	89	97	26		120	130	125	133
1927–31	112	101	24		164	147	136	144
20–1									
1907–11	—	107	20		145	117	140	131
1917–21	97	96	18		143	151	134	133
1927–31	104	99	19		163	130	129	141
22–5									
1907–11	87	106	11		185	220	144	145
1917–21	121	107	12		175	159	138	151
1927–31	113	111	17		131	129	112	124

Table 4.3 (continued)

| | | Rural | | | | | |
| | | Index | | | | | |
Age at Marriage and Year of Birth	Professional	Administrative	Clerical and Sales Median	Farmers	Transport/Communication	Tradesmen, Labourers, Prod. Proc. Workers	Others
< 20							
1907–11	*	*	—	*	*	*	*
1917–21	—	84	3.15	107	110	109	115
1927–31	—	112	2.84	121	120	127	127
20–1							
1907–11	*	*	—	*	*	*	*
1917–21	113	102	2.45	123	116	91	114
1927–31	104	99	2.76	113	107	107	114
22–5							
1907–11	—	115	2.12	125	109	113	112
1917–21	116	106	2.17	125	112	118	113
1927–31	106	95	2.66	113	106	105	106
Per Cent with 5+ Issue							
< 20							
1907–11	*	*	—	*	*	*	*
1917–21	—	104	25	157	171	166	180
1927–31	—	131	22	173	172	193	193
20–1							
1907–11	*	*	—	*	*	*	*
1917–21	133	95	21	143	134	128	146
1927–31	98	90	25	116	109	122	134
22–5							
1907–11	—	165	12	200	165	165	187
1917–21	128	106	14	159	143	165	165
1927–31	102	81	21	117	121	118	125

(—) N < 100   * Not Applicable

Note: Median issue and per cent with 5+ issue indices calculated on the basis of figures carried out to two decimal places and one decimal place, respectively.

living in other urban areas, and wives of workers in transport and communications married at ages 22–5 and living in rural areas) can probably also be explained in terms of small cell frequencies (N = 144 and 115, respectively).

But with respect to the general pattern of increases in the proportion with five or more children, the exceptions among residential/occupational groupings are as numerous as are the instances of conformity, and in no way attributable to small cell frequencies. As will be discussed in more detail presently, these would appear largely — although possibly not entirely — explicable in terms of the extension of more effective control over fertility: particularly as they pertain mostly to the partially overlapping categories of (1) rural-dwellers, (2) those marrying at younger ages, and (3) those in non-white-collar occupations.

While the general direction of fertility differences between occupational groupings remained much the same within each residential category, there was none the less a tendency towards contraction of these differences: a tendency in keeping with that already noted for the country as a whole. The direction of these differences remained essentially unchanged, but the differences themselves narrowed markedly, mainly because, within each residential category, the major increases in fertility during this period took place within those occupational categories (the white-collar) initially characterised by the lowest fertility. The contraction was particularly pronounced among those who married at age 20 and over — ages at which one could expect the effects of unintentional pregnancy on total fertility to have been relatively less.

In this contraction across occupational lines, the experience of the wives of professionals was exceptional. It does not show up much when occupational groupings are considered as a whole, but when the population is sub-divided by residence those in the professional category are seen to have increased their fertility so much during this period as to have moved — within each residential category — from a position that was either the lowest or next to the lowest (only that of the clerical and sales category was ever lower) to one that was the highest, or virtually the highest, of all. But as the professional category was composed almost entirely of Australian- and British-born, an understanding of this development requires analysis based on sub-division by nativity and religion.

Nativity and Religion

As already noted (see chapter 3), the concentration of the overseas-born in two broad occupational groupings — tradesmen, etc. and all others — very much limits the range of possible comparisons between occupational groupings within the various nativity/religion sectors of the population. Only with the Australian-born and the non-Catholics among the British-born is there sufficient occupational dispersion to permit comparisons across all seven occupational groupings. With the Italian-born and Catholic British-born, comparisons are possible to some extent across six occupations; and with the Greek-born and non-Catholic Dutch- and German-born, to a lesser extent, across five. But comparisons within nativity/religion groupings among the rest can be made for the most part only between the tradesmen, etc. and all others categories, which is hardly a worthwhile exercise given the absence of any particular pattern of association between these two (apart from a slight tendency within the younger cohorts towards higher fertility on the part of those in the particularly heterogeneous all others category), and the fact that there is nothing to compare them with within their respective nativity/religion groupings.

What few data exist for cross-occupational comparisons among other than the Australian-, British- and Italian-born (and the data for such comparisons extend over no more than the two youngest cohorts) suggest two things: (1) adherence to the general pattern of higher relative fertility among farmers and non-white-collar workers, and (2) continuation of that pattern of declining fertility previously observed when looking at these populations as a whole (see chapter 3). The latter is in marked contrast to the pattern of increasing fertility during this period among the Australian- and British-born. It is only with the German-born non-Catholics among these others that there is even a suggestion of an increase in fertility — and this only among the wives of white-collar workers, where the possibility of a spurious association cannot be ruled out because the cell frequencies are less than 200 (less than 150, for the most part) and the percentages with five or more issue (the measure in which the apparent increase shows up most) are so small (in the vicinity of 5–6 per cent) as to render them particularly susceptible to extensive *relative* change without the occurrence of more than a slight *absolute* change. Thus, even when sub-divided by occupation, the overseas-born would appear to have their own patterns of fertility — patterns characterised by continuing declines

Table 4.4: Median Issue and Percentage with 5+ Issue Born to Current Marriage, by Husband's Occupation, Nativity and Religion. Wives 40–64 Years of Age who Commenced Current Marriage Before Age 26, By Year of Birth (Australia, 1971)

Religion, Husband's Occupation and Year of Birth	Median Issue							Per Cent with 5+ Issue						
	Australia	British Isles	Italy	Netherlands	Greece	Germany	Yugoslavia	Australia	British Isles	Italy	Netherlands	Greece	Germany	Yugoslavia
Catholic														
Professional														
1907–11	2.52	—	—	—	•	—	—	27	—	—	—	•	—	—
1912–16	2.72	—	—	—	•	—	—	29	—	—	—	•	—	—
1917–21	3.03	—	—	—	•	—	—	34	—	—	—	•	—	—
1922–26	3.25	3.17	—	—	•	—	—	36	32	—	—	•	—	—
1927–31	3.62	3.14	—	—	•	—	—	42	32	—	—	•	—	—
Administrative														
1907–11	2.46	—	—	—	•	—	—	24	—	—	—	•	—	—
1912–16	2.39	—	—	—	•	—	—	20	—	—	—	•	—	—
1917–21	2.61	2.90	—	—	•	—	—	24	31	—	—	•	—	—
1922–26	2.86	2.81	2.39	—	•	—	—	28	25	18	—	•	—	—
1927–31	3.06	2.69	2.41	3.19	•	—	—	31	26	15	35	•	—	—
Clerical/Sales														
1907–11	2.27	—	—	—	•	—	—	19	—	—	—	•	—	—
1912–16	2.50	2.29	—	—	•	—	—	22	19	—	—	•	—	—
1917–21	2.47	2.33	—	—	•	—	—	23	21	—	—	•	—	—
1922–26	2.75	2.63	2.43	—	•	—	—	27	25	14	—	•	—	—
1927–31	2.97	2.68	2.25	—	•	—	—	30	24	16	—	•	—	—
Farmers														
1907–11	3.26	—	3.06	—	•	—	—	38	—	34	—	•	—	—
1912–16	3.41	—	3.18	—	•	—	—	40	—	36	—	•	—	—
1917–21	3.49	—	2.98	—	•	—	—	41	—	34	—	•	—	—
1922–26	3.57	—	2.95	—	•	—	—	43	—	27	—	•	—	—
1927–31	3.83	—	2.75	—	•	—	—	47	—	22	—	•	—	—

Table 4.4 (continued)

Religion, Husband's Occupation and Year of Birth	Median Issue							Per Cent with 5+ Issue						
	Australia	British Isles	Italy	Netherlands	Greece	Germany	Yugoslavia	Australia	British Isles	Italy	Netherlands	Greece	Germany	Yugoslavia
Catholic (continued)														
Transport/Communication														
1907–11	2.54	—	—	—	•	—	—	24	—	—	—	•	—	—
1912–16	2.67	—	—	—	•	—	—	26	—	—	—	•	—	—
1917–21	2.66	—	—	—	•	—	—	26	—	16	—	•	—	—
1922–26	2.78	3.13	2.36	—	•	—	—	29	30	11	—	•	—	—
1927–31	2.97	2.86	2.22	—	•	—	—	31	29		—	•	—	—
Tradesmen, Labourers, Prod. Proc. Workers														
1907–11	2.49	2.52	3.57	—	•	—	—	24	23	42	—	•	—	—
1912–16	2.55	2.59	3.22	4.09	•	—	2.54	24	26	36	51	•	—	23
1917–21	2.61	2.73	2.82	3.93	•	2.24	2.14	25	27	27	49	•	23	14
1922–26	2.75	2.82	2.42	3.63	•	1.84	1.79	28	29	19	43	•	10	11
1927–31	2.92	2.84	2.19	3.13	•	1.93	1.81	30	28	14	31	•	14	9
Others														
1907–11	2.63	2.77	3.51	—	•	—	2.57	28	30	42	—	•	—	30
1912–16	2.64	2.67	3.06	—	•	—	2.35	27	22	34	—	•	—	12
1917–21	2.72	2.68	2.81	4.03	•	—	—	29	26	29	51	•	—	—
1922–26	2.87	3.07	2.53	3.65	•	1.80	1.91	31	34	22	43	•	10	13
1927–31	3.06	3.13	2.40	3.08	•	2.09	2.24	33	34	18	31	•	17	14
Non-Catholic														
Professional														
1907–11	1.87	1.80	•	—	—	—	—	7	9	•	—	—	—	—
1912–16	2.05	1.88	•	—	—	—	—	9	9	•	—	—	—	—
1917–21	2.11	1.99	•	—	—	—	—	9	9	•	—	—	—	—
1922–26	2.28	2.10	•	—	—	1.66	—	11	11	•	—	—	—	—
1927–31	2.48	2.28	•	2.27	—	1.66	—	11	11	•	16	—	—	—
Administrative														
1907–11	1.91	1.81	•	—	—	—	—	9	8	•	—	—	—	—
1912–16	1.95	1.77	•	—	—	—	—	8	6	•	—	—	—	—
1917–21	2.02	1.86	•	—	—	—	—	8	8	•	—	—	—	—
1922–26	2.16	2.01	•	2.65	2.60	1.63	—	9	9	•	23	20	6	—
1927–31	2.33	2.10	•	2.48	2.36	1.87	—	11	10	•	15	11	7	—

Table 4.4 (continued)

Religion, Husband's Occupation and Year of Birth	Median Issue							Per Cent with 5+ Issue						
	Australia	British Isles	Italy	Netherlands	Greece	Germany	Yugoslavia	Australia	British Isles	Italy	Netherlands	Greece	Germany	Yugoslavia
Non-Catholic continued														
Clerical/Sales														
1907–11	1.77	1.68	•	—	—	—	—	8	7	•	—	—	—	—
1912–16	1.86	1.73	•	—	—	—	—	8	8	•	—	—	—	—
1917–21	1.91	1.85	•	—	—	—	—	8	10	•	—	—	—	—
1922–26	2.03	1.96	•	2.45	—	1.38	—	9	11	•	20	—	5	—
1927–31	2.20	2.14	•	2.24	2.21	1.60	—	11	10	•	20	7	7	—
Farmers														
1907–11	2.72	2.46	•	—	—	—	—	25	21	•	—	—	—	—
1912–16	2.69	2.50	•	—	—	—	—	23	19	•	—	—	—	—
1917–21	2.72	2.54	•	—	—	—	—	23	22	•	—	—	—	—
1922–26	2.83	2.80	•	—	—	—	—	24	28	•	—	—	—	—
1927–31	2.97	2.74	•	—	2.69	—	—	25	21	•	—	16	—	—
Transport/Communication														
1907–11	2.13	2.04	•	—	—	—	—	17	12	•	—	—	—	—
1912–16	2.16	2.00	•	—	—	—	—	15	11	•	—	—	—	—
1917–21	2.27	2.02	•	—	—	—	—	17	15	•	—	—	—	—
1922–26	2.38	2.14	•	—	—	—	—	18	16	•	—	—	—	—
1927–31	2.55	2.40	•	—	—	1.69	—	20	17	•	—	—	11	—
Tradesmen, Labourers, Prod. Proc. Workers														
1907–11	2.11	1.95	•	2.72	—	—	—	16	13	•	24	—	—	—
1912–16	2.13	1.97	•	2.82	3.00	2.22	—	15	13	•	31	32	19	—
1917–21	2.15	2.05	•	2.77	3.04	2.11	2.23	15	14	•	27	30	16	17
1922–26	2.29	2.20	•	2.64	2.63	1.81	2.12	16	15	•	26	22	12	12
1927–31	2.43	2.29	•	2.71	2.15	1.74	1.95	18	16	•	22	8	12	9
Others														
1907–11	2.14	1.96	•	3.00	3.31	1.74	—	18	14	•	34	34	20	—
1912–16	2.19	2.06	•	3.30	3.09	—	—	18	15	•	35	35	—	—
1917–21	2.26	2.11	•	2.65	3.01	2.11	—	18	19	•	30	31	15	—
1922–26	2.38	2.23	•	2.85	2.60	1.80	2.09	20	17	•	27	19	14	11
1927–31	2.55	2.39	•	2.75	2.18	2.03	1.80	21	17	•	22	11	13	7

(—) N < 100   (*) Not applicable

Table 4.5: Median Issue and Percentage with 5 + Issue Born to Current Marriage, by Husband's Occupation, Nativity, and Religion. Values for Australian-born and Relative Values for Overseas-born (Australian-born = 100). Wives 40–64 Years of Age who Commenced Current Marriage Before Age 26, By Year of Birth (Australia, 1971)

Religion, Husband's Occupation and Year of Birth	Median Issue							Per Cent with 5 + Issue						
	Australia Median	British Isles	Italy	Netherlands	Greece	Germany	Yugoslavia	Australia Per Cent	British Isles	Italy	Netherlands	Greece	Germany	Yugoslavia
Catholic														
Professional														
1907–11	2.52	—	—	—	•	—	—	27	—	—	—	•	—	—
1912–16	2.72	—	—	—	•	—	—	29	—	—	—	•	—	—
1917–21	3.05	—	—	—	•	—	—	34	—	—	—	•	—	—
1922–26	3.25	98	—	—	•	—	—	36	89	—	—	•	—	—
1927–31	3.62	87	—	—	•	—	—	42	74	—	—	•	—	—
Administrative														
1907–11	2.46	—	—	—	•	—	—	24	—	—	—	•	—	—
1912–16	2.39	—	—	—	•	—	—	20	—	—	—	•	—	—
1917–21	2.61	111	—	—	•	—	—	24	130	—	—	•	—	—
1922–26	2.86	98	84	—	•	—	—	28	90	62	—	•	—	—
1927–31	3.06	88	79	104	•	—	—	31	85	50	114	•	—	—
Clerical/Sales														
1907–11	2.27	—	—	—	•	—	—	19	—	—	—	•	—	—
1912–16	2.50	92	—	—	•	—	—	22	89	—	—	•	—	—
1917–21	2.47	94	—	—	•	—	—	23	93	—	—	•	—	—
1922–26	2.75	96	88	—	•	—	—	27	93	54	—	•	—	—
1927–31	2.97	90	76	—	•	—	—	30	80	52	—	•	—	—
Farmers														
1907–11	3.26	—	94	—	•	—	—	38	—	90	—	•	—	—
1912–16	3.41	—	93	—	•	—	—	40	—	90	—	•	—	—
1917–21	3.49	—	85	—	•	—	—	41	—	86	—	•	—	—
1922–26	3.57	—	83	—	•	—	—	43	—	63	—	•	—	—
1927–31	3.83	—	72	—	•	—	—	47	—	46	—	•	—	—

Table 4.5 (continued)

Religion, Husband's Occupation and Year of Birth	Median Issue Index							Per Cent with 5+ Issue Index						
	Australia Median	British Isles	Italy	Netherlands	Greece	Germany	Yugoslavia	Australia Per Cent	British Isles	Italy	Netherlands	Greece	Germany	Yugoslavia
Catholic (continued)														
Transport/ Communication														
1907–11	2.54	—	—	—	•	—	—	24	—	—	—	•	—	—
1912–16	2.67	—	—	—	•	—	—	26	—	—	—	•	—	—
1917–21	2.66	—	—	—	•	—	—	26	—	—	—	•	—	—
1922–26	2.78	113	85	—	•	—	—	29	102	54	—	•	—	—
1927–31	2.97	96	75	—	•	—	—	31	96	37	—	•	—	—
Tradesmen, Labourers, Prod. Proc. Workers														
1907–11	2.49	101	143	—	•	—	—	24	98	174	—	•	—	97
1912–16	2.55	102	126	160	•	86	100	24	110	151	215	•	—	55
1917–21	2.61	105	108	151	•	67	82	25	109	109	198	•	93	39
1922–26	2.75	103	88	132	•	66	65	28	104	68	155	•	37	29
1927–31	2.92	97	75	107	•	—	62	30	95	47	103	•	46	—
Others														
1907–11	2.63	105	133	—	•	—	98	28	108	154	—	•	—	110
1912–16	2.64	101	116	—	•	—	89	27	81	125	—	•	—	44
1917–21	2.72	99	103	148	•	63	—	29	92	102	177	•	—	—
1922–26	2.87	107	88	127	•	68	67	31	110	70	141	•	31	—
1927–31	3.06	102	78	101	•	—	73	33	103	54	94	•	52	—
Non-Catholic														
Professional														
1907–11	1.87	96	•	—	—	—	—	7	135	•	—	—	—	—
1912–16	2.05	92	•	—	—	—	—	9	99	•	—	—	—	—
1917–21	2.11	94	•	—	—	73	—	9	97	•	—	—	—	—
1922–26	2.28	92	•	—	—	67	—	11	106	•	—	—	46	44
1927–31	2.48	92	•	92	—	—	—	11	96	•	148	—	43	42

Table 4.5 (continued)

Religion, Husband's Occupation and Year of Birth	Median Issue							Per Cent with 5+ Issue						
	Australia Median	British Isles	Italy	Index Netherlands	Greece	Germany	Yugoslavia	Australia Per Cent	British Isles	Italy	Index Netherlands	Greece	Germany	Yugoslavia
Non-Catholic (continued)														
Administrative														
1907–11	1.91	95	•	—	—	—	—	9	86	•	—	—	—	—
1912–16	1.95	91	•	—	—	—	—	8	74	•	—	—	—	—
1917–21	2.02	92	•	—	—	—	—	8	96	•	—	—	—	—
1922–26	2.16	93	•	123	120	75	—	9	98	•	246	211	61	—
1927–31	2.33	90	•	106	101	80	—	11	96	•	139	101	64	—
Clerical/Sales														
1907–11	1.77	95	•	—	—	—	—	8	86	•	—	—	—	—
1912–16	1.86	93	•	—	—	—	—	8	100	•	—	—	—	—
1917–21	1.91	97	•	—	—	—	—	8	116	•	—	—	—	—
1922–26	2.03	97	•	121	—	68	—	9	123	•	211	—	48	—
1927–31	2.20	97	•	102	100	73	—	11	94	•	188	68	66	—
Farmers														
1907–11	2.72	90	•	—	—	—	—	25	81	•	—	—	—	—
1912–16	2.69	93	•	—	—	—	—	23	82	•	—	—	—	—
1917–21	2.72	93	•	—	—	—	—	23	97	•	—	—	—	—
1922–26	2.83	99	•	—	—	—	—	24	115	•	—	—	—	—
1927–31	2.97	92	•	—	91	—	—	25	83	•	—	63	—	—
Transport/ Communication														
1907–11	2.13	96	•	—	—	—	—	17	73	•	—	—	—	—
1912–16	2.16	93	•	—	—	—	—	15	71	•	—	—	—	—
1917–21	2.27	89	•	—	—	—	—	17	84	•	—	—	—	—
1922–26	2.38	90	•	—	—	—	—	18	88	•	—	—	—	—
1927–31	2.55	94	•	—	—	66	—	20	86	•	—	—	56	—

Table 4.5 (continued)

Religion, Husband's Occupation and Year of Birth	Median Issue Index							Per Cent with 5+ Issue Index						
	Australia Median	British Isles	Italy	Netherlands	Greece	Germany	Yugoslavia	Australia Per Cent	British Isles	Italy	Netherlands	Greece	Germany	Yugoslavia
Non-Catholic (continued)														
Tradesmen, Labourers, Prod. Proc. Workers														
1907–11	2.11	92	•	129	—	—	—	16	82	•	150	—	—	—
1912–16	2.13	92	•	132	141	104	—	15	82	•	202	211	124	—
1917–21	2.15	95	•	129	141	98	104	15	90	•	174	199	103	110
1922–26	2.29	96	•	115	115	79	93	16	96	•	162	138	77	72
1927–31	2.43	94	•	112	88	72	80	18	92	•	127	47	66	52
Others														
1907–11	2.14	91	•	140	155	81	—	18	78	•	184	185	110	—
1912–16	2.19	94	•	151	141	—	—	18	83	•	192	189	—	—
1917–21	2.26	93	•	117	133	93	88	18	103	•	163	170	84	55
1922–26	2.38	94	•	120	109	76	88	20	83	•	137	95	69	55
1927–31	2.55	94	•	108	86	80	71	21	82	•	105	53	62	32

(—) N < 100
(*) Not applicable
Note:
Median issue and per cent with 5+ issue indices calculated on the basis of figures carried out to two decimal places and one decimal place, respectively.

in fertility within all, or nearly all, occupational categories for which there are enough cases to permit a meaningful analysis (see Table 4.4).

With each of the other nativity/religion groupings (those made up of the more numerous Australian-born, Italian-born and non-Catholic British-born), the general patterns of fertility by occupation were much like those for each sector as a whole: there were increases among the Australian- and British-born, and decreases (very marked ones, at that) among the Italian-born (Table 4.4).

Because the increases that occurred were generally greater among the wives of white-collar workers, the result was a contraction of the differences between occupational groupings. But while the increases among the Catholic Australian-born occurred at the higher parities as well as at the medians, those among the non-Catholics (both Australian- and British-born) were largely confined to the middle range of parities. At the higher parities, the pattern of change among these non-Catholics was characterised more by decreases or virtual stability. Moreover, while the experience of increased fertility among the Catholic Australian-born extended even to a relatively high fertility sector like farmers and graziers — and did so with respect to both median issue and the proportions at the higher parities — the experience of increased fertility in the farmer and grazier sector among non-Catholics was confined to only small increases in median issue, with proportions at the higher parities continuing to decline. Thus, while fertility among non-Catholic Australian- and British-born wives did increase during this period, it did so in a way that entailed greater concentration around a more central value. With Australian-born Catholics, on the other hand, the increases in the proportions at the higher parities were among the more prominent manifestations of the increases in fertility that occurred within that population, generally (see Table 4.5).

With respect to differences between nativity/religion groupings within the *same* occupation categories, the general patterns were those found without the further sub-division by occupation. In medians, this amounted to (1) persistence of much the same degree of difference between the British- and Australian-born (of either religion); (2) such marked declines among the Dutch-born (both Catholic and non-Catholic) as to produce, in combination with the increases among their respective Australian-born co-religionists, almost a complete closing of the gap formerly existing between these two nativity groupings; (3) a disappearance first, and then an expansion in the opposite direction, of the difference between the Italian-born and their fellow Catholics among the Australian-born, as the fertility of the former declined and that of the latter rose; (4) a similar pattern of differences between the Greek-born and their non-Catholic co-religionists among the Australian-born; (5) further expansion of the already considerable difference between the fertility of the German-born and that of their respective Australian-born co-religionists (although there is a suggestion of stability in this difference among non-Catholics in the administrative and clerical and sales categories); and (6) further expansion, also, of the already considerable differences separating the Yugoslav-born from their Australian-born co-religionists.

But it is in the proportions at the extremes that the contrasts between nativity/religion groupings within the same occupation are most marked. This is particularly so with the proportions at the highest parities which, constituting a generally larger share of the total than is the case with the proportions at the lowest parities, are less susceptible to random fluctuation, and for that reason more reliable entities for comparison. Again using the Australian-born as the basis for comparison, the differences between the proportions with five or more issue were far in excess of those between medians. For most, this meant that the deviation from the Australian-born proportion was in a markedly lower direction; but with the Dutch-born, this comparison at the higher parities suggests not only how extensive was the fertility decline among the Dutch, but also how persistent was their previous pattern of high fertility. The proportions with five or more issue remained higher for Catholics than non-Catholics among both the Dutch-born and the Australian-born. But while the gap between the Dutch- and Australian-born proportions at these parities had, by the end of the period, all but disappeared among Catholics, it remained large among non-Catholics, even though down markedly from previous levels. Among those in the 1927−31 cohort, the percentage of Dutch-born non-Catholic wives with five or more issue was still, relative to that among Australian-born non-Catholics, 88 per cent higher in the professional, 39 per cent higher in the administrative and 27 per cent higher in the trades, etc. category. Only in the all others category did it drop to a level but 5 per cent higher.

What stands out in the association between nativity/religion groupings and fertility differences by occupation, so far as such comparisons are possible, is (1) the marked increase in fertility among the Australian-born in all occupational groupings, but particularly among Catholics in the white-collar category; (2) the lesser increases among the British-born which, while generally more pronounced among the non-Catholics than Catholics, were not enough to remove the latter from their relatively higher fertility position; (3) the continued general decline in the fertility of the other overseas-born, particularly among those (such as the Dutch-born Catholics) who were marked by especially high fertility in earlier cohorts; (4) the increased proportions with five or more issue among the Australian-born — especially Catholics in the white-collar occupations, among whom the increases in the proportions with six or more were particularly marked; (5) a general contraction of fertility differences by occupation; and (6) a general reflection within each occupational grouping of the kind of fertility differences found between nativity/religion groupings as a whole.

Schooling

The analysis of fertility differences by schooling is limited in this study by the fact that the highest schooling category is that of 'nine years or more'. This will be discussed in more detail in the next chapter, but for the present it is enough to note that such a limitation exists.

Standardised by schooling and age at marriage, the pattern of fertility differences among occupations was much as that observed without reference to schooling. At each level of schooling, the wives of farmers and graziers had the highest fertility (highest medians, highest proportions with five or more children, the lowest proportions with no more than one), and the wives of clerical and sales workers the lowest.

But there was, during the period, a considerable narrowing of the fertility gap between white-collar and industrial workers at all levels of schooling. The one exception was the pattern among wives of professional workers, whose fertility moved from a position that was relatively lower than that of the other occupational groupings (clerical and sales excepted) at the beginning of the period to one that, at its close, was relatively higher (farmers and graziers excepted). This was particularly the case with those at the higher levels of schooling who married at ages 22–5. None the less, despite this increased fertility among professionals, fertility levels among farmers and graziers continued to be the highest of all and, in addition, retained much the same positions relative to those of the other non-white-collar workers. This excess fertility on the part of farmers and graziers was particularly pronounced at the upper schooling levels, and especially in terms of the proportions at these levels who had five or more issue (see Table 4.6).

With reference to differences by schooling within each occupational category, there were two main developments: (1) a general narrowing of the range of differences, particularly among non-white-collar workers, and (2) a reversal, among those who married at ages 22-5, of the relative fertility position of those with the most schooling and those with the least. At the beginning of the period (that is, with the cohort of 1907–11) relative fertility within each occupational grouping declined with increases in schooling, but by the end of the period it had increased. However, this was only with those marrying at the upper ages (22–5); at other marriage ages the older pattern continued, although in a much attenuated form (see Table 4.7).

In short, the general pattern of fertility differences by occupation observed in association with urban–rural residence and nativity and religion can be observed as well in association with years of schooling. However, in some contrast to the situation with residence and nativity/religion, the differences associated with schooling tended to diminish: both in those between occupational groupings at the same level of schooling and those between levels of schooling within the same occupational categories. Only with farmers and graziers did fertility retain the high levels found in earlier cohorts; and only with the professionals did it undergo a marked change in relative position.

Discussion

'One's job', the Lynds wrote, over 40 years ago 'is the watershed down which the rest of one's life tends to flow. . . . Who one is, whom one knows, how one lives, what one aspires to be, these and many other urgent realities of living are patterned for one by what one does to get a living and the amount of living this allows one to buy.'[2] It should hardly come as a surprise to find, then, that the job is also related to fertility. Within European populations, the statistical evidence of this association extends back several centuries.[3]

Table 4.6: Median Issue and Percentage with 5+ Issue Born to Current Marriage, by Husband's Occupation and Wife's Schooling. Values for Clerical and Sales Workers and Relative Values for Other Occupations (Clerical and Sales = 100). Wives 40–64 Years of Age who Commenced Marriage Before Age 26, by Year of Birth and Age at Marriage (Australia, 1971)

Age at Marriage, Years of Schooling and Year of Birth	Index		Clerical and Sales Median	Median Issue		Index	
	Professional	Administrative	Median	Farmers	Transport/ Communication	Tradesmen, Labourers, Prod. Proc. Workers	Others
< 20							
Under 6							
1907–11	—	80	2.46	146	106	115	121
1917–21	92	91	2.71	124	108	110	118
1927–31	108	100	2.72	127	117	106	119
6–7							
1907–11	—	—	2.18	148	—	123	122
1917–21	110	109	2.27	145	126	123	126
1927–31	107	102	2.56	136	114	109	118
8							
1907–11	—	—	—	—	—	—	—
1917–21	106	94	2.32	122	112	109	123
1927–31	108	105	2.42	132	116	110	117
9+							
1907–11	—	—	—	—	—	—	—
1917–21	97	97	2.22	132	110	110	113
1927–31	102	99	2.40	133	110	103	110

Table 4.6 (continued)

Age at Marriage, Years of Schooling and Year of Birth	Index		Per Cent with 5+ Issue			Index		
	Professional	Administrative	Clerical and Sales Median	Farmers	Transport/ Communication		Tradesmen, Labourers, Prod. Proc. Workers	Others
20–1								
Under 6								
1907–11	—	108	1.90	155	129		138	133
1917–21	104	104	2.12	142	117		117	123
1927–31	112	108	2.31	134	112		109	119
6–7								
1907–11	—	118	1.88	151	127		129	119
1917–21	100	102	2.16	138	117		108	111
1927–31	103	101	2.38	129	111		103	110
8								
1907–11	—	110	1.94	—	—		125	115
1917–21	105	103	2.07	141	115		110	103
1927–31	109	102	2.33	130	109		103	109
9+								
1907–11	103	94	1.91	—	—		112	98
1917–21	104	99	2.06	120	102		102	103
1927–31	105	101	2.37	131	105		98	106

Table 4.6 (continued)

Age at Marriage, Years of Schooling and Year of Birth	Index			Per Cent with 5+ Issue		Index	
	Professional	Administrative	Clerical and Sales Median	Farmers	Transport/ Communication	Tradesmen, Labourers, Prod. Proc. Workers	Others
22–5							
Under 6							
1907–11	99	104	1.80	147	121	114	113
1917–21	110	110	1.86	146	117	114	119
1927–31	111	102	2.19	124	108	102	110
6–7							
1907–11	102	111	1.76	148	117	107	109
1917–21	108	104	1.91	139	109	106	106
1927–31	110	109	2.18	134	108	103	109
8							
1907–11	115	105	1.75	139	107	117	105
1917–21	116	107	1.88	136*	109	106	103
1927–31	111	102	2.36	125	103	99	103
9+							
1907–11	108	107	1.69	145	109	102	103
1917–21	115	105	1.93	134	105	96	103
1927–31	115	106	2.26	134	105	97	103

Table 4.6 (continued)

Age at Marriage, Years of Schooling and Year of Birth	Index		Per Cent with 5+ Issue			Index	
	Professional	Administrative	Clerical and Sales %	Farmers	Transport/ Communication	Tradesmen, Labourers, Prod. Proc. Workers	Others
< 20							
Under 6							
1907–11	–	83	21	205	117	146	165
1917–21	100	78	24	153	136	128	150
1927–31	126	109	23	177	157	133	160
6–7							
1907–11	–	–	22	170	–	124	126
1917–21	144	133	17	216	169	164	183
1927–31	111	102	20	189	138	131	151
8							
1907–11	–	–	–	–	–	–	–
1917–21	65	97	17	168	163	135	171
1927–31	124	108	17	191	151	142	165
9+							
1907–11	–	–	–	–	–	–	–
1917–21	96	79	17	193	143	127	140
1927–31	89	80	18	184	115	120·	127

Table 4.6 (continued)

Age at Marriage, Years of Schooling and Year of Birth	Per Cent with 5+ Issue						
	Index					Index	
	Professional	Administrative	Clerical and Sales %	Farmers	Transport/ Communication	Tradesmen, Labourers, Prod. Proc. Workers	Others
20–1							
Under 6							
1907–11	—	118	13	264	166	207	203
1917–21	90	97	16	196	137	135	159
1927–31	123	108	16	190	138	134	165
6–7							
1907–11	—	137	14	225	149	139	138
1917–21	108	93	13	217	165	138	158
1927–31	99	96	16	172	140	117	135
8							
1907–11	—	182	7	—	—	296	235
1917–21	117	80	12	215	151	123	117
1927–31	104	97	14	196	139	124	148
9+							
1907–11	57	70	14	—	—	86	86
1917–21	102	83	13	149	87	106	119
1927–31	91	79	17	151	103	99	111

Table 4.6 (continued)

Age at Marriage, Years of Schooling and Year of Birth	Index		Per Cent with 5+ Issue			Index	
	Professional	Administrative	Clerical and Sales %	Farmers	Transport/ Communication	Tradesmen, Labourers, Prod. Proc. Workers	Others
22–5							
Under 6							
1907–11	102	113	9	283	176	190	199
1917–21	128	128	9	262	171	178	211
1927–21	139	101	13	161	139	114	160
6–7							
1907–11	87	105	10	215	181	117	228
1917–21	133	96	9	226	155	132	149
1927–31	103	91	13	196	129	113	130
8							
1907–11	134	114	8	204	144	148	142
1917–21	138	106	9	228	148	140	153
1927–21	112	94	13	172	119	103	115
9+							
1907–11	95	121	8	219	161	125	117
1917–21	120	89	11	185	130	106	120
1927–31	122	89	13	187	118	101	114

(—) N = 100

Note: Median issue and per cent with 5+ issue indices calculated on the basis of figures carried out to two decimal places and one decimal place, respectively.

Table 4.7: Median Issue and Percentage with 5+ Issue Born to Current Marriage, by Husband's Occupation and Wife's Schooling. Values for Those with Eight Years of Schooling and Relative Values for Those with Other Levels of Schooling (8 Years = 100). Wives 40–64 Years of Age who Commenced Current Marriage before Age 26, by Year of Birth and Age at Marriage (Australia, 1971)

Husband's Occupation, Age at Marriage and Year of Birth	Median Issue				Per Cent with 5+ Issue			
	Index Under 6 Years	6–7 Years	8 Years Median	Index 9+ Years	Index Under 6 Years	6–7 Years	8 Years Per Cent	Index 9+ Years
Professional								
< 20								
1907–11	*	*	—	*	*	*	—	*
1917–21	100	101	2.47	87	219	218	12	147
1927–31	113	105	2.62	93	139	109	21	78
20–1								
1907–11	*	*	—	*	*	*	—	*
1917–21	101	99	2.17	99	99	97	15	89
1927–31	102	96	2.54	98	142	109	14	111
22–5								
1907–11	89	89	2.01	91	85	83	10	71
1917–21	93	94	2.19	101	96	104	12	106
1927–31	97	96	2.51	104	128	93	15	113
Administrative								
< 20								
1907–11	*	*	—	*	*	*	—	*
1917–21	114	114	2.17	100	115	135	17	80
1927–31	108	103	2.53	94	139	116	18	80

Table 4.7 (continued)

Husband's Occupation, Age at Marriage and Year of Birth	Median Issue				Per Cent with 5+ Issue			
	Index		8 Years Median	Index 9+ Years	Index		8 Years Per Cent	Index 9+ Years
	Under 6 Years	6–7 Years			Under 6 Years	6–7 Years		
Administrative								
20–1								
1907–11	96	103	2.14	84	110	146	14	73
1917–21	103	103	2.14	95	157	123	10	107
1927–31	105	101	2.38	101	134	114	13	105
22–5								
1907–11	103	107	1.83	98	110	118	9	106
1917–21	101	99	2.01	100	125	100	9	102
1927–31	97	99	2.30	104	110	98	12	98
Clerical/Sales								
< 20								
1907–11	*	*	—	*	*	*	—	*
1917–21	117	102	2.32	96	143	98	17	99
1927–31	112	106	2.42	99	137	122	17	108
20–1								
1907–11	98	97	1.94	98	169	195	7	189
1917–21	102	104	2.07	100	129	106	12	102
1927–31	99	102	2.33	102	120	116	14	128
22–5								
1907–11	103	101	1.75	97	112	129	8	100
1917–21	99	102	1.88	103	103	108	9	122
1927–31	97	96	2.26	100	102	101	13	103

Table 4.7 (continued)

Husband's Occupation, Age at Marriage and Year of Birth	Median Issue				Per Cent with 5+ Issue			
	Index Under 6 Years	6–7 Years	8 Years Median	Index 9+ Years	Index Under 6 Years	6–7 Years	8 Years Per Cent	Index 9+ Years
Farmers								
< 20								
1907–11	*	*	—	*	*	*	—	*
1917–21	120	117	2.82	104	130	126	29	114
1927–31	108	108	3.20	100	127	120	32	104
20–1								
1907–11	*	*	—	*	*	*	—	*
1917–21	103	102	2.91	85	118	106	27	71
1927–31	102	102	3.03	103	116	102	27	99
22–5								
1907–11	109	107	2.44	100	155	136	16	108
1917–21	106	104	2.56	101	119	107	20	99
1927–31	96	104	2.82	107	96	115	22	112
Transport/Communication								
< 20								
1907–11	*	*	—	*	*	*	—	*
1917–21	113	111	2.59	94	119	102	28	86
1927–31	114	105	2.80	94	142	111	25	82
20–1								
1907–11	*	*	—	*	*	*	—	*
1917–21	-103	106	2.39	88	117	116	19	59
1927–31	102	104	2.54	94	119	117	19	95

Table 4.7 (continued)

Husband's Occupation, Age at Marriage and Year of Birth	Median Issue				Per Cent with 5+ Issue			
	Index		8 Years Median	Index 9+ Years	Index		8 Years Per Cent	Index 9+ Years
	Under 6 Years	6–7 Years			Under 6 Years	6–7 Years		
Transport/Communication								
22–5								
1907–11	116	110	1.87	99	136	161	11	112
1917–21	106	102	2.04	100	119	113	13	107
1927–31	102	101	2.33	102	119	109	16	102
Tradesmen, Labourers, Prod. Proc. Workers								
< 20								
1907–11	112	106	2.53	95	128	115	24	103
1917–21	117	110	2.54	96	136	120	23	93
1927–31	109	106	2.65	93	128	112	24	91
20–1								
1907–11	108	100	2.42	88	118	91	22	55
1917–21	109	102	2.28	93	142	119	15	88
1927–31	104	102	2.41	97	129	108	17	102
22–5								
1907–11	100	93	2.04	85	143	102	11	87
1917–21	107	102	1.99	93	131	102	12	93
1927–31	100	100	2.23	98	113	110	13	101

Table 4.7 (continued)

Husband's Occupation, Age at Marriage and Year of Birth	Median Issue				Per Cent with 5+ Issue			
	Index		8 Years Median	Index 9+ Years	Index		8 Years Per Cent	Index 9+ Years
	Under 6 Years	6–7 Years			Under 6 Years	6–7 Years		
Others								
< 20								
1907–11	118	105	2.53	88	142	115	24	83
1917–21	112	100	2.86	87	125	105	29	81
1927–31	114	106	2.83	94	132	111	27	83
20–1								
1907–11	113	100	2.23	84	146	114	17	70
1917–21	123	113	2.13	100	176	143	14	104
1927–31	107	102	2.55	99	134	105	20	96
22–5								
1907–11	111	104	1.84	95	157	207	11	83
1917–21	109	100	2.03	98	143	105	13	95
1927–31	103	102	2.33	100	142	113	15	101

(—) N < 100
* Not applicable
Note:
Median issue and per cent with 5+ issue indices calculated on the basis of figures carried out to two decimal places and one decimal place, respectively.

Yet the nature of this association has been marked by discontinuity. In both its direction and its underlying causal elements, the association between occupation and fertility has exhibited a variety of changes. So far as fertility is concerned, it would appear that occupation has been less a causal element in itself than an indicator of the likely presence of certain causal elements: of some, like income and relative income, social position, life-style and levels of aspiration, that are essentially personal in nature; and of others, like ethnicity, religion and urban–rural residence, that relate more to group affiliations. In the present analysis it has been possible to adjust for some of the latter, but not for any of the former.

A further difficulty in analysing fertility differences between occupations is the heterogeneous nature of the occupational categories themselves. For example, the administrative workers category includes Members of Parliament, business executives, shopkeepers and local government meat inspectors; the transport and communications workers category, air traffic controllers, telephone switchboard operators, letter sorters and lorry drivers; the tradesmen, etc. category, carpenters, textile machine-operators, die-makers, freight-handlers, and builders' labourers; and the all others category, police and firemen, charwomen, air hostesses, bartenders, jockeys, embalmers, members of the armed forces (all ranks) and those not in the workforce.[4] So far as certain conditions customarily of major importance to decision-making about childbearing are concerned — such conditions as income, life-style and levels of aspiration, for instance — these categories are doubtless characterised more by overlap than by differentiation.

Moreover, just as people can change residences, so also can they change occupations. And as the period of childbearing normally lasts only a few years, it is by no means unlikely for a husband's ocupation during the most important years (from the standpoint of its effect on fertility) to have been different from that recorded here. While the use of broad occupational categories doubtless reduces the effect of such shifts, it can also obscure some potentially interesting detail. For example, are physicians, as is often claimed, an unusually high fertility grouping, and those in the performing arts an unusually low one? Any stability achieved by the use of broad categories can only be at the sacrifice of this kind of detail.

But while shifts may be less likely between occupational categories than between individual occupations, there is nothing immutable even about one's position within a category as broad as those used here. Take transport and communications workers, for example. Between 1961 and 1971, there was a net decrease of 9 per cent in the number of men of the 1927–36 birth cohort in this occupational category, and of 18 per cent in the number of men of the 1917–26 cohort;[5] and these, being net movements, represent the very minimum of occupational shifts involving this category of workers. As death could be expected to account for declines of about 2 and 5 per cent, respectively, there remain the questions of what occupational categories these men — 7 per cent in the one instance, 13 per cent in the other — went to, and the effect this shift had on the fertility levels associated with each. Or consider farmers and graziers, where there occurred a 24 per cent decrease between 1961 and 1971 in the 1917–26 cohort alone. What occupations did these men enter, and — more important for present purposes — to what extent did they transfer to these occupations the propensity for higher fertility associated with their former occupations? Similarly, there have been marked increases in the numbers of professionals. What occupations did these men have before, or what occupations would they have had if the distribution of employment opportunities had not changed, and what bearing, if any, does this have on either their levels of fertility or the levels of fertility recorded for the various occupational categories used here?

A related matter introducing a further difficulty into the analysis of fertility differences between occupations is the possibility that the composition of one or another occupational grouping may have changed with respect to something of significance to the determination of fertility — income or levels of aspiration, for example — for which no data are available for analysis here.

Nevertheless, despite these limitations to their analysis, fertility differences by broad occupational categories do exist in Australia and have done so for a long time. Moreover, with age at marriage held constant, these differences follow much the same pattern by urban–rural residence, schooling and (so far as cell frequencies permit analysis) nativity and religion. In whatever category of the population, farmers and graziers tended to have the highest fertility and white-collar workers — particularly those in the clerical and sales category — the lowest. There is, in short, something about fertility in association with occupation that needs to be accounted for.

But whatever that something is, it was of lesser magnitude at the end of the period than at the beginning, for the major increases in fertility during this period took place within those occupational categories formerly characterised by the lowest fertility, thereby appreciably narrowing the fertility gaps between occupations.

In all this, the pattern of fertility among Australian-born Catholic wives of professional (and, to a lesser extent, administrative and clerical and sales) workers is particularly worthy of note. The period saw increased fertility on the part of Australian-born Catholics in all occupational sectors, but at each marriage age it is the wives of professionals who experienced the largest relative gains and also the largest absolute gains, whether these gains are measured in terms of median issue or in terms of the proportion bearing five or more. This sector's gains at the upper parities were, in fact, particularly impressive, for they indicate an increase in group fertility attained not so much by means of a withdrawal from the lowest parities (zero to one) — although this did happen — as from a positive movement into the highest parities (five or more and, in particular, six or more) — and this on the part of a sector of the population already characterised by relatively high proportions at these parities. Only for their counterparts among the farmers and graziers were the corresponding proportions any higher.

Moreover, at least among the later cohorts (cell frequencies are too low for such comparisons among the earlier ones), the fertility of these Australian-born Catholic professionals actually *increased* with advancing age at marriage: thus forming a contrast with the pattern of essentially similar fertility by age at marriage among their counterparts in the other white-collar and farmer and grazier categories, and, in particular, with the pattern of *declines* with advancing marriage age within every other category of the population, Catholic and non-Catholic alike.

Explaining the observed pattern of fertility by husband's occupation thus entails accounting, in particular, for two developments: first, the general narrowing of fertility differences between occupational categories, and secondly, the contrasting expansion of those of these differences that involved Australian-born Catholic professionals. As before, the explanation can be divided in terms of physiological differences, differences in the ability and willingness to exercise control over childbearing, and differences in desired numbers of children.

If either of these developments owes anything to physiology it cannot be very much. As argued earlier, any role physiological factors might have played would have had to take the form of differences either in coital frequency or in overall levels of health and well-being of a sort to affect the likelihood of intercourse, conception or successful gestation and parturition. While such differences between occupational groupings are certainly possible, and even probable, they can hardly have accounted for more than a fraction of the fertility differences under review here. Overall fertility levels were simply too low, and the range of possible variation, in consequence, too narrow, to permit these factors to operate at more than a very marginal level. The fertility differences associated with husband's occupation — like those already observed in association with urban–rural residence, nativity and religion — are to be explained in terms of values, knowledge and attitudes, not physiology.

So how might the mix of these determinants — the mix of factors relating to the ability and willingness to exercise control over childbearing, as well as to desired numbers of children — have been altered so as to produce a general narrowing of fertility differences between occupations? One possibility is through shifts in personnel out of the occupational categories associated with one's parents, as well as out of those previously occupied by oneself; the movers taking with them into the new occupational category both the children already born (or the longer-birth intervals already undergone, if we are to consider movement from lower to higher fertility categories, as well) and certain fertility-related values, attitudes, knowledge (or ignorance, as with respect to the more reliable practice of birth control, for instance) of a sort that both adds to the heterogeneity of the mix of such causal elements within each occupational category and makes these various mixes more similar to one another. While we do not know the full extent of such shifts, we do know from the data on the net of these movements that it was more than negligible. While fertility increases occurred to some extent in all occupational categories during this period, the general movement was toward a reduction of the fertility differences associated with occupation. That the major net occupational shifts during this period were away from the category with the highest fertility (farmers and graziers) and toward those with the lowest (white-collar) certainly suggests that personnel shifts between occupational categories could have played a significant role in reducing the earlier fertility differences between them.[6]

It is even possible to reason along similar lines in accounting for the fact that the fertility of those in the farmers and graziers category also rose during this period, despite the already elevated fertility of this sector of the population at the beginning of the period. For it is not implausible to suppose that within this occupational grouping, which was the one to experience the greatest net loss in numbers over the period, those least attached to its ways of life (and, therefore, presumably least attached to its higher fertility norm as well) may have been the ones most likely to leave it for another. If this is what did, in fact, take place, the movement between occupational categories would, in this one instance, have rendered an occupational grouping more, rather than less, homogeneous, at least with respect to those of its values and patterns of life that pertain to fertility.

But while shifts in personnel between these occupational categories doubtless had something to do with removing the fertility differences between them, it is likely that a greater force in this direction came from development of a more general norm concerning the desirable (or at least acceptable) range of fertility; for this narrowing of fertility differences between occupational groupings took place not only in the population as a whole, but — so far as cell frequencies permit analysis — within the various subdivisions of the population as well. This would have resulted not so much from the introduction of greater heterogeneity into the determinants of fertility within each occupational category as from a growing similarity between these categories as to their participants' life-styles, incomes, patterns of consumption, levels of aspiration, and the like. Movements between occupations would certainly have helped this process along, but it was probably furthered even more by such developments as the extension of access to the media of mass communication and of exposure to a content in these media that was much the same everywhere (that is, the same newspaper and magazine content, the same films, the same radio and television programmes), the extension of mass advertising, greater geographic mobility, and through it all an expanding dependence on the market-place as a system for the allocation of goods and services — and increasingly the same goods and services, at that.

A third element in this reduction of the fertility differences between occupational categories is doubtless the diffusion of effective control over fertility — both the actual practice of birth control and its acceptability. The apparent pattern of this practice among the overseas-born has already been discussed (chapter 3). Sub-division by husband's occupation does nothing to alter that picture. However, among the Australian-born the pattern is less straightforward, primarily because of the tack taken by Catholics. Yet even among Catholics, the increases in proportions at the higher parities were less among those who, from the experience of the earlier cohorts, could be presumed to have practised birth control less widely or efficiently, namely, rural-dwellers, those who married at younger ages and those with husbands in non-white-collar occupations. Only among the wives of professional workers, the category characterised at the beginning of the period by the lowest proportions at the upper fertility levels — and for that reason presumably the category with the most extensive control, then, over its fertility — was there any general increase in the proportions bearing five or more children (the one exception, those who were rural-dwelling and married at ages 20–1, can be attributed to the small cell frequency: N = 103).

Turning now to the second major development requiring explanation in the pattern of fertility differences by husband's occupation, namely, the very extensive increases in the fertility of the Australian-born Catholic professionals, one finds once again a strong indication that (as already discussed in more detail in chapter 3) it was the upper income, upper status elements of the Catholic population who were the ones particularly susceptible to their Church's teaching on the family and birth control. Whatever underlay their susceptibility, it was this sector of the population that experienced the greatest gains in fertility during this period and that as a result underwent not only a marked increase in absolute fertility, but also a marked change in fertility position relative to that of the other sectors. Only its Australian-born co-religionists among the farmers and graziers ended the period with a fertility level any higher — and that by an amount very much less than at the beginning.

Nor is the movement of people from one occupational sector to another likely to have played any significant part in this transition. In order for this to have been the case, there would (because of the high fertility of these professionals) have to have been massive additions to the professional category either of those with the highest fertility propensities within the other occupational group-ings (which hardly seems likely), or of persons from the higher fertility farmers and graziers sector (which, while it doubtless happened, could hardly have done so on a scale sufficient to account for the magnitude of the change).

No, something happened among Australian-born Catholic wives of professionals (and, to a much lesser extent, of men in the other two white-collar categories) to make them desire — or at least acquiesce in having — a progeny not only more numerous than that of previous cohorts in this sector of the population, but also more numerous than that of any other sector of the population, save their Australian-born farmer and grazier co-religionists. As already suggested in chapter 3, this 'something' would appear to have been the development of a stronger sense of Catholic identity in combination with a personal economic position more favourable to the support of children.

Notes

1. See e.g. Rudolf Andorka, *Determinants of Fertility in Advanced Societies*, op. cit. pp. 61–3; and also Clyde V. Kiser, Wilson H. Grabill and Arthur A. Campbell, *Trends and Variations in Fertility in the United States*, Cambridge, Mass.: Harvard University Press (1968), pp. 185–207; Census of England and Wales (1911), vol. 13, *Fertility of Marriage*, London: General Register Office (1917); and W. D. Borrie, *Population Trends and Policies*, Sydney: Australasian Publishing Co. (1948), p. 114.

2. Robert S. Lynd and Helen Merrell Lynd, *Middletown in Transition*, New York: Harcourt, Brace & Co. (1937), p. 7.

3. Andorka, op cit., pp. 61–3.

4. Commonwealth Bureau of Census and Statistics, *Classification and Classified List of Occupations, revised: June 1971*, Canberra: Commonwealth Government Printing Office (1971).

5. Calculated from data in Australia, Commonwealth Bureau of Census and Statistics, *Census of Population and Housing, 1961*, vol. 8, Part 1, Canberra (1965), Table 54; and Australia, Commonwealth Bureau of Census and Statistics, *Census of Population and Housing, 1971*, Bulletin 8, Canberra (1972), Table 4.

6. In this connection see David Goldberg, 'The fertility of two-generation urbanites'. *Population Studies*, 12 (1959).

5 FERTILITY AND SCHOOLING

Introduction

An association between schooling and fertility has been widely observed. But it is an association not everywhere in the same direction, nor is the causal nexus invariably free of ambiguities. In some instances, schooling would appear to affect fertility through its effect on, for example, the extent of one's knowledge of the more efficacious techniques of birth control, one's levels of aspiration, or the range of behaviour over which one feels capable of exercising some degree of control. In other instances, schooling appears to be more an indicator of the existence of certain elements of some presumed causal significance to fertility, such as social class and income, the status of women, or feelings of personal independence. In most populations, this association is doubtless of both types simultaneously. Australia is surely no exception.

The 1971 census was the second Australian census to inquire into schooling (1966 being the first). The items of information collected in 1971 relate to two things, first, the highest level of schooling attended or being attended, and secondly, the trade or other formal qualifications (including tertiary level diplomas and degrees) already obtained or being worked toward. The questions asked were as follows:[1]

1. What is the highest level of schooling this person has ever attended?
2. If this person is now a child at school or a full-time or part-time student, print full name and address of school, university, college, etc.
3. Is this person now doing a course leading to a trade or other qualification? Give full name of qualification for which studying (e.g. Automotive Engineering Certificate, B.Econ., etc.)
4. Since leaving school has this person obtained a trade or other qualification (e.g. trade or apprenticeship certificate, diploma, degree)? Full name of qualification(s) (e.g., Fitter and Turner's Certificate, Diploma in Public Health, B.Eng. (Civil), etc.). Main field of training or study (e.g. bricklaying,

146

nursing, carpentry, economics, sociology, physics, electrical engineering, etc.). Name of training or educational institution(s) at which above qualification was obtained (e.g. Sydney Technical College; University of Melbourne).

For the first of these questions, respondents were given the following instructions:

If schooling was completed several years ago, in another state or overseas, give the grade which is most nearly the same.
If now attending school give the present grade.

Respondents were also instructed to tick one of the following boxes:

Primary School   Secondary School

Grade or Form   Grade or Form

Never
Attended   Kindergarten or   1 2 3 4 5 6 7 8 9
School   1 2 3 4 5 or 6

☐   ☐   ☐☐☐☐☐☐☐☐   ☐

Because education systems differ among the Australian states, the question on schooling was varied appropriately in the schedules used in the different states, and a procedure developed for assigning grades (or forms) in each state or territory to an approximately comparable level.[2]

There is an obvious emphasis on trade qualifications and apprenticeships, but given the small proportion (well under 10 per cent even in more recent cohorts) who embark upon tertiary studies this is probably to be expected. Certainly there is little likelihood of its introducing any bias into the analysis. But the same cannot be said of the shift from years of schooling *completed* on the 1966 schedule, to years of schooling *ever attended* on the 1971 schedule, for this introduces a further risk of upward bias to that already to be expected from respondents' sometimes claiming more schooling than they actually had.

The sub-categories of schooling chosen for this analysis are four: (1) fewer than six years; (2) six to seven years; (3) eight years; and (4) nine years or more. As with the other decisions about categorisation for this study, this one for schooling was determined on the basis of its apparent significance in the Australian setting.

Obviously, some items of information had to be sacrificed so that others could be included, and some decisions had to be made in the absence of any clear idea of their consequences. But the decision made about categories of schooling, while it incorporated the major breaks in the Australian school system, turns out to have been less than satisfactory; not so much because it limits the present analysis as because it limits the possibilities for comparisons with future generations. To commence the highest category at a level as low as nine years was not a wise decision. Were there the opportunity to do this tabulation again, I would choose to combine the fast-disappearing lowest category (fewer than six years) with the equally fast-disappearing next to lowest category (six to seven years), retain the next category (eight years), and then make two or three categories out of the uppermost one (nine years or more). This would employ the same number of categories (or add no more than one) while introducing further detail into the information on those at the upper levels where the largest proportionate gains in schooling have been taking place, and where they seem likely to continue to take place for some time into the future. The distribution by schooling of the population under study, together with more recent cohorts, is presented below, with the nine years or more category appropriately sub-divided so as to show what opportunities for future comparisons have been lost because of the system of categorisation used here (Table 5.1).

Findings

General

Throughout the period under consideration (that represented in the fertility of the cohorts of 1907–11 to 1927–31), there was an almost consistently negative association between schooling and fertility. Those with the least schooling had the highest fertility, and those with the most schooling had the lowest — whether the schooling referred to is the wife's or the husband's. The only exceptions are in the proportions at the lowest parities (zero to one) where there came to be so few (around 15 per cent with the cohort of 1917–21, 10 per cent with the cohort of 1927–31) as virtually to wipe out altogether the differences between schooling categories, while at the same time, allowing a greater likelihood of some variation in rank order between them.

But while this generally inverse relation persisted, the differences

Table 5.1: Women 15–64 Years of Age, by Number of Years of School Attendance, by Age (Australia, 1971)

Year of Birth	1952–56		1947–51		1937–46		1927–36		1917–26		1912–16		1907–11	
Age in 1971	15–19		20–24		25–34		35–44		45–54		55–59		60–64	
Years of School Attendance (1971)	No.	%	No.	%	No.	%	No.	%	No.	%	No.	%	No.	%
0–5 years[a]	6 228	1.67	13 201	2.51	47 556	5.82	61 041	8.56	53 862	7.93	27 841	9.80	29 003	12.27
6–7 years[b]	16 689	4.49	44 852	8.54	124 965	15.29	157 216	22.04	219 747	32.35	105 120	37.02	95 733	40.49
8 years[c]	39 953	10.74	62 258	11.85	124 911	15.29	131 267	18.40	132 354	19.49	50 948	17.94	38 936	16.47
9 + years, of whom:														
9[d]	117 792	31.67	166 068	31.62	250 092	30.60	182 096	25.52	131 042	19.29	44 659	15.73	29 521	12.49
10[e]	103 662	27.87	98 054	18.67	106 023	12.97	74 980	10.51	54 450	8.02	18 293	6.44	12 847	5.43
11–12[f]	86 211	23.18	103 093	19.63	108 636	13.29	79 698	11.17	70 877	10.44	30 639	10.79	24 880	10.52
Tertiary														
Non-degree	1 175	0.32	26 708	5.09	39 868	4.88	19 151	2.68	11 479	1.69	4 553	1.60	4 090	1.73
BA+	196	0.05	10 960	2.09	15 154	1.85	7 988	1.12	5 411	0.80	1 898	0.67	1 437	0.61
Total	371 906	100.00	525 194	100.00	817 205	100.00	713 437	100.00	679 222	100.00	283 951	100.00	236 447	100.00

a For Queensland, South Australia, Northern Territory and Western Australia, includes those with six years.
b 7–8 years in Queensland, South Australia, Northern Territory and Western Australia.
c Nine years in Queensland, South Australia, Northern Territory and Western Australia.
d Ten years in Queensland, South Australia, Northern Territory and Western Australia.
e Eleven years in Queensland, South Australia, Northern Territory and Western Australia.
f Twelve years in Queensland, South Australia, Northern Territory; 12–13 years in Western Australia.

declined considerably. This shows up particularly well in the pattern of ratios. The difference between medians declined about three-quarters among wives and two-thirds among husbands; that between the proportions with five or more children by more than half; and that between the proportions with no more than one child (which, because of the smaller base percentage, was subject to greater relative variation), by nearly 60 per cent among wives, and 90 per cent among husbands.

This narrowing of fertility differences by schooling — whether of wives or husbands — came about entirely through increases in fertility, for no schooling category experienced a reduction in fertility during this period — quite the contrary, in fact. At one extreme, the least schooling category, which had the highest fertility at the beginning of the period (the highest median, the highest proportion with five or more issue, and the lowest proportion with no more than one) increased its median issue slightly (by less than 10 per cent), retained the same proportion with five or more issue, and underwent a decline of more than a third in the proportion with no more than one child. At the other extreme the most schooling category, which had the lowest fertility at the beginning of the period, had, by the end of the period, increased its median issue by nearly a third and its proportion with five or more issue by nearly a half, while experiencing a decrease of more than a half in its proportion with no more than one child. The result was a virtual disappearance of the differences by schooling with respect to both the median and the proportion at the lowest parities, and more than a halving of this difference at the highest parities.

Standardisation by age at marriage does little to alter this general pattern: within each age at marriage category fertility was still negatively associated with schooling, and a marked decline over the period took place in the fertility differences associated with different levels of schooling.

However, standardisation by age at marriage does show that these differences tended to be greater at the earlier marriage ages and, moreover, that the differences associated with age at marriage, although declining during the period, were consistently less at each successively higher level of schooling. Within the cohort of 1927–31, for example, the median issue of wives with nine or more years of schooling who married before age 20 was only 4 per cent higher than the comparable figure for wives who married at ages 22–5, while among those with fewer than six years of schooling the excess was much higher — 29 per cent. The pattern was the same in the cohort of 1907–11, only there the comparable figures were 20 and 43 per cent, respectively.

Urban–Rural Residence

Sub-division by urban–rural residence shows much the same pattern of differences, that is a negative association between fertility and schooling (whether wife's or husband's schooling) within the earlier cohorts, a general contraction of these differences over successive cohorts, and a pattern of greater differences among those who married at the younger ages. But among those who married at ages 22–5, the earlier negative association between fertility and schooling had disappeared altogether by the end of the period, giving way among other urban- and rural-dwellers to no association at all and, among metropolitan-dwellers, to an association that was slightly positive with respect to median issue and hardly in evidence with respect to the proportions at the highest parities (see Table 5.2).

With differences by residence within each category of schooling the situation was markedly stable. Rural-dwellers always had the highest fertility and metropolitan-dwellers the lowest, but in addition the relative fertility differences between residential groupings remained at much the same level within each category of schooling. Although the differences by schooling narrowed, they did so at a pace roughly the same within each residential category. The relative fertility differences associated with urban–rural residence persisted within each schooling category — just as they did with respect to such other sub-divisions of the population as those by nativity/religion and husband's occupation.

Nativity and Religion

Comparisons between different nativity/religion categories are limited, predictably enough, by small frequencies in some of the categories, particularly among the older cohorts and at the higher schooling levels. But they are also limited — and perhaps more significantly so — by uncertainty concerning the comparability of school systems in different countries, not merely as to curriculum but also as to social significance. Quite apart from what one may have learned in the process, does having undergone, say, six or seven years of schooling signify a different status position or a different relative life-style in Greece than in the Netherlands (or

Table 5.2: Median Issue and Percentage with 5+ Issue Born to Current Marriage, by Residence and Years of Schooling. Wives 40–64 Years of Age who Commenced Current Marriage before Age 26, by Year of Birth and Age at Marriage (Australia, 1971)

Age at Marriage and Year of Birth	Median											
	Metropolitan				Other Urban				Rural			
	<6 Years	6–7 Years	8 Years	9+ Years	<6 Years	6–7 Years	8 Years	9+ Years	<6 Years	6–7 Years	8 Years	9+ Years
<20												
1907–11	2.67	2.47	2.38	2.02	3.16	2.82	2.63	2.43	3.68	3.20	2.93	2.48
1917–21	2.81	2.59	2.44	2.27	3.15	2.98	2.81	2.70	3.56	3.33	2.86	2.73
1927–31	2.72	2.62	2.52	2.39	3.32	3.16	2.95	2.86	3.63	3.50	3.19	2.97
20–1												
1907–11	2.31	2.05	2.08	1.88	2.65	2.61	2.49	2.06	3.07	2.82	2.84	2.34
1917–21	2.32	2.18	2.09	2.02	2.62	2.63	2.47	2.38	3.00	2.92	2.76	2.45
1927–31	2.38	2.35	2.35	2.33	2.80	2.73	2.64	2.70	3.09	3.09	2.98	2.91
22–5												
1907–11	1.89	1.81	1.80	1.70	2.22	2.15	2.05	1.97	2.60	2.44	2.39	2.28
1917–21	1.98	1.93	1.94	1.95	2.30	2.28	2.24	2.19	2.68	2.61	2.55	2.47
1927–31	2.13	2.15	2.22	2.31	2.56	2.53	2.53	2.61	2.84	2.91	2.79	2.90

Table 5.2 (continued)

Age at Marriage and Year of Birth	Per Cent with 5+ Issue											
	Metropolitan				Other Urban				Rural			
	<6 Years	6–7 Years	8 Years	9+ Years	<6 Years	6–7 Years	8 Years	9+ Years	<6 Years	6–7 Years	8 Years	9+ Years
<20												
1907–11	28	23	21	18	37	33	25	25	45	37	33	19
1917–21	29	23	20	18	34	33	29	27	42	38	32	31
1927–31	26	22	20	18	37	33	28	25	43	39	32	28
20–1												
1907–11	21	16	14	10	28	25	20	14	35	31	27	22
1917–21	19	14	12	12	25	24	19	18	32	30	26	19
1927–31	18	15	14	15	27	23	21	21	32	29	26	25
22–5												
1907–11	13	11	9	8	19	15	13	13	25	19	18	15
1917–21	13	10	10	10	18	16	15	15	24	21	20	18
1927–31	13	12	12	13	21	19	17	19	26	26	22	23

among the Greek-born in Australia than among their Dutch-born counterparts)? And, if so, does this have any influence on fertility? That the data at hand permit no answer to such questions does not lessen their significance, but it does mean that, for present purposes, it is necessary to assume relative comparability among the different national school systems — at least so far as their significance for fertility among nativity groupings in Australia is concerned.

The Catholic:non-Catholic difference in fertility already observed in association with other attributes is also found in association with schooling. Whatever the nativity/schooling category under consideration, the fertility of Catholics nearly always exceeded that of non-Catholics. What few exceptions there were can readily be explained in terms of small cell frequencies ($100 < N < 200$). In both median issue and the proportion at the highest parities, the Catholic:non-Catholic difference was least among the Yugoslav- and German-born and greatest among the Dutch-born. It remained much the same among the others — except for those Australian-born with nine or more years of schooling, among whom there was an increase between successive cohorts within each age at marriage category, most particularly the highest (22–5) (see Table 5.3). This increase among the Australian-born was, in fact, most marked at the highest parity of all: six or more, where the Catholic:non-Catholic ratio increased by two-thirds, rising from the already high level of 468 for the 1907–11 cohort to 785 for the 1927–31 cohort (non-Catholic percentage = 100), as against an increase of less than a quarter (from 191 to 235, respectively) over the same period at exact parity five. Moreover, this was entirely the result of increases in fertility among Catholics, for, far from declining, the fertility of the corresponding group of non-Catholics also increased during this period, but to a much lesser extent, and from a base already much lower.

Within the Catholic population itself, the only nativity groupings to evince the overall negative pattern of association between fertility and schooling were the British- and Italian-born; and even with these there was some fluctuation, particularly among the former. With the Australian-born, the slightly negative association in earlier cohorts had, by the middle of the period, turned slightly positive so far as median issue is concerned, and U-shaped with respect to the proportion in the upper parities; while among the Dutch-, German- and Yugoslav-born the pattern of association was

Table 5.3: Catholic:Non-Catholic Ratio (Non-Catholic = 100) for Median Issue and Percentage with 5+ Issue Born to Current Marriage, by Nativity and Years of Schooling. Wives 40–64 Years of Age who Commenced Current Marriage before Age 26, by Year of Birth (Australia, 1971)

Years of Schooling and Year of Birth	Median Issue					Per Cent with 5+ Issue				
	Australia	British Isles	Netherlands	Germany	Yugoslavia	Australia	British Isles	Netherlands	Germany	Yugoslavia
< 6 years										
1907–11	130	128	—	—	—	132	162	—	—	—
1912–16	113	123	147	—	—	135	180	162	—	—
1917–21	111	127	132	—	91	130	162	161	—	114
1922–26	110	132	119	102	83	133	186	129	74	76
1927–31	111	129	114	104	98	129	185	113	68	105
6–7 years										
1907–11	125	136	—	—	—	186	191	—	—	—
1912–16	129	141	—	—	—	189	212	—	—	—
1917–21	124	134	159	—	—	191	190	187	—	—
1922–26	122	127	143	98	—	190	188	196	76	—
1927–31	118	120	114	111	—	171	179	154	136	—
8 years										
1907–11	132	—	—	—	—	236	—	—	—	—
1912–16	132	127	—	—	—	209	156	—	—	—
1917–21	133	147	—	101	—	263	275	—	—	—
1922–26	132	132	—	90	—	265	201	—	95	—
1927–31	131	124	108	—	—	248	187	113	117	—
9+ years										
1907–11	129	144	—	—	—	241	311	—	—	—
1912–16	130	138	—	—	—	259	228	—	—	—
1917–21	138	135	168	—	—	304	229	260	—	—
1922–26	142	137	129	113	98	314	225	181	124	203
1927–31	146	127	130	111	111	349	209	207	142	180

(−) N < 100

Note:
Median and per cent with 5+ issue indices calculated on basis of figures carried out to two decimal places and one decimal place, respectively.

essentially irregular — very likely owing to both the relatively small cell frequencies (100 < N < 200) in many instances and the fact that different marriage ages (all under 26, however) had to be combined in an effort to maximise these frequencies (Table 5.3).

Thus it is that the generally negative association between fertility and schooling was most common among the non-Catholic population. In fact among them this association existed within each nativity grouping throughout the period, whether the measure under consideration is median issue or the proportion at the highest parities; and so far as can be determined from smaller cell frequencies, it did so within each age at marriage category as well. The only exception is among the Australian-born in the highest schooling category who had married at the upper ages (22–5), for these wives, like their Catholic counterparts (but to a much lesser extent, and at a much lower level of fertility) had, by the middle of the period, increased their fertility sufficiently to produce an overall pattern that was slightly U-shaped.

As this suggests, the range of relative differences across schooling categories was not the same within the different nativity/religion groupings. Yet, in spite of the marked differences among them in overall levels of fertility, the lowest schooling category's excess over the highest schooling category among the non-Catholic Australian-, British-, Dutch- and German-born was, by the end of the period, very much the same (about 10 per cent) with respect to median issue; and, considering the possibility of variation in the fact of small percentages to begin with, not so very different with respect to the proportion at five or more parity (ranging from an excess of about 100 per cent among the Australian-born and 80 per cent among the Dutch- and German-born, down to one of about 50 per cent among the British-born). Only among the Yugoslav- and Greek-born did those with the least schooling have a median issue markedly higher than that among those with the most schooling (28 per cent higher among the Yugoslav-born, 18 per cent among the Greek-born); while, at the upper parities, where it was these two nativity groupings that had the smallest proportions, the excess in the lowest schooling category was but 76 per cent among the Yugoslav-born and a *negative* 10 per cent among the Greek-born (see Table 5.4).

Within the various schooling categories the pattern of differences between nativity/religion groupings was as much as that observed with respect to other attributes: the large gaps between the

Table 5.4: Median Issue and Percentage with 5+ Issue Born to Current Marriage, by Nativity and Religion, together with Values for Those with Fewer than Six Years of Schooling Relative to Values for Those with 9+ Years of Schooling (9+ = 100). Wives 40–64 Years of Age who Commenced Current Marriage before Age 26, by Year of Birth (Australia, 1971)

Religion, Country of Birth, and Year of Birth	Median Issue		Per Cent with 5+ Issue	
	< 6 Index	9+ Median	< 6 Index	9+ %
Catholic				
Australia				
1907–11	111	2.40	127	22
1912–16	101	2.60	113	24
1917–21	93	2.87	88	35
1922–26	87	3.23	84	36
1927–31	84	3.59	77	42
British Isles				
1907–11	103	2.58	93	29
1912–16	99	2.56	125	21
1917–21	105	2.60	108	25
1922–26	107	2.79	118	28
1927–31	112	2.75	131	26
Italy				
1907–11	—	—	—	—
1912–16	—	—	—	—
1917–21	131	2.16	144	19
1922–26	132	1.88	190	11
1927–31	119	1.95	148	10
Netherlands				
1907–11	—	—	—	—
1912–16	—	—	—	—
1917–21	96	4.00	95	50
1922–26	114	3.09	109	38
1927–31	98	3.15	100	31
Germany				
1907–11	—	—	—	—
1912–16	—	—	—	—
1917–21	—	—	—	—
1922–26	94	1.78	91	9
1927–31	101	1.86	89	12
Yugoslavia				
1907–11	—	—	—	—
1912–16	—	—	—	—
1917–21	—	—	—	—
1922–26	121	1.53	153	7
1927–31	113	1.71	103	10

Table 5.4 (continued)

Religion, Country of Birth, and Year of Birth	Median Issue		Per Cent with 5+ Issue	
	< 6 Index	9 + Median	< 6 Index	9 + %
Non-Catholic				
Australia				
1907–11	110	1.86	232	9
1912–16	117	2.00	217	9
1917–21	115	2.08	206	10
1922–26	111	2.28	197	11
1927–31	110	2.46	207	12
British Isles				
1907–11	117	1.79	178	9
1912–16	111	1.85	159	9
1917–21	111	1.93	152	11
1922–26	112	2.03	143	12
1927–31	110	2.17	148	12
Netherlands				
1907–11	—	—	—	—
1912–16	118	2.66	139	26
1917–21	123	2.38	154	19
1922–26	123	2.39	154	21
1927–31	112	2.42	182	15
Greece				
1907–11	—	—	—	—
1912–16	—	—	—	—
1917–21	—	—	—	—
1922–26	—	—	—	—
1927–31	118	1.87	190	5
Germany				
1907–11	—	—	—	—
1912–16	—	1.60	—	12
1917–21	—	1.77	—	10
1922–26	105	1.57	154	7
1927–31	108	1.67	184	8
Yugoslavia				
1907–11	—	—	—	—
1912–16	—	—	—	—
1917–21	—	—	—	—
1922–26	142	1.56	408	4
1927–31	128	1.54	176	6

(−) N < 100

Note:
Median and per cent with 5+ issue indices calculated on basis of figures carried out to two decimal points and one decimal point respectively.

Australian- and Dutch-born in earlier cohorts had narrowed considerably by the later cohorts, and those between the Australian-born and the Italian-, Yugoslav- and Greek-born had reversed; the fertility of British-born wives continued at about the same level as that of Australian-born, and the fertility of German-born continued at a much lower level (Table 5.5).

Two things stand out about these differences, both of them testifying to the high fertility of Australian-born Catholics and particularly those with the most schooling in the later cohorts: first, these fertility differences by nativity were greater among Catholics than non-Catholics, using the fertility of the Australian-born as the basis of comparison; and secondly, by the end of the period, the differences between nativity/religion groupings were greatest at the highest schooling level, most particularly among Catholics, in consequence of the marked increases in fertility among those of them who were Australian-born.

Among non-Catholics alone one other thing stands out, namely, the persistence (although to a steadily narrowing degree with successive cohorts) of a much higher proportion of Dutch-born at the uppermost parities.

Husband's Occupation

Fertility differences in association with wife's schooling also existed within each husband's occupation category. At the beginning of the period (i.e. with the fertility of the 1907–11 cohort) the pattern of this association was generally inverse, and at each age at marriage. But by the end of the period (i.e. with the cohort of 1927–31) this had given way in places (particularly among those married at higher ages) either to no real pattern of association at all (as with the wives of husbands in the administrative, clerical and sales, transport and communications categories) or to a reversal of the earlier negative association (as with the wives of professional workers in particular, but also to a modest extent with those of farmers and graziers). Only among the wives of non-white-collar industrial and commercial workers (still the substantial majority of all workers, of course) did the usual negative association of fertility with schooling persist to the end of the period — but it did so to a much more limited extent at the end than at the beginning of the period. For example, among wives married at ages 22–5 whose husbands were in the trades, etc. occupational category, the median issue of those with fewer than six years of schooling exceeded the median issue of

Table 5.5: Ratio of Value for Overseas-born to Value for Australian-born (Australian-born = 100) for Median Issue and Percentage with 5+ Issue Born to Current Marriage, by Religion and Years of Schooling. Wives 40–64 Years of Age who Commenced Current Marriage before Age 26, by Year of Birth (Australia, 1971).

Religion, Years of Schooling and Year of Birth	Median Issue							Per Cent with 5+ Issue						
	Australia	British Isles	Italy	Netherlands	Greece	Germany	Yugoslavia	Australia	British Isles	Italy	Netherlands	Greece	Germany	Yugoslavia
Catholic														
< 6 Years														
1907–11	100	100	123	—	•	—	99	100	96	136	—	•	—	98
1912–16	100	96	115	175	•	—	96	100	98	118	211	•	—	66
1917–21	100	103	106	145	•	—	82	100	100	103	180	•	—	69
1922–26	100	107	89	126	•	60	66	100	110	67	138	•	28	38
1927–31	100	102	77	103	•	62	64	100	105	47	97	•	32	32
6–7 Years														
1907–11	100	103	—	—	•	—	—	100	91	—	—	•	—	—
1912–16	100	104	101	—	•	—	—	100	103	109	—	•	—	—
1917–21	100	106	90	164	•	—	—	100	102	66	212	•	—	—
1922–26	100	104	83	144	•	69	67	100	106	53	176	•	37	24
1927–31	100	100	73	108	•	70	59	100	105	43	114	•	52	33
8 Years														
1907–11	100	—	—	—	•	—	—	100	—	—	—	•	—	—
1912–16	100	94	84	—	•	—	—	100	76	77	—	•	—	—
1917–21	100	108	76	—	•	—	—	100	126	49	—	•	—	—
1922–26	100	102	61	—	•	66	—	100	96	28	—	•	34	—
1927–31	100	95	61	96	•	55	61	100	91	28	86	•	39	24
9+ Years														
1907–11	100	108	—	—	•	—	—	100	132	—	—	•	—	—
1912–16	100	98	—	—	•	—	—	100	88	—	—	•	—	—
1917–21	100	91	75	139	•	55	47	100	82	63	166	•	26	21
1922–26	100	86	58	96	•	52	48	100	79	30	106	•	27	23
1927–31	100	77	54	88	•	—	—	100	61	24	74	•	—	—

Table 5.5 (continued)

Religion, Years of Schooling and Year of Birth	Median Issue							Per Cent with 5+ Issue						
	Australia	British Isles	Italy	Netherlands	Greece	Germany	Yugoslavia	Australia	British Isles	Italy	Netherlands	Greece	Germany	Yugoslavia
Non-Catholic														
< 6 Years														
1907–11	100	102	•	146	162	–	–	100	78	•	154	148	–	–
1912–16	100	88	•	134	127	–	–	100	73	•	176	147	–	–
1917–21	100	90	•	122	127	–	100	100	80	•	145	138	51	78
1922–26	100	89	•	116	104	65	87	100	79	•	143	93	51	66
1927–31	100	88	•	100	82	67	73	100	73	•	110	38	59	39
6–7 Years														
1907–11	100	95	•	–	–	–	–	100	89	•	–	–	–	–
1912–16	100	96	•	158	–	114	–	100	92	•	256	–	144	–
1917–21	100	98	•	129	–	103	–	100	102	•	216	–	110	–
1922–26	100	100	•	122	94	86	–	100	107	•	171	83	92	–
1927–31	100	98	•	111	83	75	–	100	100	•	126	37	66	–
8 Years														
1907–11	100	91	•	–	–	–	–	100	95	•	–	–	–	–
1912–16	100	98	•	–	–	–	–	100	102	•	–	–	–	–
1917–21	100	99	•	135	–	92	–	100	121	•	244	–	169	–
1922–26	100	102	•	127	–	85	–	100	127	•	218	–	95	–
1927–31	100	101	•	116	–	80	–	100	120	•	189	–	83	–
9+ Years														
1907–11	100	96	•	–	–	–	–	100	102	•	–	–	–	–
1912–16	100	93	•	133	–	80	–	100	100	•	275	–	126	–
1917–21	100	93	•	114	–	85	–	100	109	•	194	–	100	–
1922–26	100	89	•	105	–	69	68	100	110	•	183	–	65	32
1927–31	100	88	•	98	76	68	63	100	102	•	125	41	67	45

(–) N < 100
(*) Not applicable
Note:
Median issue and per cent with 5+ issue indices calculated on the basis of figures carried out to two decimal places and one decimal place, respectively.

Table 5.6: Difference between Highest and Lowest Values Associated with Years of Schooling. Median Issue and Percentage with 5+ Issue Born to Current Marriage, by Husband's Occupation and Age at Marriage. Wives 40–64 Years of Age, by Year of Birth (Australia, 1971)

Age at Marriage and Year of Birth	Range of Medians						
	Professional	Administrative	Clerical/Sales	Farmers	Transport/Communication	Tradesmen, Labourers, Prod. Proc. Workers	Others
< 20							
1907–11	—	—	—	—	—	0.43	0.76
1917–21	0.34	0.31	0.49	0.55	0.49	0.54	0.70
1927–31	0.51	0.35	0.32	0.27	0.55	0.41	0.58
20–1							
1907–11	—	0.41	0.06	—	—	0.49	0.64
1917–21	0.06	0.16	0.10	0.53	0.43	0.37	0.49
1927–31	0.13	0.12	0.07	0.08	0.17	0.08	0.22
22–5							
1907–11	0.13	0.16	0.11	0.21	0.32	0.32	0.30
1917–21	0.18	0.05	0.07	0.16	0.14	0.27	0.23
1927–31	0.21	0.16	0.08	0.31	0.04	0.05	0.08

Table 5.6 (continued)

Age at Marriage and Year of Birth	Range of Per Cent with 5+ Issue						
	Professional	Administrative	Clerical/Sales	Farmers	Transport/Communication	Tradesmen, Labourers, Prod. Proc. Workers	Others
< 20							
1907–11	—	—	—	—	—	6.6	14.2
1917–21	13.2	9.1	7.5	13.8	9.1	9.9	13.0
1927–31	12.6	10.5	6.1	8.5	15.0	8.6	13.5
20–1							
1907–11	—	9.9	7.0	—	—	13.9	13.3
1917–21	1.6	5.6	3.6	12.5	10.8	8.2	11.0
1927–31	5.9	4.4	3.8	4.6	4.5	4.9	7.6
22–5							
1907–11	3.0	0.9	2.2	8.6	6.8	6.4	13.6
1917–21	1.2	2.3	1.9	4.0	2.5	4.6	6.3
1927–31	5.0	1.5	0.4	3.3	3.0	1.8	6.3

those with nine or more years by 18 per cent in the cohort of 1907–11, as against only 2 per cent in the cohort of 1927–31. With respect to the proportions with five or more issue, the comparable figures were 65 and 12 per cent, respectively. What had been a clearly negative association between fertility and schooling a generation earlier — standardised for age at marriage and husband's occupation — had, by the end of the period, either all but disappeared or become, instead, a very slight association in the opposite direction (or occasionally a slightly U-shaped one).

Throughout, the range of fertility differences by wife's schooling varied inversely with age at marriage: within each occupational category these differences were greatest among those married below age 20, and generally least among those married at 22–5 (see Table 5.6).

With respect to the range of fertility differences across all seven occupational groupings, those associated with wife's schooling (standardised for age at marriage) show a general pattern of declining differences as one moves from: lower to higher levels of schooling, lower to higher ages at marriage, and earlier to later cohorts (see Table 5.7). It is more in evidence when farmers and graziers are excluded, and in median issue than in the proportions at the higher parities, but the pattern is there, none the less. The main exceptions are where the wives of professionals had the highest median issue of all — that is, in the later cohorts among wives with at least eight years of schooling.

Husband's Schooling

At the most general level, fertility was associated with husband's schooling in much the same way as with wife's. The two patterns of association were, in fact, virtually identical. But what happens when husband's and wife's schooling are considered together? Are there, among wives with a given amount of schooling, systematic fertility differences on the basis of husband's schooling? For example, among wives with nine or more years of schooling, was the fertility of those whose husbands also had at least nine years of schooling consistently different from that of wives whose husbands had fewer than six? By and large, it was. During the period under consideration, a generally inverse relation obtained between fertility and *husband's* schooling within each category of *wife's* schooling; and similarly, between fertility and *wife's* schooling within each category of *husband's* schooling. Thus it was that

Table 5.7: Difference between Highest and Lowest Values Associated with Husband's Occupation, Farmers and Graziers Included and Excluded. Median Issue and Percentage with 5+ Issue Born to Current Marriage, by Schooling and Age at Marriage. Wives 40–64 Years of Age, by Year of Birth (Australia, 1971)

Age at Marriage and Year of Birth	Range of Medians								Range of Per Cent with 5+ Issue							
	Includes Farmers				Excludes Farmers				Includes Farmers				Excludes Farmers			
	<6	6–7	8	9+	<6	6–7	8	9+	<6	6–7	8	9+	<6	6–7	8	9+
< 20																
1907–11	1.60	1.04	—	—	1.00	0.51	—	—	21.8	15.3	—	—	13.5	5.8	—	—
1917–21	0.89	1.03	0.54	0.71	0.72	0.60	0.54	0.28	12.9	19.5	12.2	15.7	12.2	13.9	12.2	15.5
1927–31	0.74	0.91	0.78	0.80	0.51	0.45	0.41	0.25	17.5	17.9	15.1	15.0	13.6	10.3	10.8	4.9
20–1																
1907–11	1.05	0.96	—	—	0.72	0.54	0.43	0.43	20.5	16.2	—	—	13.4	9.4	16.1	6.0
1917–21	0.85	0.77	0.84	0.44	0.41	0.37	0.32	0.08	17.0	11.3	14.3	8.3	10.9	6.2	6.3	4.5
1927–31	0.78	0.70	0.70	0.74	0.43	0.27	0.22	0.15	14.6	12.0	13.0	12.5	10.6	6.9	5.2	5.5
22–5																
1907–11	0.87	0.85	0.69	0.76	0.39	0.30	0.29	0.16	15.7	14.0	8.0	9.6	8.5	14.0	3.7	5.1
1917–21	0.86	0.74	0.68	0.66	0.36	0.18	0.31	0.29	14.6	11.8	11.1	10.2	10.0	5.2	6.6	4.4
1927–31	0.53	0.74	0.56	0.77	0.22	0.19	0.25	0.35	8.1	12.6	9.4	13.2	8.0	3.9	2.5	4.5

(—) N < 100

fertility was highest where both spouses had fewer than six years of schooling, and lowest where both had more than nine — whether the measure is median issue or the proportion with five or more. This was the general case in all cohorts and within each wife's age at marriage category; the one notable exception was among wives married at ages 22–5 in the 1927–31 cohort among whom there were no systematic differences so far as median issue was concerned, although the pattern with respect to proportion with five or more issue was the same as elsewhere.

However, there was a narrowing of these differences over the period — particularly among those couples in which the wife was at least 20 years of age at time of marriage — in consequence of fertility increases among those in the highest schooling category. In median issue, the difference between couples at the two extremes — that is, the difference between those in which both spouses had at least nine years of schooling and those in which neither spouse had more than five — declined from 0.95 issue with the 1907–11 cohort to 0.62 issue with the 1927–31 cohort for couples where the wife was under 20 at time of marriage, as against a decline from 0.67 to 0.23 among those where the wife was 20–1 at time of marriage, and from 0.39 to 0.12 where she was 22–5. In the proportion with five or more issue the pattern was much the same: a decline of only 1 per cent (from 16 to 15 per cent) between the cohorts of 1907–11 and 1927–31 where the wife was under 20 at marriage, as against one from 15 to 8 per cent over the same period among those where the wife was 20–1 at the time of marriage, and from 10 to 2 per cent where she was 22–5.

The variation by husband's schooling tended to be somewhat greater than that by wife's — both in median issue and in the proportion at the upper parities — but the difference was never more than negligible. So far as fertility was related to schooling, it was so in roughly equal measure among both husbands and wives, when standardised, respectively, for the schooling of the other spouse.

Because of the uncertainty about the comparability of schooling received overseas, and also because of the occupational and residential concentration of the overseas-born, the association of fertility with husbands' and wives' schooling considered together is best assessed by focusing more narrowly on the Australian-born alone, in particular on those of the Australian-born who were living in metropolitan areas, so as to control for residence while retaining large enough cell frequencies to permit comparisons by religion and age at marriage.

Doing this reveals some deviation from the pattern followed by the population as a whole, primarily because of the clear difference between the patterns of Catholics and non-Catholics. While the pattern among non-Catholic wives married before age 20 (standardised for age and age at marriage) followed that of the general population — with fertility being inversely related to spouse's schooling — the pattern among their Catholic counterparts (on the basis of the relatively few cells for which frequencies are large enough to permit analysis) was more often one of little or no association, or else a U-shape. At higher marriage ages, the non-Catholic pattern continued to consist of a relatively inverse association so far as the proportion with five or more issue is concerned, and either no association or else a slightly positive one at the highest schooling level with respect to median issue. With Catholics, however, the association at the higher marriage ages was nearly always positive or at least U-shaped, whether the variable is median issue or the proportion with five or more, and whether the association is with wife's or husband's schooling.

Nor was there any tendency toward a narrowing of these differences among Catholics, although such a tendency did exist among non-Catholics in most sectors. Table 5.8 is illustrative of the difference between Catholics and non-Catholics in this regard. Deviations from the general inverse pattern are particularly notable among Catholics at higher schooling levels in the most recent cohort, whether it is variation in association with husband's or with wife's schooling that is under consideration. Deviations from the general pattern also occurred among non-Catholics in the same categories, but here it was to only a very limited extent. In general, the association of schooling with fertility was virtually nil among non-Catholics, while among Catholics it was markedly positive (see Table 5.9).

The variation with respect to both median issue and the proportion with five or more issue was slightly more by wife's schooling than by husband's among Catholics. Among non-Catholics there was no difference respecting the median and, as with Catholics, somewhat more variation by wife's schooling with respect to the proportion at the highest parities.

Table 5.8: Differences with Respect to Median Issue and Proportion with 5+ Issue. Values for Couples in which Both Spouses have 9+ Years of Schooling Subtracted from Corresponding Values for Couples in which Neither Spouse has more than Five Years of Schooling. Metropolitan-dwelling Couples in which Wife is Australian-born, by Wife's Year of Birth, Age at Marriage and Religion (Australia, 1971)

Age at Marriage	Year of Birth	Differences between:			
		Medians		Per Cent with 5+	
		Catholic	Non-Catholic	Catholic	Non-Catholic
< 20	1907−11	—	0.70	—	8.6
	1917−21	0.12	0.44	− 1.9	14.9
	1927−31	0.01	0.48	5.1	18.1
20−1	1907−11	—	0.30	—	8.9
	1917−21	− 0.21	0.26	− 1.9	10.1
	1927−31	0.13	0.00	16.2	8.6
22−5	1907−11	− 0.16	0.08	0.3	6.4
	1917−21	− 0.55	− 0.05	− 11.2	3.7
	1927−31	− 1.21	− 0.30	− 22.2	3.6

Discussion

The association of fertility with level of schooling ran the gamut in Australia during the relatively short period represented by the childbearing of the cohorts of 1907−31, moving from a markedly negative association at the beginning of the period to little if any association at the end, particularly among those marrying at ages 20−5. In this, the one real exception was with Australian-born Catholics, among whom an association that, at the beginning of the period, was either negative (as with those married before age 22) or nil (as with those married at ages 22−5) had, by the end of the period, shifted to one that was either U-shaped (with those married before age 20) or markedly positive (with all the others) (see Table 5.10). In each instance, these changes resulted from increases in fertility within those sectors of the population in which fertility had been relatively low; in no instance did they result from declines within sectors where fertility had been relatively high.

Moreover, where it occurred, the observed narrowing of the fertility differences associated with schooling can hardly have owed

Table 5.9: Median Issue and Percentage with 5+ Issue, by Schooling of Spouse. Metropolitan-dwelling Couples in which Wife is 40–64 Years of Age and was Married at Age 22–5, by Wife's Religion (Australia, 1971)

Median Issue

Wife's Schooling	Catholic					Non-Catholic				
Husband's Schooling:	<6	6–7	8	9+	Ratio: lowest/highest	<6	6–7	8	9+	Ratio: lowest/highest
<6	2.39	2.56	2.71	2.67	0.88	2.07	2.12	2.15	2.12	0.96
6–7	2.55	2.40	2.53	2.92	0.82	2.05	2.00	2.09	2.20	0.91
8	2.74	2.69	2.85	3.25	0.83	2.04	2.00	2.03	2.22	0.90
9+	3.11	3.16	3.23	3.60	0.86	2.17	2.20	2.19	2.37	0.92
Ratio: lowest/highest	0.77	0.76	0.78	0.74		0.94	0.91	0.93	0.89	

Per Cent with 5+ Issue

Wife's Schooling	Catholic					Non-Catholic				
Husband's Schooling:	<6	6–7	8	9+	Ratio*: lowest/highest	<6	6–7	8	9+	Ratio*: lowest/highest
<6	20	25	26	24	0.74	12	13	11	13	0.85
6–7	22	18	22	28	0.65	12	9	8	9	0.67
8	25	25	27	34	0.72	10	7	6	7	0.63
9+	32	33	33	42	0.76	7	8	8	8	0.87
Ratio*: lowest/highest	0.61	0.54	0.65	0.57		0.61	0.52	0.56	0.55	

* Calculated with figures carried out to one decimal place

Table 5.10: Median Issue and Percentage with 5+ Issue, by Years of Schooling. Australian-born Wives Married before Age 26, by Year of Birth, Age at Marriage and Religion (Australia, 1971)

Age at Marriage	Year of Birth	Median Issue					Per Cent with 5+ Issue				
Years of Schooling:		< 6	6–7	8	9+	Ratio: < 6/9+	< 6	6–7	8	9+	Ratio*: < 6/9+
Catholic < 20	1907–11	3.16	2.89	2.73	2.47	1.28	36	32	30	25	1.44
	1927–31	3.42	3.19	3.06	3.37	1.01	40	35	33	39	1.02
20–1	1907–11	2.78	2.65	2.92	2.33	1.19	29	29	28	20	1.44
	1927–31	2.98	2.91	3.12	3.59	0.83	31	30	32	43	0.74
22–5	1907–11	2.34	2.46	2.50	2.40	0.98	22	25	24	22	1.03
	1927–31	2.78	2.80	3.05	3.62	0.77	27	27	31	43	0.63
Non-Catholic < 20	1907–11	2.85	2.64	2.44	2.14	1.33	32	26	19	18	1.75
	1927–31	3.20	2.85	2.65	2.62	1.22	35	26	21	19	1.88
20–1	1907–11	2.43	2.23	2.20	1.92	1.27	23	18	15	10	2.27
	1927–31	2.67	2.50	2.39	2.50	1.07	23	17	13	14	1.71
22–5	1907–11	1.97	1.88	1.85	1.81	1.09	14	10	8	7	1.99
	1927–31	2.39	2.26	2.21	2.42	0.99	18	13	9	10	1.70

* Calculated from percentages carried out to one decimal place

anything to changes in category of schooling subsequent to the completion of childbearing. An adult may undertake additional schooling, but few in the populations under study here are likely to have done so to the extent necessary to put them into a higher category, for adult schooling in Australia consists principally of the acquisition of secondary or tertiary qualifications by those already in the highest schooling category used here (nine or more years). However, to the extent that such shifts did take place, the result would have been a lessening of fertility differences between categories, simply because all changes of category would, of necessity, have been in the same upward direction.

The association of fertility and schooling can be of three general types: (1) fertility — particularly the timing of childbearing — can affect the level of schooling; (2) schooling, in turn, can affect fertility; and (3) the two can be related (non-causally) in consequence of the relation each bears to some condition which one or the other presumably indicates the existence of. That a particular association may involve elements of all three types simultaneously does not make analysis any easier. Moreover, confusion is engendered by the frequent failure, first to distinguish between the relation schooling may bear, respectively, to intended and unintended fertility; secondly, to differentiate clearly between schooling as a direct cause, as an indirect cause, and as merely an indicator of the existence of other causes; and thirdly, and related to this, the failure to recognise that in those societies (and Australia is not one of them) in which one or another sector of the population virtually monopolises a particular level of schooling, this level of schooling will either have no causal connection with fertility or, at most, serve only to reinforce a fertility pattern originating from a set of determinants quite removed from schooling.

The type of association in which the direction of causation is from fertility to schooling is of little moment here. Such association is doubtless possible, particularly when childbirth evokes the response of leaving school earlier than would otherwise have been the case. But in an analysis like the present one, where the highest schooling category begins at a level as low as nine years, and where children commence school at age five or six, the instances in which childbearing could have affected the level of schooling recorded here are surely so few that this direction of causation can be safely ignored.

The second type of association, in which the direction of

causation is from schooling to fertility, is more important. An association of this type can be either direct or indirect and, as already noted, is in most populations — Australia's included — doubtless something of both.

Schooling can directly affect fertility by giving information concerning both the desirability (or possibly undesirability, if the system of schooling is Catholic) of controlling births and the means appropriate to that end. It can affect age at marriage (a factor that, in the present analysis, is standardised for) and also opportunity (and, especially among women, incentive) to participate in the workforce.

Indirectly, schooling can raise or redirect aspirations in ways that make control over fertility more desirable; it can bring the individual into contact with alternative ways of looking at the world, or with alternative sets of peer-group pressures; and, while one could expect a competitive system of schooling to turn out 'losers' who defined themselves as less than capable of coping with life, and therefore less than capable also of fully controlling their fertility, it appears that additional schooling — competitive or not — results instead more frequently in development of a sense of being able to exercise some measure of control over the course of one's life — presumably including one's fertility.

Particularly in populations characterised by relatively high fertility differences in formal schooling are likely to be associated with differences in knowledge about modern techniques of birth control, access to these techniques, and willingness to use them, together with the presence of those conditions of life, levels of aspiration, and the like that determine interest in controlling fertility in the first place. Much research remains to be done, and there are some maddening inadequacies in study design (such as the common failure to standardise for age at marriage, or to separate analytically the variables relating to intent and belief from those relating to demographic processes) in some of the research that has been done, but differences in schooling in such populations do seem to be generally associated with quite marked differences in fertility.[3]

But in populations of relatively low fertility it is different. Here, fertility differences associated with schooling tend to be narrow, particularly if knowledge of birth control is fairly general and one focuses on essentially behavioural aspects by holding age at marriage constant. Moreover, while the association of schooling with fertility in such populations may be causal — either directly or indirectly — its more important association is likely to be not as a causal factor, but as an *indicator* of the presence or absence of certain causal factors.

As such, schooling, like husband's occupation, is frequently used as a proxy for a variety of fertility-related (and often mutually reinforcing) conditions: social status, life-style and living conditions, levels of aspiration (both for oneself and for one's children), income and relative income, for example. In fact, for want of better information, schooling and occupation are often combined to form an indicator of social status, particularly in modern societies. An example is afforded by the categories of schooling and occupation used here, which, while very broad, none the less lend themselves to an interesting comparison between the fertility levels of what may be taken as two very general social extremes within the Australian population: (1) the 'highest', namely, that consisting of wives with nine or more years of schooling who married at ages 22–5 and whose husbands were professional workers; and (2) the 'lowest', namely, that consisting of wives with fewer than six years of schooling who married before age 20 and whose husbands were in the tradesmen, etc. occupational category. The reasons for including age at marriage in this categorisation are first, that in modern societies early marriage is more often associated with lower status origins; and secondly, early marriage tends to restrict one's opportunities for social advancement, particularly through the limits it imposes on the acquisition of further schooling or training and, among women, on the acquisition of experience in the labour market.

A comparison of the fertility of these two extremes shows a marked decrease taking place in the difference between them. By the end of the period it was only in the proportion at the highest parities that there was any very great difference, and even there this had been reduced by more than half. Apart from a decline in the proportion with no more than one child (a decline of only 3 per cent) the fertility of the 'lowest' status grouping hardly changed; the narrowing of the gap between 'highest' and 'lowest' arose entirely out of increased fertility among those in the 'highest' status grouping (see Table 5.11).

As with the explanation of group fertility differences associated with husband's occupation (chapter 4), explanation of comparable differences associated with years of schooling entails accounting, in particular, for two things: (1) the general narrowing of the

'Table 5.11: Selected Fertility Measures of Those in 'Highest' and 'Lowest' Social Status Groupings. All Wives Married before Age 26, by Year of Birth (Australia, 1971)

Birth Cohort	Median Issue			Per Cent with 0–1 Issue			Per Cent with 5 + Issue		
	Status Grouping		Ratio:	Status Grouping		Ratio:	Status Grouping		Ratio:
	Highest	Lowest	Highest/lowest	Highest	Lowest	Highest/lowest	Highest	Lowest	Highest/lowest
1907–11	1.83	2.84	0.64	20.5	11.0	1.86	7.3	30.3	0.24
1917–21	2.22	2.98	0.74	12.6	9.1	1.38	12.7	31.3	0.41
1927–31	2.61	2.88	0.91	7.1	8.0	0.89	16.4	30.1	0.54

differences associated with the various levels of schooling (whether husband's or wife's); and (2) the contrasting expansion of those differences involving Australian-born Catholics at the highest levels (again, whether based on husband's or wife's schooling).

The explanatory variables can, again, be categorised under three broad headings: (1) differences in physiology; (2) differences in the ability and willingness to exercise control over childbearing; and (3) differences in desired numbers of children.

Physiological differences of a sort to affect the likelihood of intercourse, conception or gestation and successful parturition may well have existed among persons at various levels of schooling but, as with other attributes, their role in determining the fertility differences observed in association with different levels of schooling can hardly have been important. As already noted, overall fertility levels were simply too low — and the range of possible variation, in consequence, too narrow — to permit these factors to operate at more than a very marginal level.

Nor is another physiological difference — the experience of child mortality and the consequent incentive to have an additional child in compensation — likely to have been of any particular significance either. This is frequently cited as a factor supporting higher fertility among those in lower social strata (for which lower levels of schooling are taken as a proxy); but while mortality differences by social strata do exist in Australia (as elsewhere), they do so over a very narrow range so far as strata as broadly defined as those under consideration here are concerned, although there are, admittedly, no data by which to make a comparison specifically on the basis of parents' schooling.[4]

Ruling out physiological differences as an explanation leaves differences in the ability and willingness to control fertility, and differences in desired numbers of children. It seems reasonable to suppose that the diffusion of effective control over fertility already deemed to have played a major role in the narrowing of fertility differences associated with residence, nativity and husband's occupation would have taken place also in association with schooling. But there is no evidence to support this view because no schooling category experienced a decline in fertility over the period under consideration. The narrowing of fertility differences associated with schooling came about entirely through increases in fertility. Given that it is, after all, the same population in each instance — whether the basis for comparison is husband's occupation or nativity — the conclusion must be that fertility increased simultaneously with the extension of control over it; that birth control was becoming what its advocates always claimed it was — control, and not solely prevention. The only other possibility is that those taking part in the numerical expansion at the higher schooling levels (and the corresponding contraction at the lower) brought with them some measure of the relative ignorance of birth control presumably associated with the lower schooling levels of their parents. While this may have taken place to some extent, it could hardly have done so, given the pattern of narrowing group fertility differences associated with other attributes, to the extent necessary to account for more than a fraction of the changes that occurred.

If, then, there was no lessening of the ability to control fertility — only, at most, a possibility of a slight change in its distribution among persons at the different levels of schooling — what of the willingness to exercise this ability? Might this not have declined? It would appear that it did, particularly among Australian-born Catholics in the higher schooling categories; and in this fact would seem to lie the main explanation for the markedly higher fertility increases of this sector of the population, for in the fertility pattern exhibited in relation to schooling there is much the same suggestion as that previously observed in relation to other attributes (chapters 3 and 4): namely, that the upper income, upper status elements of the Catholic population were particularly susceptible to their Church's essentially pro-natalist teaching on the family and birth control during that period (from around the late 1940s through the 1960s) when this teaching seems to have been disseminated with particular vigour. As was developed more fully in chapter 3, this greater susceptibility appears to have resulted from the combination of two factors within this sector of the population: a generally stronger sense of Catholic identity and a personal economic position generally more favourable to the support of children. Australian-born, upper-status Catholics were both more willing to follow — or at least acquiesce in — the demands of their church's teaching so far as these pertained to fertility, and they were better able to abide the higher fertility consequences of doing so.

But while much of this presumably stronger sense of Catholic identity on the part of upper-status Catholics may be supposed to have originated in the particular character of their position within a religious minority (see chapter 3), there can be little doubt that it also owed much to their schooling itself, for the great majority of Australian Catholic women with nine or more years of schooling acquired at least some of that higher schooling within the Catholic school system. Probably no fewer than 75 per cent did so.[5] This means that these women were likely to have been brought most forcefully into contact with the generally pro-natalist Catholic teaching and ideals about appropriate female roles, birth control and the like at precisely those ages that are of particular significance in the development of adult self-awareness and identity. It is not that those Catholics with less schooling lacked experience of Catholic schools, but rather that this experience was greater among those Catholics with more schooling overall — and that it was undergone at a particularly important stage in their lives so far as the consequences for fertility are concerned.

This is not to say, of course, that the higher fertility among upper-level Catholics owed nothing to a desire for more children — that it all derived from a greater ignorance of the more effective methods of birth control or a lesser willingness to put these methods to use. Certainly differences in desired numbers of children could play an important part in creating group fertility differences like those observed here, and undoubtedly did so in this instance. But it must be recognised that desire for children is a matter of degree, that it can fluctuate over time, and — perhaps of particular significance in the case of upper-level Catholics — that the distinction between actually desiring a child and merely acquiescing in its birth, while perfectly clear at a theoretical level, is not always so clear at the level of actual behaviour, particularly if there is some ethical uncertainty about limiting births. Solely on the basis of their exposure to Catholic pro-natalism, one could expect these upper-level Catholics to have aspired to relatively high fertility. But whether they actually wanted the number of births they had in excess of those born to either their non-Catholic counterparts or their co-religionists at lower levels of schooling is another matter. Both the rapidity of the increase and the cohorts most affected suggest the operation of something beyond simply the desire for more children.

With the rest of the population (non-Catholics and lower-level Catholics) the trend toward a narrowing of the fertility differences associated with schooling, in consequence of increased fertility within those groupings originally characterised by relatively low fertility, can be attributed to four simultaneous developments:

(1) the further extension of effective control over fertility; (2) possibly some transfer of higher fertility norms into the upper schooling levels as a result of increased proportions remaining longer in school; (3) a desire for more children on the part of those in what were initially the lowest fertility sectors of the population; and (4) overall, a growing similarity between different social strata concerning the limits of acceptable and desirable family size, the ability to keep one's procreation within these limits and the particular determinants of fertility behaviour likely to be experienced.

Notes

1. Australia, Commonwealth Bureau of Census and Statistics, *Census of Population and Housing* (1971), Bulletin 1, Part 8, p. xii.
2. Ibid., p. xiv.
3. Susan H. Cochrane, *Fertility and Education: What Do We Really Know?* Baltimore: Johns Hopkins University Press (1979).
4. See Gouranga La Dasvarma, *Differential Mortality in Australia, with Special Reference to the Period 1970–1972*, PhD thesis in demography, Australian National University (1980), chapters 6 and 7, and p. 189.
5. Estimated by combining two sets of data (1) unpublished data supplied by the Australian Bureau of Statistics showing 19.3 per cent of the 343,700 girls attending secondary school in 1964 to be enrolled in Catholic schools, and (2) data from the 1961 census (vol. viii, *Statistician's Report*, Canberra (1967), p. 213), showing 24.8 per cent of girls ages 15–19 reporting their religion as Catholic. Assuming (not altogether correctly) that all girls attending Catholic secondary schools were Catholics, produces an estimate of 77.8 per cent as the proportion of Catholic girl secondary pupils who were attending Catholic schools.

6 FERTILITY AND WIFE'S PARTICIPATION IN THE LABOUR FORCE

Introduction

Over the 17-year period 1954 to 1971, labour force participation in Australia increased markedly among women, while declining slightly among men. Among persons 15–64 years of age, it was 42 per cent for women and 87 per cent for men in 1971;[1] 33 and 93 per cent, respectively, ten years earlier;[2] and 29 and 94 per cent, respectively, at the beginning of the period, in 1954.[3]

While there was little association with marital status among men (when standardised for age), the association with marital status among women was considerable. For example, in 1971, the labour force participation rate among 25–34-year-old women was almost 2½ times as high for the unmarried as for the married (76 per cent vs. 33 per cent, respectively); and among those 45–54 years of age, more than half again as high (58 per cent vs. 36 per cent, respectively).[4]

Within the study population, consisting of wives who commenced their current marriages before the age of 26, the proportions in the labour force at each level in 1971 were as follows:

Age	Year of Birth	Per Cent in Labour Force	No.
60–4	1907–11	10	6 863
55–9	1912–16	22	22 852
50–4	1917–21	31	45 985
45–9	1922–26	39	81 323
40–4	1927–31	43	99 582

Censuses do not ask directly whether someone is in or not in the labour force. Determination of labour force status — and also of employment status, which underlies it — is made subsequent to enumeration on the basis of the respondent's answers to questions about activities in the labour market during some specified period, usually the week preceding the date of the census. In the 1971 Australian census, the pertinent questions were these:

179

14. (a) Did this person have a full- or part-time job, or business or farm of any kind last week?
    Tick 'yes' even if this person was temporarily absent from a job because of sickness, holidays, industrial dispute, etc.
    Tick 'no' if this person did not have a job or did only unpaid housework.

(b) Did this person do any work at all last week for payment or profit?
    Tick 'yes' even if this person was working only part-time or helping without pay in a family business.
    Tick 'no' if this person did not work or did only unpaid housework.

(c) Was this person temporarily laid off by his employer without pay for the WHOLE of last week?

(d) Did this person look for work last week?
    Looking for work means being registered with the Commonwealth Employment Service, or approaching a prospective employer, or placing or answering advertisements, or writing letters of application, or awaiting the results of recent applications.

15. How many hours per week does this person usually work in the job or jobs held last week?

16. In the job held last week, was this person
    A wage or salary earner?
    Conducting own business but not employing others?
    Conducting own business and employing others?
    A helper not receiving wages or salary?

17. (a) What is the full trading name of this person's own or employer's business?

(b) What is the full name of the Division, or Branch, or Section (if any) in which he works?

(c) What is the full address of the Division, or Branch, or Section (if any) or business at which he works?

(d) What kind of industry, business or service is carried out at that address?

18. What was this person's occupation (kind of work) last week?

Those classified as 'in the labour force' were, during the week preceding the census, either employed, temporarily unemployed or looking for work — the determination in each instance being made on the basis of the respondent's answers to Question 14. But as not everyone answered Question 14: to ensure that everyone would none the less have a labour force status, a coding procedure had to be adopted. This was as follows:

(a) Check the answers to Questions 15 to 18. If these indicate that the person has a genuine occupation, industry or place of work, regard the person as *in the labour force* and *employed*. If, however, there are answers to Questions 15 to 18 which indicate, for example, that the person is a pensioner or a full-time student, then the person is not in the labour force.

(b) If there are no satisfactory answers to Questions 15 to 18, examine the answer to Question 2 (Usual Major Activity) for the person. If the first box (working in a job, trade, business or profession) has been ticked, the person is *in the labour force* and *employed*. Otherwise the person is *not in the labour force*.[5]

The concept of the labour force is both broad and narrow: broad, because it takes very little employment to classify one as being in the labour force; narrow, because the definition of 'work' underlying the concept is strictly economic in nature, being work 'for payment or profit', whatever the effort entailed or the value (economic or otherwise) of the result. Doing one's *own* housework, for example, is not a labour force activity; being paid to do someone *else's* is. Similarly, studying as a student is not a labour force activity, but studying as a trainee in some company's management programme is.

To such questions relating to concept can be added others relating to enumeration. For example, whether one has actually looked for work in the period specified is essentially a matter of self-assessment, although the Australian census (in contrast to the American) does at least offer guidelines on the census schedule itself. Something along the same lines can also be said concerning self-assessment as an unpaid worker in a family enterprise: some who for one reason or another do not qualify may none the less answer in a way that puts them into this category, while others who do qualify may answer in a way that does not. Respecting the latter, the wives of pieceworkers in the American clothing industry in the early years of this century are a possible case in point. Jaffe has suggested[6] that they may have viewed the work they did on clothes brought home by their husbands not as work, but simply as part of the normal duties of a working-class wife.

Overall is the problem of the 'discouraged worker', that is, the unemployed person not looking for work, in the belief (correct or incorrect) that no work is available. In an effort to estimate the effect of this 'discouraged worker' phenomenon on unemployment levels reported for the United States in 1970–72, Abraham and Jaffe applied the age and sex-specific proportions employed and unemployed during a previous period of 'near-full' employment (1968–69) in order to obtain expected 'full employment' levels against which to compare the actual levels for the period under consideration. With adjustments for seasonal variation and the upward trend in female labour force participation, they estimated actual unemployment in the total civilian population at a level some 21 per cent higher than that reported by the Bureau of Labor Statistics (BLS) (7.6 per cent in the first quarter of 1972 as against the BLS estimate of 6.3 per cent); and unemployment specifically among women as 23 per cent higher (8.1 *vs.* 6.6 per cent).[7] An even greater discrepancy was found some years later in Australia. Using much the same approach, including incorporation of an adjustment for long-term upward movement in age-specific labour force participation rates — this time among men as well as women — Sheehan and Stricker calculated that, in August 1979, actual unemployment rates were some 67 and 108 per cent higher, respectively, for men and women than those reported in the Australian Bureau of Statistics' labour force survey (8 *vs.* 4.8 per cent among men, 11.5 *vs.* 5.8 per cent among women).[8]

Despite such uncertainties concerning concept and the accuracy of coverage based on it, labour force status, however defined, has been widely observed to be closely associated with fertility. On average, the fertility of women participating in the labour force is notably lower than that of women who are not, even when standardised for marital status and, by restricting analysis to wives who have borne at least one child, for parental status as well. Australia is no exception.

Findings

As already noted, the pattern of labour force participation within the study population in 1971 was that reached after a period of marked increases in such participation among women generally. This change toward greater participation probably occurred in all sectors of the population, but the evidence strongly suggests that it was more extensive at the younger ages, for the 1971 participation rates within the study population were almost invariably higher with each successively younger cohort. The pattern was general throughout the population, at every parity level within each nativity grouping (see Table 6.1) and, so far as can be determined from the few data available, among both Catholics and non-Catholics. Although less marked at the higher parities than at the lower, the increases between successive cohorts were sizable among wives at all parities.

Although a part of this pattern of decreasing participation at successively older ages can doubtless be attributed to age-related retirement, most of it must derive, instead, from the general increase that occurred in the participation of women in the labour force. This is what took place over no greater period than the five years between the censuses of 1961 and 1966.

Age	Per Cent Increase in Labour Force Participation
60–4	24
55–9	22
50–4	25
45–9	32
40–4	36

Source:
United Nations, *Demographic Yearbook 1964*, Table 8; and *Demographic Yearbook 1972*, Table 8.

Participation increased over the period within each successive cohort through ages 55–9. And that there is more to the age pattern of this participation than can be accounted for in terms of normal attrition through retirement may be seen in the overall changes that have occurred in that pattern, as well as in the variety of these patterns among different populations and different sectors within populations.

But these changes taking place *between* cohorts in the patterns of wives' participation in the labour force seem to have been accompanied by no particular change *within* cohorts in the pattern of

Table 6.1: Percentage in the Labour Force. Wives 40–64 Years of Age who Commenced Current Marriage before Age 26, by Year of Birth, Nativity and Specified Numbers of Children Born to Current Marriage (Australia, 1971)

Children Born to Current Marriage	Year of Birth	Australia	British Isles	Italy	Netherlands	Greece	Germany	Yugoslavia
0	1907–11	10	12	—	—	—	—	—
	1912–16	20	33	—	—	—	—	—
	1917–21	31	44	—	—	—	—	—
	1922–26	41	60	49†	—	—	60	—
	1927–31	50	66	64	—	—	61	72†
1	1907–11	10	12	9†	—	—	—	—
	1912–16	20	29	27	—	—	—	—
	1917–21	30	45	39	28†	—	47†	62
	1922–26	38	55	60	47†	—	62	71
	1927–31	45	65	63	53	75	63	—
5	1907–11	10	11	5	—	—	—	—
	1912–16	19	29	13	19	11†	—	—
	1917–21	27	37	27	33	27†	—	—
	1922–26	33	46	27	29	44	49†	28†
	1927–31	30	45	36	35	54†	41	59†

(—) N < 100
† 100 < N < 150

fertility associated with this participation. Within each category of the population for which cell frequencies are high enough to permit comparison, fertility continued to be consistently lower among wives recorded as in the labour force than among wives recorded as not in the labour force; or, to put it another way, within each cohort, labour force participation was consistently higher at successively lower parities. This was so whatever the sector of the population under consideration. There is some suggestion, at least among the Australian- and British-born, where the cell frequencies are high enough to permit comparisons among all age groupings, that the negative association between fertility and participation in the labour force increased with successively younger cohorts. This could be expected to take place with a growing acceptance of the suitability of a wife's having a job — which would presumably mean shifting to a situation in which the employment of wives was relatively less of a response to necessity, and relatively more a response to choice. But the differences are not very great and, moreover, those for Italian-born, among others, so far as the paucity of data permits analysis, seem to run in a contrary direction.

So as to avoid distortion arising out of the geographic concentration of the overseas-born, analysis by religion/nativity was restricted to those living in metropolitan areas. Among wives in this category, we find generally higher participation rates among the overseas-born and generally lower ones among the Australian-born: a pattern that holds at every parity level, even among the childless, and that also holds among both Catholics and non-Catholics (see Table 6.2). Only with the Dutch-born and the older wives among the Italian- and Greek-born did rates of participation approximate the relatively low ones of the Australian-born.

Within the lower age range, participation rates were much the same among the various categories of overseas-born (excepting the Dutch-born, whose relatively low rates approximated those of the Australian-born); at the higher ages — so far as can be ascertained from the small cell frequencies available — the differences were greater, mainly the result of particularly low rates among the Italian- and Greek-born. The wider and overlapping age ranges necessary to produce large enough cell frequencies may have introduced some distortion, but the general pattern of higher rates at successively younger ages holds within each sector. But while the differences by age are particularly marked among the Italian- and

Table 6.2: Percentage in the Labour Force. Metropolitan-dwelling Wives who Commenced Current Marriage before Age 26, by Year of Birth, Religion, Country of Birth and Selected Issue from Current Marriage (Australia, 1971)

Religion	Parity	Year of Birth	Australia	British Isles	Italy	Greece	Netherlands	Germany	Yugoslavia
Catholic	0	1907–16	18	–	–	*	–	–	–
		1912–21	30	–	22	*	–	–	–
		1917–26	44	–	45	*	–	–	–
		1922–31	54	74†	58	*	–	60†	73†
		1927–31	57	–	64	*	–	–	–
	2	1907–17	19	39	16	*	–	–	19†
		1912–21	30	44	31	*	–	–	38†
		1917–26	39	55	50	*	44†	59	56
		1922–31	47	60	57	*	50	58	62
		1927–31	50	60	59	*	49	56	64
	4	1907–16	18	30	11	*	–	–	–
		1912–21	28	42	22	*	25†	–	–
		1917–26	35	45	35	*	32	–	45†
		1922–31	39	52	40	*	34	52	57
		1927–31	40	57	41	*	34	57	62

Table 6.2 (continued)

Religion	Parity	Year of Birth	Australia	British Isles	Italy	Greece	Netherlands	Germany	Yugoslavia
Non-Catholic	0	1907–16	17	25	*	—	—	—	—
		1912–21	27	36	*	—	—	—	—
		1917–26	38	55	*	—	—	63	—
		1922–31	48	65	*	—	—	64	—
		1927–31	53	68	*	—	—	64	—
	2	1907–16	17	24	*	14	27	39	—
		1912–21	27	40	*	24	35	49	—
		1917–26	36	51	*	49	38	52	50
		1922–31	43	58	*	67	45	57	61
		1927–31	46	61	*	72	48	61	64
	4	1907–16	16	22	*	7	19†	—	—
		1912–21	25	35	*	19	31	—	—
		1917–26	33	45	*	39	36	51	43†
		1922–31	37	50	*	51	38	47	55
		1927–31	39	51	*	56	40	41	—

(—) N < 100
† 100 < N < 150
* Not applicable

Greek-born, there is at least a suggestion that the rates of participation among the German-born may have changed only a little (Table 6.2).

So far as comparative levels of participation among Catholics and non-Catholics are concerned, the differences within the various nativity groupings were minimal — again, so far as small cell frequencies permit analysis along this dimension. Nevertheless, with the exception of the higher parity wives among the Dutch-born, participation rates among Catholics were consistently higher than those among non-Catholics — if only by a few percentage points. Nor does there appear to have been any change in this Catholic:non-Catholic difference with successive cohorts, or even any tendency for this difference to be greater among wives at some parities rather than others.

Given the situation respecting cell frequencies, additional sub-division in terms of schooling is meaningful only among the Australian-born (Table 6.3). Still confining analysis to metropolitan-dwellers, we see that the pattern already observed without any sub-division by schooling is repeated within each schooling category, namely, a higher proportion in the labour force at successively younger ages, irrespective of parity; an inverse association between parity and participation; and (except at the higher schooling levels among those at the higher parities) a level of participation among Catholics that is consistently higher than that among non-Catholics (although not, generally, very much higher). So far as any association with schooling itself is concerned, there is, as has been found elsewhere,[9] a general tendency for participation to increase with increased schooling: this, in the present study, within each age/religion/parity category.

Discussion

In contrast to the other attributes used in this analysis, labour force status is subject to considerable change over the course of one's lifetime. Especially is this the case with married women, among whom participation in the labour force is closely associated with the number and timing of births and, in particular, with the presence or absence of young children in the household.

It is conceivable that the pattern of labour force participation at an earlier stage of life could help shape that at a later one, for

Table 6.3: Percentage in Labour Force. Australian-born Metropolitan-dwelling Wives who Commenced Current Marriage before Age 26, by Year of Birth, Religion, Schooling and Selected Issue from Current Marriage (Australia, 1971)

Parity	Year of of Birth	Catholic				Non-Catholic			
		Years of Schooling				Years of Schooling			
		6	6-7	8	9+	6	6-7	8	9+
0	1907-11	9†	—	—	—	9	12	9	14
	1912-16	19	23†	—	—	19	23	22	23
	1917-21	35	37	—	—	26	32	36	37
	1922-26	48	49	50†	59†	39	45	46	48
	1927-31	53	56	63	58†	42	53	58	60
2	1907-11	10	11	11	16	8	12	11	12
	1912-16	22	26	25	25	18	21	24	22
	1917-21	33	34	36	37	26	30	33	36
	1922-26	37	43	49	45	34	44	42	44
	1927-31	43	49	52	54	39	45	48	51
4	1907-11	9	9	9†	11†	7	11	10	15
	1912-16	22	21	21	29	15	18	23	26
	1917-21	31	28	32	36	24	28	31	37
	1922-26	32	36	40	42	30	33	37	42
	1927-31	34	36	43	45	32	36	40	45
5	1907-11	9	11†	—	—	8	7	11†	11†
	1912-16	16	20	20†	28†	19	20	20	23
	1917-21	21	30	31	33	24	27	31	30
	1922-26	28	32	35	41	29	32	33	43
	1927-31	28	33	37	40	31	34	35	41
6+	1907-11	8	8	—	—	5	11	—	—
	1912-16	16	21	19	23†	16	20	20	28
	1917-21	23	27	26	28	19	25	28	31
	1922-26	24	26	28	31	22	27	29	35
	1927-31	25	24	29	29	25	26	29	35

(—) N < 100
† 100 < N < 150

example, by providing (or not providing) experience, contacts with possible employers, a sense of being able to obtain and hold a job, different levels of aspiration relating to life-style or social relations, and alternative role models. But there is no way of knowing whether this obtained with the population under consideration here, for the data at hand refer only to the situation at the time of the census, and not to that during the period of actual or potential childbearing. These women could have both entered and withdrawn from the labour force many times during the period leading up to that reported on here. All we know is who was or was not in the labour force at the time of the census. We do not know who was in the labour force at some previous time, and no longer is, as contrasted with somebody who was never in; the duration of labour force participation; the relative extent of full- and part-time participation; the timing of this participation with respect to the period of childbearing; or the significance of such participation in these women's lives.

Nor do we know — with respect to either degree or direction — the actual causal association between labour force status and fertility: whether participation in the labour force is *negatively* associated with fertility because women with fewer children have more time to participate, or restrict their fertility in order to participate; or whether labour force participation is perhaps sometimes *positively* associated with fertility because women with more children have greater financial need, or are better able to afford more children because of their earnings, or have more time for such participation through being able to shunt housekeeping and child-care responsibilities onto their older children.

What we do know from these data is, first, that there were differences between the labour force participation rates of the different nativity/religion groupings, and that the pattern of these differences seems to have remained fairly consistent between cohorts. Participation in the labour force, like fertility itself, would thus appear to be one of those cultural differences separating the Australian-born from those born overseas.

We also know, at least so far as the Australian-born are concerned, that participation in the labour force is positively associated with schooling. Thus, the highest participation rates are among those with the most schooling and fewest children, and the lowest are among those with the least schooling and the most children. The relative degrees of importance cannot be specified, but it would appear from this that the employment of wives — predictably enough — is a function of both opportunities and competing demands on one's time. Those with more schooling would presumably have greater opportunities in the job market, while those with more children would presumably face greater demands on their time and energies. The differential between these extremes would be reduced to the extent that economic pressures associated with having a more numerous progeny encouraged higher parity women to enter the labour market. The specific effect of such pressures cannot be ascertained from the data at hand, but we can acknowledge that these contrary pressures doubtless exist.

As already noted, the pattern of somewhat higher participation on the part of Catholic wives in general obtained, as well, within the more specific schooling categories. Because the Catholic excess tended to be more pronounced at the younger ages, probably much of its origin lies in the greater likelihood that an Australian-born Catholic at these ages will have at least one parent born overseas and, therefore, be adhering in some measure to a higher participation norm associated with overseas birth. However, this general pattern of higher participation among Catholics tended to decrease with advancing parity, particularly among those in the highest schooling category, to the point where, with wives of 6 + parity, there was no difference at all among those with fewer than nine years of schooling, and a difference in the opposite direction (that is, toward higher participation rates among non-Catholics) among those with nine or more years of schooling (see Table 6.3). As one can infer from the fertility differences already observed between Australian- and overseas-born wives that the highest fertility wives among the Australian-born (either Catholic or non-Catholic) are least likely to have overseas-born parents, this would appear to be yet another indication that it is among the younger cohorts of higher status Australian-born Catholics that one finds the greatest degree of adherence to their Church's teaching — not just on birth control but more particularly in the present instance on the role of wife and mother. Doubtless, a variety of conditions is operating — including the likely possibility that the proportion with young children in this uppermost and open-ended parity category may be higher among Catholics than among non-Catholics. But the pattern of participation does also suggest a greater adherence on the part of this particular sector of the Catholic population to teaching relating to the wife/mother role that defines employment outside the home as a not altogether acceptable activity for mothers. Even if they had no young children, adherence to this teaching in the past could have affected enough of these mothers' views of themselves, and their experience and skills, to account for the direction of the Catholic: non-Catholic differential at this level, and also for the differential

between these Catholics and their co-religionists at other parities.
More general conditions of the labour market, of qualifications and competing interests, underlie all the relations observed here. But while the specific causal connections between fertility and participation in the labour force cannot be specified with the types of data at hand, there is none the less a strong suggestion in these data that differences in norms relating to the wife/mother role — differences between different sectors of the population and between generations — have been prime determinants of the pattern of women's participation in the labour force in Australia.

Notes

1. Calculated from data in Australia, *Census of Population and Housing, 1971*, Bulletin 5, 'The Labor Force', Part 9, Canberra (1972), Table 1.
2. Calculated from data in Australia, *Census of the Commonwealth of Australia, 1961*, vol. 8, 'Statistician's Report', Canberra (1967), pp. 278–9.
3. Calculated from data in Australia, *Census of the Commonwealth of Australia, 1954*, vol. 8, 'Australia', Canberra (1975), Tables 45 and 46.
4. Calculated from data in Australia, *Census of Population and Housing, 1971*, Bulletin 5, Table 1.
5. Information supplied by Australian Bureau of Statistics.
6. A. J. Jaffe, 'Trends in the participation of women in the working force'. *Monthly Labor Review*, 79 (1956), p. 565.
7. William J. Abraham and A. J. Jaffe, 'A note on alternative measures of unemployment and the shortfall in employment, 1970–2'. *New York Statistician*, 23 (1972), pp. 2–5.
8. Australian Bureau of Statistics, Labour Force Survey, August 1979; and P. J. Sheehan and P. P. Stricker, *Dimensions of Unemployment*, Institute of Applied Economic and Social Research, University of Melbourne, forthcoming, chapter 1. Cited in Peter Sheehan, *Crisis in Abundance*, Ringwood, Vic.: Penguin (1980), pp. 40–1.
9. See e.g. G. G. Cain, *Married Women in the Labor Force: An Economic Analysis*, Chicago: University of Chicago Press (1966); W. G. Bowen and T. A. Finegan, *The Economics of Labor Force Participation*, Princeton: Princeton University Press (1969); and A. J. Jaffe and Jeanne Clare Ridley, *Employment of Women and Fertility*, Bethesda, Maryland: National Institute of Child Health and Human Development (1976).

7 THE PERVASIVE SIGNIFICANCE OF AGE AT MARRIAGE

Introduction

In the determination of fertility, marital status is important only to the extent that it affects the likelihood of conceiving and carrying a pregnancy to term; only, that is, to the extent that the married behave differently from the unmarried with respect to the three stages of reproduction: intercourse, conception and gestation/parturition.

The 1971 census is, therefore, of particular significance, for it may be the last Australian census for some time to provide data on age at marriage (derived, as already noted, by combining data given on age and duration of marriage) from which one might expect to draw a reasonably accurate picture of the distribution of the female population with respect to (1) age at commencement of regular sexual relations and (2) the age period over which childbearing is most widely accepted and, for that reason, over which a pregnancy is most likely to be allowed to run its course. This is because Australians, like other European populations, have in recent years undergone marked changes in standards and practices relating to (1) premarital sexual behaviour, (2) the use of contraception by unmarried women, and (3) access to abortion and the willingness to avail oneself of this procedure. The evidence for these changes takes a variety of forms: survey data showing increases in the proportions having sexual relations at younger ages,[1] liberalisation of laws on abortion and increases in the recorded incidence of legally-induced abortion,[2] changes in laws and practices relating to the provision of contraceptive advice and materials to the unmarried, declines in the proportions married at very young ages (simultaneously with the liberalisation of access on the part of the unmarried to contraception and abortion), increases in the extra nuptial birth rate among women in the upper ages,[3] and material from both official and unofficial sources (supplemented by one's own everyday observations) documenting an increase in the extent of cohabitation without the formalisation of such unions by marriage.[4]

Table 7.1: Median Issue and Percentage with 5+ Issue Born to Current Marriage. Wives 40–4 and 50–4 Years of Age, by Specified Age at Commencement of Current Marriage (Australia, 1971) (selected categories)

Selected categories	Wives Aged 40–4									Wives aged 50–4								
	Age at Marriage					Per Cent Decrease to Age 25 from Age		Age at Marriage		Age at Marriage					Per Cent Decrease to Age 25 from Age		Age at Marriage	
	17	19	21	23	25	17	19	27	29	17	19	21	23	25	17	19	27	29
Residence:																		
Metropolitan	2.77	2.48	2.33	2.24	2.09	25	16	1.90	1.66	2.80	2.48	2.12	1.98	1.86	34	25	1.73	1.52
Rural	3.73	3.29	2.97	2.89	2.75	26	16	2.48	2.26	3.93	3.09	2.84	2.58	2.48	37	20	2.34	1.99
Labour Force:																		
In	2.66	2.40	2.28	2.18	2.02	24	16	1.78	1.46	2.85	2.44	2.14	1.99	1.89	34	23	1.81	1.54
Not In	3.38	2.93	2.67	2.55	2.40	29	22	2.16	1.91	3.13	2.76	2.36	2.17	2.02	35	27	1.86	1.66
Schooling Less than																		
6 Years	3.20	2.84	2.57	2.36	2.18	32	23	1.90	1.75	3.20	2.86	2.43	2.21	2.03	37	29	1.82	1.56
6–7 Years	3.10	2.70	2.50	2.34	2.21	29	18	1.91	1.64	2.99	2.68	2.32	2.08	1.95	35	27	1.84	1.58
8 Years	2.93	2.61	2.44	2.36	2.21	25	15	1.99	1.69	2.81	2.43	2.18	2.07	1.95	31	20	1.93	1.70
9+ Years	2.58	2.48	2.47	2.46	2.32	10	7	2.14	1.85	2.59	2.21	2.10	2.10	1.98	24	10	1.81	1.63
Birthplace & Religion:																		
Australia:																		
Catholic	3.51	3.11	3.08	3.09	2.92	17	6	2.59	2.25	3.41	3.06	2.68	2.63	2.51	26	15	2.34	2.09
Non-Catholic	3.13	2.71	2.44	2.32	2.17	31	20	1.93	1.67	3.00	2.63	2.24	2.01	1.90	37	28	1.80	1.60
British Isles:																		
Catholic	—	3.26	2.86	2.82	2.57	—	21	2.59	2.15	—	3.33	2.61	2.74	2.47	—	26	2.61	—
Non-Catholic	2.87	2.44	2.25	2.10	1.94	32	20	1.85	1.66	2.82	2.32	2.00	1.89	1.77	37	24	1.68	1.51
Greece	2.76	2.44	2.33	2.10	1.89	32	23	1.80	1.62	—	—	—	—	—	—	—	—	—
Italy	2.64	2.43	2.37	2.16	1.98	25	19	1.91	1.80	3.29	3.01	2.71	2.75	2.29	30	24	1.88	1.79

Median Issue

Table 7.1 (continued)

	Wives Aged 40-4									Wives aged 50-5								
	Age at Marriage					Per Cent Decrease to Age 25 from Age		Age at Marriage		Age at Marriage					Per Cent Decrease to Age 25 from Age		Age at Marriage	
	\<── Per Cent with 5+ Issue ──\>																	
Selected categories	17	19	21	23	25	17	19	27	29	17	19	21	23	25	17	19	27	29
Residence:																		
Metropolitan	28	19	15	13	11	60	42	9	7	28	21	14	11	10	65	52	9	7
Rural	45	35	27	24	22	51	38	17	14	45	33	28	22	20	60	41	17	14
Labour Force:																		
In	24	17	13	11	10	59	42	7	4	24	21	14	11	11	65	49	10	8
Not In	39	29	22	19	16	58	44	13	10	39	27	18	15	13	62	51	11	8
Schooling:																		
Less than 6 Years	37	29	22	18	14	63	53	11	8	37	30	21	17	15	61	51	12	10
6–7 Years	32	23	18	16	15	55	38	10	9	32	25	17	12	12	63	52	11	8
8 Years	30	21	16	15	12	59	41	10	7	30	19	13	13	11	66	43	11	7
9+ Years	22	19	17	16	13	38	29	11	8	22	17	12	12	12	53	31	9	7
Birthplace and Religion:																		
Australia:																		
Catholic	41	34	33	33	29	29	14	23	19	41	32	26	24	24	41	24	21	17
Non-Catholic	33	23	15	12	10	71	58	8	6	33	24	15	10	9	72	61	8	6
British Isles:																		
Catholic	—	35	28	23	21	—	41	21	15	—	40	22	24	20	—	49	21	12
Non-Catholic	28	19	13	11	7	74	61	6	6	28	18	12	10	7	75	60	8	6
Greece	26	15	8	5	6	78	61	4	4	26	—	—	—	—	—	—	—	—
Italy	24	19	17	11	8	65	57	6	5	24	32	26	26	18	52	43	13	7

(—) N < 100

And yet, a negative association between wife's age at marriage and lifetime fertility persists as a common research finding,[5] and Australia — at least through the childbearing experience of the birth cohort of 1931 — is no exception. The negative nature of this association in Australia has, in fact, been remarkably consistent, not only within the various sectors of the population, but also between successive marriage ages within those sectors.

Findings

General

With one exception (and a particularly interesting exception it is), all sectors of the Australian population under study here (that is, in the birth cohorts 1907–31) evince a persistent decline in lifetime fertility with each increase in age at marriage. This is seen in both median issue and the proportions at the higher parities (see Table 7.1). The fertility of wives who commenced their current marriages at, say, age 20 was consistently higher than that of those who married at age 21, and lower than that of those who married at age 19. Similarly for each of the other ages, fertility in the next higher age was consistently lower, and in the next lower age consistently higher.

Within this pattern of successively lower fertility at each higher age at marriage, the extent of the decrease between successive ages tended to be somewhat greater at both the lower marriage ages (17 to 19, for example) and the higher (say, 25 to 29). But the overall pattern of lower fertility with each advance in marriage age persisted throughout.

The relative differences associated with age at marriage were predictably greater at the extremes of parity than in the middle ranges. But it is to be noted that, for the population as a whole, this gap narrowed with successive cohorts — as the proportions at the higher parities rose among those marrying later and, concurrently, the proportions at the very highest parity (6+) fell among those marrying earlier (Table 7.2).

Although nearly every sector of the population evinces this general pattern, there were some differences among them in extent. These differences were greater for those not in the labour forces than for those who were; for those with less schooling than for those with more; and at least among the Australian-born, for non-Catholics than for Catholics (Table 7.1).

Table 7.2: Percentages with Specified Numbers of Children Born to Current Marriage among Wives Married at Ages 20 and 24, together with Ratio of these Two Percentages at Each Parity (Wives Married at Age 20 = 100). Selected Categories by Year of Birth (Australia, 1971)

Year of Birth	Age at Marriage	Children Born to Current Marriage						
		0	1	2	3	4	5	6+
1907–11	24	7.0	15.4	29.3	22.4	13.4	6.1	6.3
	20	3.3	12.0	24.7	21.3	14.6	8.9	15.2
	ratio	212	128	119	105	92	69	41
1917–21	24	5.9	12.4	31.1	23.8	14.0	6.3	6.4
	20	3.0	10.3	26.4	23.6	15.8	9.2	11.7
	ratio	197	120	118	101	89	68	55
1927–31	24	4.7	8.3	28.5	26.8	17.0	7.8	6.8
	20	2.4	7.1	26.2	25.6	18.4	9.8	10.4
	ratio	196	117	109	105	92	80	65

Although grouped data on marriage age make it possible to observe a broader spectrum of the population, the introduction of such data does not alter the general picture: fertility continued to be consistently lower at successively higher ages at marriage, and the extent of this difference continued to be greater at the upper parities than at those in the middle range.

The Exception

The one exception is upper-status Australian-born Catholic wives. Yet, even with them, the exception lies only with those in the most recent cohorts — so pervasive is the influence of age at marriage. The earlier cohorts show the same pattern as that of the other sectors, albeit in a generally more attenuated form (Table 7.3). But by the end of the period (that is, with the cohort of 1927–31), the earlier negative association between fertility and age at marriage had given way to a positive association instead: in median issue and also in the proportions with five or more, and in some instances six or more.

For example, the ratio in median issue between those married at

Table 7.3: Median Issue and Percentage with 5+ Issue Born to Current Marriage, with Ratio between Values for Highest and Lowest Marriage Ages (Value for Lowest = 100). Australian-born Wives, by Religion, Year of Birth, Schooling and Husband's Occupation (Australia, 1971)

Age at Marriage:		Median Issue				Per Cent with 5+ Issue			
		Under 20	20−1	22−5	Ratio	Under 20	20−1	22−5	Ratio
Schooling	Year of Birth								
< 6 Years									
Catholic	1907−11	3.16	2.78	2.34	74	36	29	22	61
	1917−21	3.20	2.70	2.41	75	36	28	21	60
	1927−31	3.42	2.98	2.78	81	40	32	27	67
Non-Catholic	1907−11	2.85	2.43	1.97	69	32	23	14	45
	1917−21	3.02	2.46	2.07	69	33	21	14	43
	1927−31	3.20	2.67	2.39	75	35	23	18	50
6−7 Years									
Catholic	1907−11	2.89	2.65	2.46	85	32	29	25	78
	1917−21	3.23	2.75	2.55	79	36	28	24	65
	1927−31	3.19	2.91	2.80	88	35	30	27	78
Non-Catholic	1907−11	2.64	2.23	1.88	71	26	18	10	39
	1917−21	2.71	2.30	1.97	73	26	16	10	38
	1927−31	2.85	2.49	2.26	79	26	17	13	48
8 Years									
Catholic	1907−11	2.73	2.92	2.50	92	30	28	24	79
	1917−21	3.15	2.70	2.65	84	34	27	25	76
	1927−31	3.06	3.12	3.05	100	33	32	31	94
Non-Catholic	1907−11	2.44	2.20	1.85	76	19	15	8	41
	1917−21	2.41	2.17	1.95	81	19	12	8	42
	1927−31	2.64	2.39	2.21	84	21	13	9	43
9+ Years									
Catholic	1907−11	2.47	2.33	2.40	97	25	20	22	85
	1917−21	3.11	2.93	2.82	91	33	29	30	91
	1927−31	3.37	3.59	3.62	107	39	43	43	108
Non-Catholic	1907−11	2.14	1.92	1.81	85	18	10	7	40
	1917−21	2.44	2.14	2.03	83	19	11	9	45
	1927−31	2.62	2.50	2.42	92	19	14	10	55
Husband's occupation:									
Professional									
Catholic	1907−11	—	—	2.62	—	—	—	27	—
	1917−21	—	3.00	2.98	—	—	34	33	—
	1927−31	2.85	3.54	3.74	131	32	40	44	139

Table 7.3 (continued)

Age at Marriage:	Year of Birth	Median Issue				Per Cent with 5+ Issue			
		Under 20	20–1	22–5	Ratio	Under 20	20–1	22–5	Ratio
Husband's Occupation:									
Non-Catholic	1907–11	—	2.10	1.80	—	—	9	6	—
	1917–21	2.32	2.20	2.09	90	15	10	9	56
	1927–31	2.66	2.47	2.46	92	18	12	10	53
Administrative									
Catholic	1907–11	—	—	2.47	—	—	—	22	—
	1917–21	2.58	2.68	2.59	100	25	24	24	96
	1927–31	3.00	3.07	3.06	102	31	30	30	98
Non-Catholic	1907–11	2.17	2.07	1.84	85	16	14	7	44
	1917–21	2.33	2.11	1.96	84	17	10	7	39
	1927–31	2.56	2.37	2.25	88	18	11	8	44
Clerical and Sales									
Catholic	1907–11	2.12	2.40	2.26	107	24	21	18	74
	1917–21	2.69	2.59	2.40	89	26	24	21	80
	1927–31	2.96	2.94	3.00	101	30	30	30	100
Non-Catholic	1907–11	2.26	1.86	1.68	74	18	10	6	35
	1917–21	2.34	2.04	1.83	78	18	11	6	34
	1927–31	2.46	2.27	2.07	84	16	12	8	48
Farmer and Grazier									
Catholic	1907–11	3.64	3.25	3.14	86	45	39	36	80
	1917–21	3.82	3.60	3.34	87	47	43	37	80
	1927–31	3.86	3.76	3.86	100	48	45	48	99
Non-Catholic	1907–11	3.50	2.88	2.53	72	42	31	19	46
	1917–21	3.19	2.87	2.55	80	34	26	18	53
	1927–31	3.38	3.00	2.78	82	37	25	19	53
Transport and Communication									
Catholic	1907–11	—	—	2.39	—	—	—	22	—
	1917–21	2.94	2.80	2.50	85	33	28	22	67
	1927–31	3.18	2.99	2.82	89	36	31	28	77
Non-Catholic	1907–11	2.39	2.38	1.96	82	21	21	14	64
	1917–21	2.82	2.38	2.01	71	31	19	12	39
	1927–31	2.96	2.55	2.29	77	29	19	14	48
Trades, etc.									
Catholic	1907–11	2.86	2.71	2.27	79	28	27	21	74
	1917–21	3.16	2.61	2.44	77	33	26	21	65
	1927–31	3.23	2.91	2.78	86	36	30	26	74

Table 7.3 (continued)

		Median Issue				Per Cent with 5 + Issue			
Age at Marriage:		Under 20	20–1	22–5	Ratio	Under 20	20–1	22–5	Ratio
	Year of Birth								
Husband's Occupation:									
Trades, etc.									
Non-Catholic	1907–11	2.66	2.37	1.88	71	26	20	11	41
	1917–21	2.77	2.28	1.92	69	27	17	11	39
	1927–31	2.84	2.43	2.21	78	27	17	12	45

(−) N < 100
Note:
Median issue and per cent with 5 + issue ratios calculated on the basis of figures
carried out to two decimal places and one decimal place, respectively.

ages 22–5 and those married before age 20 went from 0.74 among
Australian-born Catholic wives with fewer than six years of
schooling in the cohort of 1907–11 to 0.81 among their counterparts in the cohort of 1927–31, but among those with nine or more
years of schooling the change was from 0.97 to 1.07; with respect to
the proportion with five or more issue, the comparable changes
were from 0.61 to 0.67 and from 0.85 to 1.08, respectively (calculated on the basis of percentages carried out to one decimal place).
Among Australian-born non-Catholics, by way of contrast,
comparable changes in the median were from 0.69 to 0.75 among
those with fewer than six years of schooling, and from 0.85 to 0.92
among those with nine or more; in the proportions with five or
more issue, the respective changes among Australian-born non-
Catholics were from 0.45 to 0.50 and from 0.40 to 0.55 — a
narrowing of the range, but a continuation of the pattern of
negative association, none the less.

It was much the same by husband's occupation. Among the non-
Catholic Australian-born, the usual negative pattern of association
between fertility and age at marriage obtained in all occupational
groupings within each cohort. But among the Catholic Australian-
born, age at marriage, by the time the cohort of 1927–31 is
reached, remained negatively associated with fertility only among
manual industrial workers. Among farmers and graziers, and also
white-collar workers, the association had become essentially nil;
and among professional workers it had become markedly positive.

By the cohort of 1927–31, the fertility level of Australian-born Catholic wives married at ages 22–5 to husbands in the professional occupation category had become second only to that of their counterparts among the wives of farmers and graziers married either before age 20 or at ages 22–5; and then by only 3 per cent (or 0.12 of a child) in the case of median issue (3.74 *vs.* 3.86 per cent) and only 7 per cent (or 3.2 percentage points) in the case of the proportion with five or more (44.4 *vs.* 47.6 per cent) (Table 7.3). The pattern of association between fertility and age at marriage among upper-status Australian-born Catholics was at variance with that in every other sector of the population.

Discussion

Introduction

Given the nature of the association between age and female fecundity, it is to be expected that a negative association would exist between lifetime fertility and wife's age at marriage in populations exercising little direct control over childbearing.[6] But that a similarly negative association should also exist in populations where control over childbearing is substantial is not so readily anticipated, for here the role of differences in female fecundity can hardly be more than minimal. One might reasonably suppose, in fact, that the control of fertility would reduce such an association (at least among those who married at the more fecund ages) precisely through removing that part of it that derived from higher than average fecundity among those marrying at successively younger ages.[7] Yet this has not proved to be the case, for a strong negative association between fertility and wife's age at marriage is also found in a number of prominently contracepting populations — the American and British, for example — no less than the Australian. Age at marriage, it would seem, can signify quite different things in different populations, and presumably also quite different things among different persons within the same population. The task here, then, is to enumerate what these different things could be: what it is about different ages at marriage that could give rise to *fewer* offspring among women who marry *later*, and to *more* offspring among women who marry *earlier* — particularly, though not exclusively (for while its data are more comprehensive and detailed, Australia is, in this regard, but part of a larger whole), with respect to their relative importance to the pattern observed in Australia.

What age at marriage offers as a variable in the analysis of fertility is the element of time. Certain factors of potential significance to fertility can come into being only over time: changes in physiology, and also in status, values, attitudes and self-concept, for example. What data on age at marriage afford is the possibility of categorising a population on the basis of at least the time its members have had in which to experience such changes. However crudely, these data afford sub-divisions in terms of time to develop, time to experience, time to change. Something of the same possibility is also afforded by data on years of schooling, but not with the same degree of consistency, nor for more than a restricted period of the life-cycle. So far as census-type data are concerned, there is no substitute for age at marriage as a vehicle through which to introduce the element of time.

Just what fertility-determining conditions — whether at the specific level of a particular individual or at the more general level of an entire population — might be indicated by age at marriage is not something readily subjected to detailed analysis. The conditions are several and varied, and for only a few of them is information available in a form suited to determining either whether they were present in a given instance or, if they were present, the role they may have played in accounting for a particular level of fertility. It will have to suffice here to present a list of these various conditions and then proceed to an assessment, so far as possible, of the role each seems likely to have played in producing the particular pattern of negative associations between fertility and age at marriage observed in the data at hand. Twenty such conditions can be specified, as follows:

1. Factors affecting the physiological possibility of bearing children:
(a) Physiological ability to conceive
(b) Physiological ability to carry a pregnancy to term
(c) Coital frequency

2. Factors related to selection, whether of persons with different orientations toward childbearing, or of persons with different physiological possibilities for bearing children:
(d) 'Forced' marriages
(e) Self-selection for the parental role

3. Factors affecting the ability and willingness to control child-bearing:

A. Knowledge and skill
(f) Knowledge and experience of contraception
(g) Knowledge of abortion and experience with obtaining one
B. Values and outlook, definition of the self
(h) Willingness to use birth control
(i) Unwillingness to bear children at more advanced ages

4. Factors affecting the desired number of children:

(j) Experience of roles that could lead to defining oneself more broadly than as a spouse/parent
(k) Involvement with a wider range of interpersonal contacts and role models (with respect to persons directly involved with childbearing)
(l) Existence of means for the satisfaction of one's needs alternative to those associated with children
(m) Existence of interests that could compete with children for the allocation of time and energy
(n) Existence of interests that could compete with children for the allocation of money
(o) Existence of tastes, the satisfaction of which could be presumed to be threatened or restricted by the presence of children
(p) Existence of tastes for a 'higher' standard of childcare

5. Demographic experience:

(q) Experience of contraceptive failure
(r) Increase in the desired number of children
(s) Experience of death of a child at a time when one still has the physiological capacity to bear another as a 'replacement'
(t) Remarriage

Possible Factors

(a) Physiological ability to conceive. Differences in physiological ability to conceive would appear to have played but a negligible role in causing the observed association between fertility and marriage age in Australia. The fertility differences associated with age at marriage are simply too great to permit of explanation in terms of a condition that must surely vary by relatively small degrees between successive ages. Moreover, the pattern of the association between

Table 7.4: Measures of Coital Frequency per Month, by Age and Duration of Marriage. Random Sample of Melbourne Wives (1971)

Marriage duration and age grouping	Per Cent Stated Monthly Frequency			Total %	Median Monthly Frequency	Ns	
	Less than 8 times	8–15 times	16+ times			Responding	Not Responding
Married less than 5 years							
Under 20	17	25	58	100	20	24	6
19–20	8	31	40	99	16	38	8
20–21	19	48	33	100	12	79	14
21–22	28	44	28	100	12	104	28
22–23	30	44	26	100	10	110	27
23–24	25	48	28	101	10	115	22
24–25	23	55	22	100	10	94	19
25–26	25	54	21	100	10	61	9
26–27	27	46	27	100	9	48	10
27–28	28	56	15	99	8	46	6
28–29	26	65	10	101	8	31	2
29–31	32	57	11	100	8	28	7
Married 5–9 Years							
Under 25	25	44	31	100	12	32	7
24–25	25	45	30	100	12	53	12
25–26	26	55	20	101	10	86	18
26–27	28	59	13	100	9	101	19
27–28	33	55	12	100	9	97	16
28–29	37	49	13	99	10	89	19
29–30	34	54	12	100	8	83	20
30–31	33	54	13	100	10	70	18
31–32	33	51	16	100	8	51	13
32–33	41	50	9	100	8	32	7
33–35	50	42	8	100	7	36	11

Table 7.4 (continued)

Marriage duration and age grouping	Per Cent Stated Monthly Frequency				Median Monthly Frequency	Ns	
	Less than 8 times	8–15 times	16+ times	Total %		Responding	Not Responding
Married 10–14 Years							
Under 31	41	43	16	100	8	44	8
30–31	38	44	17	99	8	52	9
31–32	40	44	16	100	8	80	10
32–33	39	47	13	99	8	89	14
33–34	37	53	11	101	8	95	17
34–35	48	44	7	99	8	96	19
35–36	45	47	7	99	8	99	22

age at marriage and completed fertility is not altogether in conformity with that presumed to exist between age and sterility, for the
observed declines in fertility commence at younger ages than do
those estimated for the onset of sterility and, moreover, they
proceed at a faster pace.[8]

That the inability to conceive as a consequence of *voluntary*
causes should also increase with age derives not from any direct
causal associations between the two, but simply from the fact that a
longer span of years affords a greater opportunity to experience
those conditions (breast-feeding excepted) that might give rise to
it.[9]

(b) Ability to carry a pregnancy to term. As the ability to avoid
spontaneous foetal wastage seems to follow quite closely the age
pattern of infecundity from involuntary causes,[10] the role of
spontaneous foetal wastage in determining the differences in
lifetime fertility related to the marriage ages under consideration
here must be no less negligible than that of age-related infecundity.
While it must be recognised that early childbearing can damage the
female reproductive system, and in that way lower a woman's
ultimate fertility, by either impairing her ability to conceive or
increasing the likelihood that she will experience a foetal death, this
seems of little moment in the Australian population, where
childbearing at the lowest ages is infrequent and (what is probably
of greater significance) levels of health among teenagers are fairly
high. But to the extent that early childbearing does damage the
reproductive system, its presence would lessen, not increase, the
negative association between fertility and age at marriage.

(c) Coital frequency. Coital frequency is the one physiological
factor that would appear to be of some significance in accounting
for the observed association between fertility and age at marriage in
Australia, although the degree of this significance, in any
numerical sense, is impossible to determine. The range of individual variation is doubtless considerable, but it is widely accepted
that coital frequency generally declines with advancing age — a
view supported by the pattern of coital frequencies, standardised
for duration of marriage, reported by a random sample of
Melbourne wives in 1971 (see Table 7.4).[11] This may result from
physiological ageing processes in the male, as Kinsey and his
associates have claimed,[12] or in the female, or possibly from some

non-physiological process instead. To anticipate somewhat factors (d) and (e) below, it may also result from earlier marriages being selective of persons who are less inclined to defer sexual gratification and who, for that reason, would be more likely to experience higher frequencies of coitus. But whatever the origin, the implication is the same: those who married at the younger ages would have been married at ages associated with *higher* frequences of coitus; and those at the older ages, at ages associated with successively *lower* frequencies.

Conception can take place only at certain times in the menstrual cycle. The pattern of intercourse, therefore, greatly influences the probability that conception will occur.[13] Moreover, it certainly seems reasonable to suppose that there is no age-related pattern of coitus in which those with less ability to conceive would tend to concentrate their coital activity into periods of maximum ovulation. It follows that the likelihood of conception will be positively associated with the frequency of coitus and, since coital frequencies on average decline with age, that one way in which ageing will affect fertility will be through its association with lower frequencies of coitus.

(d) 'Forced' marriages. 'Forced' marriages are those that take place (or of which the timing is advanced) because the bride is pregnant. In any population in which marriages take place some years after puberty, the share of such marriages in the total of all marriages can be expected to decline as marriage age advances, at least within the major childbearing ages. Table 7.5 illustrates the point for Australia.

This decline in the proportion of apparently 'forced' marriages as one proceeds from lower to higher marriage ages can contribute to a negative association between fertility and age at marriage in two ways: first, through reducing the proportion of the childless in successively younger age at marriage categories, and secondly, through selecting for earlier marriage a higher proportion of those who are either physiologically or temperamentally more inclined to higher fertility. The first does not properly belong to the present analysis because its bearing on the fertility of any age at marriage category is only in the manner of a statistical artefact. By definition, a 'forced' marriage will be of 0-parity only if the pregnancy that gave rise to it fails — through induced abortion, miscarriage or stillbirth — to eventuate in a live birth. Thus, among

Table 7.5: Percentage of Legitimate First Births* Occurring within Seven Months of Marriage, by Age of Mother (Australia, 1975)

Age of Mother	Per Cent Duration less than seven months	Per Cent Duration Not Stated	Total First Births
16	86.7	1.4	723
17	74.0	.8	2022
18	63.7	.4	3856
19	40.7	.3	5066
20	24.7	.2	6137
21	15.4	.1	6951
22	10.1	.1	7497
23	6.5	—	8176
24	5.2	.1	7969
25	4.2	—	7195
26	4.7	—	6224
27	4.8	—	5066
28	5.1	—	4203
29	5.5	.1	2736
30	7.0	.2	1983
31	6.1	.2	1474
32	6.4	.1	1068
33	6.7	.1	817
34	10.0	.2	590
35	10.8	.2	453
36	9.3	.3	367
37	14.3	1.1	272
38	10.7	1.0	206
39	11.0	—	146
40–4	12.2	1.5	263

* Nuptial confinements

Source:
Calculated from Australian Bureau of Statistics, *Births 1975*, Table 14.

any set of marriages, the higher the proportion 'forced', the lower the incidence of childlessness and, correspondingly, the higher the average lifetime fertility. To circumvent the bias this introduces into interpretation of the association between fertility and age at marriage, analysis can be confined to mothers. An example is provided in Table 7.6 relating to 40–4-year-old wives who married at ages 20 and 24. In this particular instance, the elimination of 0-parity wives makes little difference, nor does it alter the pattern of group differences in fertility — as may be seen from the ratios between the higher and lower values associated with the various attributes specified.

Table 7.6: The Contrast between Measures of Fertility Based on All Wives and Those Based on Mothers Only. Median Issue and Percentage with 5+ Issue Born to Current Marriage among Wives 40–4 Years of Age who Commenced Current Marriage at Ages 20 and 24 (Australia, 1971) (Selected Categories)

| | Married at Age 20 | | | | | | Married at Age 24 | | | | | |
| | Median Issue | | | Per Cent with 5+ Issue | | | Median Issue | | | Per Cent with 5+ Issue | | |
	All Wives	Mothers	Per Cent Increase	All Wives	Mothers	Per Cent Increase	All Wives	Mothers	Per Cent Increase	All Wives	Mothers	Per Cent Increase
Residence:												
Metropolitan	2.38	2.43	2	16.4	16.9	3	2.17	2.27	5	12.1	12.8	6
Rural	3.10	3.14	1	30.5	31.1	2	2.79	2.85	2	22.9	23.7	3
Ratio:												
Higher ÷ Lower	1.30	1.29		1.86	1.84		1.29	1.26		1.89	1.85	
Schooling:												
Less than 6 Years	2.65	2.71	2	24.1	24.8	3	2.21	2.34	6	15.3	16.3	7
9+ Years	2.45	2.51	2	17.9	18.4	3	2.41	2.47	2	14.5	15.0	3
Ratio:												
Higher ÷ Lower	1.08	1.08		1.35	1.35		1.09	1.06		1.06	1.09	
Husband's occupation												
Clerical and Sales	2.38	2.44	3	16.1	16.6	3	2.17	2.28	5	12.4	13.1	6
Farmers and Graziers	3.10	3.13	1	29.0	29.4	1	2.81	2.87	2	22.4	23.0	3
Ratio:												
Higher ÷ Lower	1.30	1.28		1.80	1.77		1.29	1.26		1.81	1.76	
Religion (Australian-born):												
Catholic	3.07	3.13	2	32.8	33.5	2	3.05	3.15	3	31.3	32.6	4
Non-Catholic	2.55	2.59	2	18.3	18.7	2	2.26	2.34	4	10.9	11.4	5
Ratio:												
Higher ÷ Lower	1.20	1.21		1.79	1.79		1.35	1.35		2.87	2.86	

So far as 'forced' marriages' being selective of persons of higher potential fertility is concerned, it can be noted that, at any age and any level of coital frequency and contraceptive efficiency, the more fecund women will be the ones more likely to conceive and, for that reason, the ones more likely also to be parties to 'forced' marriages. To the extent that such marriages are selective as to fecundity, it follows that, other things being equal, the category with the higher proportion of 'forced' marriages will also be the one with the higher average fertility.

But physiological selectivity may be only one type of selectivity associated with 'forced' marriage. It is not inconceivable that such marriages are also selective of certain personality types associated with higher fertility — whether this higher fertility is deliberately sought or merely accepted as the result of forces perceived as being largely beyond one's control. However, in introducing the idea of selectivity on other than physiological grounds, we are moving into considerations embodied in the next factor.

(e) Self-selection for the parental role. From the perspective of an economist (and with some resort to an economist's terminology), De Tray has written:

> When couples marry, they do so, not simply for the sake of being married, but in order to have access to certain consumption patterns not available to them if they remained single. A prime example is the production and consumption of 'own children'. From this perspective, the demand for marriage is derived from couples' desires for, among other things, having and raising their own children. Thus, far from being a predetermined or exogamous variable with respect to fertility, age of marriage . . . may well be *a function of* a couple's demand for children. Couples who want, on average, relatively large numbers of children will marry early in order to increase the probability of attaining that goal, while couples who want small families will marry late in order to reduce fertility.[14]

If this seems to posit rather more consciously thought-out behaviour than is likely to be the case in actual circumstances, it is none the less possible that, whether or not their marriages were 'forced', those who married at younger ages had in their number a higher proportion who wanted to play not only the conjugal, but also the parental role; less desirous of playing some alternative or competing role; and, just possibly, even fonder of children.

Along these same lines, the Hoffmans have written that one value children have for potential parents may be 'biologically based', which, they continue, 'does not mean that all persons are equal in this regard, . . . that having children is a biological necessity,' or that 'the biological value is more compelling than the social ones', only that this biological value 'may be one of the many factors that affect the motivation to have children . . .'.[15] If there is such a value, it would seem to be of a type particularly likely to lead those more affected by it to marry earlier, thereby securing to themselves a longer period of potential childbearing, with higher ·average fertility as a consequence.

But that this could have been of much significance in the Australian situation seems unlikely. For one thing, few even of those at the highest fertility levels had fertility anything like what may be presumed to have been physiologically possible for persons commencing regular intercourse at the ages at which these women married. For another, the declines in fertility with advancing age at marriage tended to be proportionally less among those sectors with generally higher fertility than among those with generally lower: the upper levels of fertility recorded here were not so high that their attainment depended on one's getting an early start on procreation.

(f) Knowledge and experience of contraception. Just as getting older is associated with the acquisition of knowledge and experience in general, so also can it be assumed to be associated specifically with the acquisition of knowledge and experience of conception. Unless we make the implausible assumption that the timing of marriage is somehow dependent upon having this knowledge or experience beforehand, it follows that, within any given birth cohort, successively higher ages at marriage will be associated with successively lower incidences of unwanted (or better still, unintended) births, and therefore with successively lower fertility.

However, it is important to relate this to birth cohorts in order to take account of probable differences among generations. While it seems likely that in most populations, younger generations will know more about birth control than did their predecessors when they were at the same age, this knowledge (and experience as well) can be expected to accumulate over time, with the result that, within any given birth cohort, the average bride who married at, say, 18 will have been less informed or experienced on her wedding day than her counterpart who married at 20, who in turn will have been less informed or experienced than her counterpart who married at 25. And because the ages of grooms are closely related to those of their brides, one can also expect more knowledge or experience of contraception among the grooms of older brides than among those of younger ones.

(g) Knowledge of abortion and experience of obtaining one. Similarly, and with the same consequences for fertility, because of the reduction it would entail in unintended births, ageing can be expected (again, within any given birth cohort) to be associated also with greater knowledge of abortion and greater experience with obtaining one. This experience (whether direct or indirect — the latter through the experience of an acquaintance or friend) is particularly worth noting because of the ethical and legal constraints so frequently associated with obtaining an abortion. Familiarity with, for example, the earliest symptoms of pregnancy, the bureaucratic maze one may have to work through to procure an abortion, the defences one can fall back on to overcome the guilt feelings so often engendered or intensified by the administrative and professional personnel one must work through[16] — each a kind of experience that can only accumulate with age — is bound to have its effect on reducing the incidence of unintended births with advancing age.

Yet during the childbearing period of the women under consideration here, the availability of abortion in Australia was severely limited — certainly the availability of legal abortion and, in all likelihood, of illegal abortion as well. Except, then, for some of the overseas-born (and not necessarily for them, either), differences in knowledge or experience of abortion are not likely to have played much of a role in determining the pattern of fertility under consideration here. It could be a different matter with the next generation however.

(h) Willingness to use birth control. Growing older can also be expected to be positively associated with the willingness to use birth control — whether contraception, abortion or sterilisation — again with a corresponding decrease in the incidence of unintended births. Some support for this contention is provided by opinion polls undertaken in the United States over the 1962–70 period

(before the liberalisation of abortion laws there) which show quite consistent declines with age in the proportion of women respondents expressing *dis*approval of legislation to legalise abortion.[17] There may be several causal elements at work here, but the most important is doubtless the age-associated accumulation of pertinent experience. To the extent that morality hinges on circumstances, one could expect to find a more accepting view of contraception and (particularly) abortion among those who have had more opportunity to experience — directly or indirectly — the kinds of undesirable circumstances these practices are presumed to forestall or mitigate.

Related to the principle that morality hinges on circumstances, and offering probably greater support for the expectation that growing older will be accompanied by a greater willingness to use birth control, is the way in which people so frequently come to define themselves differently with respect to certain ethical principles and patterns of behaviour. Seldom is the change sudden; usually it is a gradual process involving nothing more than the slight, often imperceptible extension of one's behaviour into what was previously a normatively unavailable sector along the range of possible behaviour.[18] A good example (and one with some bearing on the topic under discussion here) is supplied by Rains's description of how women in the American setting often drift into premarital sexual experiences:

> Most girls in the course of the lives prior to marriage alter their moral standards and sexual behaviour, generally becoming more permissive. This process can be viewed as an anticipation of marriage, as a coming to some terms with intimacy and sexuality.
> . . .
> While many girls do manage to come to an open and unconflicted acceptance of premarital sexual intercourse, most are not likely to have began their dating careers with this view and will have experienced uncertainty in reaching this view. . . .
> The central feature of premarital sexual careers is the experience of coming to view as acceptable what was previously viewed as unacceptable, of acting in ways which are not yet acceptable to oneself but which will come to be acceptable.[19]

Later marriage affords more time for such changes in standards and behaviour to take place; and, in doing so, for a cohort of brides who are more accepting of birth control and more experienced in its practice to come into being, with the reduction of unintended pregnancies as one consequence.[20]

(i) Unwillingness to bear children at more advanced ages. Like other human behaviour, childbearing takes place within a framework of norms. In the case of childbearing, these norms may define not only the socially acceptable range of family sizes but also the appropriate age-range for bearing children. In some societies, the upper limit to the range of appropriate childbearing ages may be expressed indirectly, as with the disapproval of additional childbearing once one has reached the status of mother-in-law or grandparent. In others, the expression may be more direct. But either way, there is likely to be some normative discouragement of childbearing at the higher ages (however 'higher' may be defined). The consequences of this for the association between fertility and age at marriage lie simply in the fact that those who marry later reach these ages at shorter marriage durations, and therefore after fewer years of possible childbearing.

That the operation of such a norm has an effect on the timing of childbearing and, through that, on fertility as well, is suggested by a comparison between populations exercising, respectively, relatively extensive and relatively slight control over procreation. One such comparison (using period rather than the more precisely appropriate cohort data) is provided in Table 7.7.

Related to this normative aspect is the possibility of a personal reluctance, particularly on the part of women, to bearing children at more advanced ages because of the (not altogether groundless) fear of undesirable physiological consequences for oneself or one's child.

(j) Experience of role that could lead to defining oneself more broadly than as a spouse/parent. Because ageing is associated with the opportunity to play different roles, it can be assumed that the higher a person's age at marriage, the more likely is that person to have had experience of a sort to expand self-definition. I have in mind here experiences like having job, travelling or undertaking university studies, any of which could broaden one's horizons and lead to the development of aspirations for the fulfilment of which children might be of little or no value, if not an actual hindrance.

Table 7.7: Birth Rate of Women Aged 35–9 as a Proportion of the Birth Rate of Women Aged 20–4. Selected Countries with (Respectively) Extensive and Slight Control over Fertility (mid-1960s)

Countries with Extensive Control over Fertility		Countries with Slight Control over Fertility	
Australia	19	Chile	63
Austria	20	Costa Rica	67
Bulgaria	10	Ecuador	71
Czechoslovakia	14	Guatemala	63
Denmark	23	Philippines	66
East Germany	17		
Hungary	15		
Japan	19		
USA	22		

Source:
United Nations, *Demographic Yearbook 1969*, Table 18.

(k) Involvement with a wider range of interpersonal contacts and role models (with respect to persons participating in childrearing). Related to factor (j) is the likelihood that those who postponed marriage would have accumulated a wider range of acquaintances, with one result being that a smaller and possibly less significant — in the sense of its involving interaction with 'significant others' [21] — proportion of their social intercourse would have been taken up with persons whose lives were at the time extensively concerned with the bearing and rearing of children. This could be expected to have lessened peer pressure to undertake, or continue with, child-bearing and, in that way, to have been conducive to lower eventual fertility.

(l) Existence of means for the satisfaction of one's needs alternative to those associated with children. As one grows older — at least to a point well beyond that defined by the childbearing ages — there would seem to be an increased likelihood of developing a variety of means to the satisfaction of one's needs (for example, for affection, response, approval, intellectual stimulation, self-respect). Of particular significance here is the fact that the longer marriage and childbearing are postponed, the greater is the likelihood that the bearing and rearing of children will not figure prominently among these means. This is not to say that this state of affairs will continue once childbearing has started, but only that the degree to which

the bearing and rearing of children serves, or is expected to serve, as a means to the satisfaction of one's needs may be lessened by the presence of other, alternative means to the same ends.

Of course, the development of means to one's ends — not to mention the development of some of the ends themselves — depends on the opportunities afforded. The Hoffmans provide an example:

> The economic setting — whether the social class or the rural–urban dimension — may affect fertility behavior not just through its effect on the child's economic value but also because the life-style associated with it may affect the noneconomic value of the child. Thus lower-class Americans may desire more children . . . because they have fewer alternative sources of the noneconomic values children provide. Children may be the lower-class man's only opportunities to feel effective, to have a sense of personal worth, to have power over another. The lower-class wife may find an affectionate response in her children that is lacking in her husband.[22]

But some opportunities of potential importance to childbearing are age-related. For example, the extent to which one actually has the opportunity of obtaining a rewarding job frequently depends on one's years of experience and training — something early marriage often restricts or, particularly in the case of women, forecloses altogether.

(m) Existence of interests that could compete with children for time and energy. As one grows older (again, up to a point) there is the further likelihood of having developed interests the satisfaction of which is rendered more difficult by the demands childcare can make upon time and energy (emotional as well as physical). Travel, participation in sport, playing an instrument, painting, reading, involvement in community activities, party-giving, having a career are examples that come readily to mind. Their development is frequently associated with growing older; their satisfaction, almost inevitably impeded to some extent by the presence of young children.

(n) Existence of interests that could compete with children for money. Growing older can also be associated with the development

of interests the satisfaction of which is rendered more difficult by the economic costs associated with the bearing and rearing of children. Interest in travel figures here, too, as would such other interests as the possession of expensive goods and services, and attendance at concerts and the theatre.[23]

(o) Existence of tastes, the satisfaction of which could be presumed to be threatened or restricted by the presence of children. Quite apart from questions of income or of demands upon one's time, growing older can be associated also with the acquistion of tastes (for example, for quiet, cleanliness, tidiness, aesthetically-pleasing accommodation) that the presence of children in one's household may make it more difficult to satisfy.

(p) Existence of tastes for a 'higher' standard of childcare. This is a different kind of taste. It relates to the likelihood that there will be some expansion over time (and therefore with ageing) in what one defines as necessary or at least desirable expenditure to make upon one's children — whether this expenditure is in terms of money or parental time and psychic energy.[24] This expansion may derive from improvements in one's income or from one's introduction to 'higher' standards through the experience of higher schooling, both of which are usually age-related. But it can also derive from an age-related rise in aspirations associated with nothing more than a general expansion of (or coming into contact with) the culture of privatism and consumerism — aspirations, for example, for giving one's children additional years of formal schooling, getting their teeth straightened, giving each child a room of his or her own, making trips that involve the whole family . . . the list is a long one in any affluent society.

(q) Experience of contraceptive failure. This is self-explanatory. Other things being equal, the earlier one marries, the longer the period of risk of contraceptive failure sudsequent to having borne all the children one may wish to have had.

(r) Increase in the desired number of children. Because child-bearing is irreversible, a change in the desired number of children — once one's initial goal has been achieved — can have only one effect on ultimate fertility, and that is to increase it. As with the possibilty of contraceptive failure (factor (q)), the younger one's

age at marriage, the longer the period during which one is physiologically capable of increasing the number of one's children in response to a change of mind.

(s) Experience of the death of a child at a time when one still has the physiological capacity to bear another as a 'replacement'. The younger one's age at childbearing (which would, of course, be related to one's age at marriage), the longer the period over which one might experience the death of a child and simultaneously (given the association of age with fecundity) be in a position to compensate for that death by bearing an additional child. A 30-year-old mother whose third (and what had beforehand been considered her last) child is run over and killed at the age of five has an average of some 10–15 more years in which to attempt with some expectation of success to bear a 'replacement', with approximately the first five of those years being ones of fairly high fecundity. Her 35-year-old counterpart, by way of contrast, has only about 5–10 years for the same purpose — with none of these years likely to be characterised by high fecundity. However, child mortality levels in Australia are fortunately low enough to ensure that the numerical importance of this factor — whatever its importance in individual circumstances — will not have been very great.

(t) Remarriage. As pointed out in chapter 1, the effect of remarriage subsequent to divorce or widowhood has been essentially eliminated from this analysis by means of the restriction to wives married before age 26. However, it is worth considering the likely role of remarriage because of recent trends in Australia pointing to an increasing incidence of divorce and remarriage, and the movement of these phenomena into the younger ages.

What might be the significance of remarriage to the association between fertility and age at marriage is unclear. It seems reasonable to suppose that future childbearing on the part of persons (particularly women) entering into second marriages — simply because of likely childbearing in their previous marriages — would be less than that of their age peers entering, instead, upon first marriages. Add to this the fact that within any particular birth cohort (in order to remove any bias associated with rapid changes in marriage patterns between generations) higher marriage ages are more likely to accompany second marriages, it follows that one could expect the increasing proportion of remarriages as one proceeds from lower to higher marriage ages to account for at least some of the negative association observed between fertility and marriage age.

However, in one sense, this line of argument is inappropriate to an attempt to enumerate the factors that might account for a negative association between fertility and age at marriage. Particularly where fertility is subject to extensive control, there is likely to be an upper-limit norm to the number of children considered suitable for a woman to bear. Any mixing of the fertilities of first marriages and remarriages would thus increase the apparent fertility difference between categories containing different proportions of first and subsequent marriages, because it would negatively bias the fertility of those categories having the higher proportions in remarriages.

But just as the effects of 'forced' marriages can be minimised by excluding the childless from the analysis, so also can the significance of remarriage to any observed association between fertility and wife's age at marriage be assessed by separately analysing different portions of the population: in the present instance, by separating the once-married from the more-than-once-married, for example. This cannot be done with Australian data, which pertain only to the current marriage, but it can be done with American. For example with age at marriage held constant, we find that among American women of essentially completed childbearing in 1970 (i.e. at ages 35–44), those in one — presumably continuous — union (i.e. married once, husband present) did indeed have a generally higher lifetime fertility than did those married more than once.[25] But the difference was only 3 per cent higher overall among Whites, and but 9 per cent higher among Blacks, which suggests that younger ages at dissolution of marriage (primarily in consequence of a higher incidence of divorce), especially if combined with possibly shorter intervals between the cessation of one marriage and the commencement of another, may eventually eliminate this difference altogether. In fact, it is just possible that it may even produce one in the opposite direction; for it is not altogether unreasonable to suppose that where fertility is low (where, that is, the difference in average family size between relatively 'high' and relatively 'low' fertility couples is on the order of only two to three children), and romantic love is considered the most appropriate basis for marriage, second marriages could be associated with higher, not lower, lifetime fertility on the grounds that, irrespective of the number of children born to their first marriages, remarried couples would want to have children in their second marriages as tangible proof of their love, or as a kind of cement to bind these new unions together. This is at least suggested by Lauriat's finding that remarried women in the United States did, in fact, 'tend to make up for the fertility they presumably would have experienced had they remained in their previous marriage'.[26] If fertility is low, such behaviour would not be likely to add more than one or two children to the number a woman could have been expected to bear had she remained in the first marriage. Thus, while her total fertility from all marriages combined would be higher, it would seldom exceed the upper normative limit.

The More Important Factors

Each of these factors doubtless played some part in creating the observed pattern of association between fertility and age at marriage. But there can be no question that some played a far less important role than others, and that with some, the role played was hardly more than negigible.

Factor (t) (remarriage) was effectively ruled out of the present analysis, as were factors (a) (physiological ability to conceive) and (b) (physiological ability to carry a pregnancy to term).

With respect to 'forced' marriages (factor (d)), it can be noted that, while these are more likely to figure among marriages entered into at younger rather than older ages, there is little to suggest that this had more than a very minor effect on the fertility differences under consideration here. Nor is there anything to suggest that any significant part in the origin of these differences was played by self-selection for the parental role (factor (e)).

While factor (g) (knowledge of abortion and experience with obtaining one) is likely to have acquired a fair degree of significance subsequently, it is not likely to have played much of a role in determining the pattern of fertility under discussion here. The changes in law and morality necessary in Australia before abortion could become a factor of any real significance in the control of fertility were not forthcoming until too late to permit abortion to have any perceptible effect on the fertility behaviour of the cohorts under consideration here.

Factor (s) (experience of death of a child at a time when one still has the physiological capacity to bear another as a 'replacement'), given the generally low mortality levels in Australia, can hardly have played more than a very minor role. Factor (p) (existence of tastes for a 'higher' standard of childcare) probably played a somewhat greater role, although its significance is hard to separate from that of factors (m)–(o), that relate more directly to the interests of parents themselves. Yet even here, if only because, during the period of childbearing under consideration, so many of the things a parent might aspire to as representing a 'higher' standard of childcare were, in Australia, either relatively little known (e.g. orthodontia, psychological counselling), or relatively little sought after (e.g. tertiary schooling), or relatively inexpensive (e.g. family vacations, outdoor recreation), it seems quite possible that factor (p) actually had little bearing on the pattern of fertility differences observed. It may be different in the future, however.

Factors (c) (coital frequency), (f) (knowledge and experience of (contraception), (h) (willingness to use birth control), (i) (unwillingness to bear children at more advanced ages) and (r) (increase in the desired number of children) probably played an inbetween role: one of more than negligible, but not primary, significance in accounting for the observed association between fertility and age at marriage. The range of marriage ages used here (that is, up to 26) and the range of observed fertility levels were both too narrow for any of these factors to have been of more than moderate significance.

This leaves factors (j)–(o), plus factor (q). The experience of contraceptive failure (factor (q)) doubtless played some role in accounting for the negative association between fertility and age at marriage: but less so among Catholics than non-Catholics, as the lesser fertility differences associated with marriage age among Catholics would indicate; and less so, also, with increasing knowledge of birth control and improvement in its practice, as the declining differences with successively younger cohorts would indicate.

With differences in physiology, selection, demographic experience and the ability and willingness to control childbearing offering either no explanation, or only a very partial one, for the observed fertility differences associated with age at marriage, explanation must finally focus on differences in desired numbers of children — as these differences may be presumed to have developed out of differences in opportunities or experiences in consequence of the postponement of marriage; that is, out of the experience of roles that could lead to defining oneself more broadly than as a spouse/parent (factor (j), the experience of a wider range of interpersonal contacts and roles with respect to persons directly engaged in childrearing (factor (k)), development of means for the satisfaction of one's needs alternative to those associated with children (factor (l)), and development of interests and tastes likely to compete with children for one's time, energy, and money (factors (m)–(o)).

The relative significance of these six factors is impossible to determine, but that they were, as a group, the most important ones in the situation under discussion seems, for the reasons already adduced, to be beyond question. Wives marrying later had generally fewer children than wives marrying earlier, not so much because they were unable to have more, or because they were better able to control their fertility, or because they had a different set of demographic experiences. They had fewer children because, on average, they wanted fewer children; and they wanted fewer children because even the least postponement of marriage enabled them — again, on average — to develop alternative ways of thinking about themselves, to acquire non- or even anti-familial interests and tastes, to develop alternative means to the satisfaction of needs others might expect childbearing to fulfil, and to become more involved at the interpersonal level with persons not so immediately or exclusively concerned with children and child-bearing.

Much the same line of reasoning can be applied to the association between fertility and the *timing* of childbearing — specifically between fertility and a mother's age at first birth. There are no data on this for Australia, but it seems reasonable to suppose that Australian experience is much like that of the United States, where a close inverse relation has been observed.[27] The one likely difference in explanation, given the finding of a higher average number of 'unwanted' children among those who were younger when they bore their first child,[28] is that factors (f) and (g) (pertaining to the ability to control childbearing) probably play a major role in causing the inverse association between fertility and age at *first birth*, while, as suggested above, their role in effecting the inverse association between fertility and *age at marriage* is probably only minor.

Husband's Age at Marriage

Nearly all the 20 factors enumerated could pertain in some measure to husbands as well as wives. But with the exception of factor (c) (coital frequency) — where the Melbourne findings previously referred to show no difference between male and female patterns — the associations would be much less pronounced. Male fecundity is substantially less directly associated with age than is female fecundity;[29] while, given European norms of childcare, whether or not one is a parent holds far less behavioural significance for men than it does for women. In fact, this sex differential holds, as well, for whether or not one is married. The difference in status and role expectations between single and married is far greater for women than for men[30] — which particularly enhances the relative significance for women (as compared with men) of factors (j) and (k) (relating to the experience of alternative roles) and (m)–(o) (relating to the acquisition of competing interests and tastes).

Apart from coital frequency, I should expect that with men the most significant of these 20 factors would be those relating to self-selection for the parental role (factor (e)), the existence of means for the satisfaction of one's needs alternative to those associated with children (factor (l)), the existence of tastes for a 'higher' standard of childcare, (factor (p)), experience of the death of a child (factor (s)) and remarriage (factor (t)). But with none of these is the association with husband's age at marriage likely even to approximate that with the wife's: marriage and parenthood are simply so much more significant to women's day-to-day lives than they are to men's.

The Exception

The one exception — the positive, rather than negative, association between age at marriage and lifetime fertility among upper-level Australian-born Catholics — would seem to support the line of reasoning already offered (in chapter 3) in explanation of the higher fertility of upper-level Australian-born Catholics, in general. For one thing, both fertility patterns are a feature of only the more recent cohorts, which suggests that they were at least partly a response to something that arose or intensified during the 1950s and 1960s. I have suggested that this something was the particular emphasis and publicity given at the time to pro-natalist Catholic teaching on contraception and abortion, and possibly on women's roles as well. Moreover, so far as distribution by occupation is concerned, the two patterns are something found only in the white-collar groupings, and, most particularly, in the professions, which suggests that it was the upper-stratum Catholic who was most receptive to this pro-natalist teaching. I have argued (again, in chapter 3) that this greater receptivity derived from two characteristics of upper-strata Catholics: a greater consciousness of their Catholic identity, and a better financial basis for coping with the added burdens of additional progeny.

Finally, something of particular significance so far as its association with age at marriage is concerned, is the fact that the Australian-born upper-level Catholics who married later were the ones most likely to have attended Catholic schools (see chapter 4) — in particular, Catholic high schools — at precisely those ages when young people are most likely to be in process of defining themselves in general, and working out their own individual versions of adult sex roles in particular. While this took place among all sectors of the society, in the cohorts under consideration here it is only among the upper-level Australian-born Catholics that it was likely to have been prominently associated with the daily possibility of exposure to Catholic pro-natalism.

Notes

1. See e.g. Stefania Siedlecky, *Sex and Contraception before Marriage: A Study of Attitudes and Experience of Never-Married Youth in Melbourne, Australia,* Australian National University, Department of Demography, Australian Family Formation Project Monograph no. 7, Canberra (1979); and Melvin Zelnik and John F. Kantner, 'Sexual activity, contraceptive use and pregnancy among metropolitan-area teenagers: 1971–1979'. *Family Planning Perspectives,* 12 (1980).

2. Christopher Tietze, 'Statistical and health aspects of abortion'. In United Nations, *Population Studies,* 57, *Papers of the World Population Conference, Bucharest, 1974,* vol. 2 (1975); and Christopher Tietze and Sarah Lewit, 'Legal abortions'. *Scientific American,* 236 (1977).

3. Calculated from data in Australian Bureau of Statistics, *Births 1973,* Canberra (1975), Table 9.

4. Erland Hofsten, 'Non-marital cohabitation — how to explain its rapid increase, particularly in Scandinavia'. International Union for the Scientific Study of Population, *Economic and Demographic Change: Issues for the 1980s. Proceedings of the Conference, Helsinki 1978,* vol. 3, Liège (1979).

5. See e.g. Lincoln H. Day, 'Differential fertility in Australia'. In International Union for the Scientific Study of Population, *International Population Conference, London, 1969,* Liège (1971); vol. III; Joan Busfield, 'Age at marriage and family size: social causation and social selection hypotheses'. *Journal of Biosocial Science,* 4 (1972); and Charles F. Westoff, 'The yield of the imperfect: The 1970 national fertility study'. *Demography,* 12 (1975).

6. See e.g., World Fertility Survey, *Fiji Fertility Survey 1974,* 'Principal Report', Suva: Bureau of Statistics (1976), pp. 60–1; and World Fertility Survey, *Encuesta Nacional de Fecundidad, Colombia 1976,* 'Resultados generales', Bogotá: Departamento Administrativo Nacional de Estadistica (1977), p. 48.

7. D. V. Glass and Eugene Grebenik, *The Trend and Pattern of Fertility in Great Britain*. Papers of the Royal Commission on Population. Vol. vi, London: Her Majesty's Stationery Office (1954), pp. 96–7.

8. For estimates of the pattern of association between age and sterility in response to involuntary causes, see Louis Henry, 'Some data on natural fertility'. *Eugenics Quarterly*, 8 (1961), pp. 81–91; Louis Henry, 'French statistical research in natural fertility'. In Mindel C. Sheps and Jeanne Clare Ridley (eds), *Public Health and Population Change*, Pittsburgh: University of Pittsburgh Press (1965), pp. 333–50; P. Vincent, *Recherches sur la fécondité*, Paris: Presses Universitaires de France (1956) (cited in Henry, 'French statistical research in natural fertility', pp. 345–6; and Ansley J. Coale, 'Factors associated with the development of low fertility: An historic summary'. United Nations, *World Population Conference, Belgrade, 1965*, vol. ii, New York: United Nations (1967), pp. 205–9.

9. Sterilisation in response to voluntary factors can arise either directly out of a sterilisation procedure itself, or indirectly from induced abortion, amenorrhea associated with breastfeeding, or the application of certain drug or radiation therapies in the treatment of disease. Of these, only induced abortion is likely to have played any role at the ages under consideration here, and that one of hardly any numerical significance. While sterilisation in consequence of legally-induced abortion does exist, it seems to be at a level no more than 'roughly corresponding to the incidence of secondary sterility after confinement' (J. Lindahl, *Somatic Complications Following Legal Abortion*, Stockholm: Svenska Bokforlaget (1959), p. 150. Cited in Christopher Tietze, 'Induced abortion and sterilization as methods of fertility control'. In Sheps and Ridley (eds), *op. cit.*, p. 410).

10. Sam Shapiro, Ellen W. Jones and Paul M. Densen, 'A life table of pregnancy terminations and correlates of foetal loss'. *Milbank Memorial Fund Quarterly*, 40 (1962), pp. 15–17.

11. It might be noted that to the extent these respondents' replies were in terms of current practice, the age-associated differences would be somewhat reduced in consequence of lower coital frequencies around periods of childbirth — something that, given the age pattern of childbearing, would affect younger respondents more than older.

12. Alfred Kinsey *et al.*, *Sexual Behavior in the Human Female*, Philadelphia: W. B. Saunders (1953), p. 353.

13. Jay H. Glasser and Peter A. Lachenbruch, 'Observations on the relationship between frequency and timing of intercourse and the probability of conception'. *Population Studies* 23 (1968), p. 407. See also John C. Barrett and John Marshall, 'The risk of conception on different days of the menstrual cycle'. *Population Studies*, 23 (1969), pp. 455–61, and esp. Table 3.

14. Dennis N. De Tray, 'Age of marriage and fertility: a policy review', *Pakistan Development Review*, 16 (1977), p. 92 (italics in original).

15. Lois Wladis Hoffman and Martin L. Hoffman, 'The value of children to parents'. In James T. Fawcett (ed.), *Psychological Perspectives on Population*, New York: Basic Books (1973), p. 46.

16. What Luker writes of the situation in the United States is probably a close approximation to what has obtained in Australia. See Kristin Luker, *Taking Chances: Abortion and the Decision Not to Contracept*, Berkeley: University of California Press (1975), chapter 3.

17. Judith Blake, 'Abortion and public opinion: the 1960–1970 decade'. *Science*, 171 (1971), pp. 542–4; and Elise F. Jones and Charles F. Westoff, 'Attitudes towards abortion in the United States in 1970 and the trend since 1965'. In Charles F. Westoff and Robert Parke Jr (eds), *Demographic and Social Aspects of Population Growth*, vol. i of Commission on Population Growth and the American Future, *Research Reports*, Washington, DC: US Government Printing Office

(1972), esp. Tables 4 and 6. But see also some contrary evidence from a small local sample in Australian Capital Territory Legislative Assembly, Standing Committee on Education and Health, Report no. 26, *Pregnancy Termination*, Canberra: Australian Capital Territory Legislative Assembly (1977).

18. Lincoln H. Day, 'Models for the causal analysis of differences in fertility: utility, normative, and drift'. In Lado T. Ruzicka (ed.), *The Economic and Social Supports for High Fertility*, Canberra: Department of Demography, Australian National University, and the Development Studies Center, Australian National University (1977), pp. 496–9.

19. Prudence Mors Rains, *Becoming an Unwed Mother: A Sociological Account*, Chicago: Aldine-Atherton (1971), pp. 10, 12–13.

20. See e.g. George S. Masnick and Joseph A. McFalls Jr, 'A new perspective on the twentieth-century American fertility swing'. *Journal of Family History*, 1 (1976).

21. George Herbert Mead, *Mind, Self and Society*, Chicago: University of Chicago Press (1934).

22. Hoffman and Hoffman, 'The value of children to parents', *op. cit.* p. 61. See also Lincoln H. Day and Alice Taylor Day, 'Family size in industrialized countries: An inquiry into the social-cultural determinants of levels of childbearing', *Journal of Marriage and the Family*, 31 (1969), pp. 242–51; and Lincoln H. Day and Alice Taylor Day, *Too Many Americans*, Boston: Houghton Mifflin (1964), pp. 229–30, 238–42.

23. Factors (m) and (n) represent the two varieties of what have been termed 'opportunity costs'. For a summary discussion, see Warren C. Robinson and David E. Horlacher, 'Population growth and economic welfare'. New York: Population Council: *Reports on Population/Family Planning*, no. 6 (1971), esp. pp. 21–5.

24. For a perceptive discussion of the importance of these kinds of tastes to the determination of fertility in a contracepting society, see Judith Blake, 'Are babies consumer durables? — a critique of the economic theory of reproductive motivation'. *Population Studies*, 22 (1968), pp. 5–25.

25. US Bureau of the Census, *Census of Population: 1970*. Subject Reports. Final Report PC(2)–3A. *Women by Number of Children Ever Born*, Washington, DC: US Government Printing Office (1973), Table 26. See also Patience Lauriat, 'The effect of marital dissolution on fertility'. *Journal of Marriage and the Family*, 31 (1969), p. 487.

26. Lauriat, ibid., p. 488.

27. Harriet B. Presser, 'The timing of the first birth, female roles and black fertility'. *Milbank Memorial Fund Quarterly*, 49 (1971); Phillips Cutwright, 'Timing the first birth: does it matter?'. *Journal of Marriage and the Family*, 35 (1973); Larry L. Bumpass, Ronald R. Rindfuss and Richard B. Janosik, 'Age and marital status at first birth and the pace of subsequent fertility'. *Demography*, 15 (1978); and James Trussell and Jane Menken, 'Early childbearing and subsequent fertility'. *Family Planning Perspectives*, 10 (1978).

28. Trussell and Menken, op. cit., Table 9, p. 216.

29. Robert E. Kennedy Jr, *The Irish: Emigration, Marriage, and Fertility*, Berkeley: University of California Press (1973), p. 175; Barbara A. Anderson, 'Male age and fertility results from Ireland prior to 1911'. *Population Index*, 41 (1975), pp. 561–7.

30. Alice Taylor Day, *Formal Egalitarianism — Private Traditionalism: The Position of Women in Australia*, PhD thesis, Australian National University, Canberra (1978), esp. chapters 7, 9, 11 and 12.

8 CONCLUSIONS AND IMPLICATIONS

Introduction

One could expect the study of group fertility differences in a country like Australia to contribute to an understanding of three aspects of demographic behaviour that are of both immediate and long-range concern to modern, western societies, namely: the causes of different patterns of childbearing, the political and social consequences of these differences, and the implications these differences may have for social policy. And because the data are unusually detailed one could expect further that the study of fertility differences specifically in Australia would be a particularly rich source of this understanding.

As it happens, this is largely the case — but less so with causation than with political and social consequences, and the implications for social policy. The causes of different patterns of childbearing, especially where fertility is subject to a large measure of direct control, remain very largely the conundrum they have always been.

Causation

What can be said, in general, concerning the causes of a particular pattern of childbearing is essentially what can be said, in general, of the causes of *any* social behaviour:

(a) A variety of factors will have been at work, some supporting the behaviour in question, others impeding it.

(b) These factors will have consisted of a variety of elements in the physical environment (including the individual actor's physiological attributes), the social environment (consisting of institutional structures and norms, and also of other human beings with whom the actor interacts — both directly and indirectly), and the personality structures (that is, the respective sums of their psychic predispositions to act) of both the individual actor and those with whom he or she interacts.

(c) The particular factors involved — and the significance of each — will have been different for different actors; different at

227

different periods of time (e.g. different in times of war as contrasted with times of peace, in periods of relatively full employment as contrasted with periods of widespread unemployment); and different at different stages in the actor's lifetime (e.g. different for 0-parity as against 1-parity women, for 25-year-olds as against 35-year-olds, for mothers whose youngest child was still at home as against mothers whose youngest was in school all day).

(d) Related to this is the fact that, in any particular behavioural situation, there is seldom, if ever, only one possible behaviour. Instead, there is usually a whole range of possibilities; the particular possibility followed in any specific instance being the result of an interacting combination of various elements in the environment (both physical and social); the personality structures of the actors involved; these actors' 'definitions of the situation'; and finally chance.

(e) Conscious choice between alternative behaviours in any behavioural situation is a matter of degree, varying from the one extreme of a careful weighing of the costs and benefits attributable to a given action to the other extreme of a virtually complete absence of any such consideration.

(f) Human behaviour is a process taking place in time, what happens at one stage or period having an effect on what happens later.

(g) A given condition can have a variety of different origins (as, for example, the cessation of childbirth after two children).

(h) Similarly, a particular causal element may give rise to a variety of consequences, depending on the other elements mixed with it in the causal brew.

(i) Specifically with respect to fertility, a given pattern will necessarily have been the result of interaction: between persons of the opposite sex of course, but also — both directly and indirectly — between potential parents and what is likely to have been a considerable variety of others, possibly ranging from close relatives and friends all the way to the personalities presented over the media of mass communication. Focusing on only one member of a couple, or even on just the couple itself, to the exclusion of others in the society, is to run the risk of missing a potentially significant causal element. For example, quite apart from any other supports there might have been, a society in which two out of three women will have had at least five births must surely, *by that fact alone*, provide greater encouragement (or at least less discouragement) to further childbearing among 4-parity women than would a society in which this ratio was but 1 out of 20 instead.

(j) Finally, and again specifically with respect to fertility, whatever the factors in the causal equation, they will inevitably have worked through the intermediate variables of intercourse, conception, gestation and parturition. That is, they must have affected the timing and frequency of intercourse; the likelihood of conception; and the likelihood that a product of conception would survive long enough to eventuate in a live birth.

These are elemental points, applicable generally — with the exception of the last two — to every type of social behaviour. But they are at a very high level of generality. They provide an overall framework for understanding social behaviour, but tell us nothing about the behaviour of particular individuals in given circumstances: neither as to the identities of the various causal elements that may have been at work, nor the relative degrees of their significance. Nor is the situation much improved even when these principles are applied to a source of data as rich as that under discussion here. We still know nothing as to why one particular woman bore four children and another two; nor, with any great assurance, why the parity distribution took one form in one sector of the population, and another form in another (although, in this latter case, the data do permit both the development of a number of interpretations that appear likely, and the reasonable rejection of others that do not).

In the present instance, the data permit no assessment whatever of the possible role played by the physical environment in determining the observed group fertility differences, and only a very limited assessment of the role of physiological differences. But as neither of these factors could have played any significant role in accounting for the observed differences, the absence of data by which to make a proper assessment of their role constitutes no real limitation to our understanding.

More serious is the fact that these data also contain nothing on a variety of other factors — self-confidence, group-identification, marital adjustment, satisfaction with life, hopes, fears, religiosity, social mobility, past experience; nothing even on income or on liking for children — that might be expected, however subject to change over one's lifetime, to have been of particular significance to fertility in a population exercising widespread direct control over its childbearing. Apart from present income, such information —

relating to numbers of people large enough to permit meaningful analysis — can be obtained, if at all, only by means of large-scale sample surveys. It is not something to be obtained through census taking.

If social scientists can profitably use census data, so much the better. But governments conduct censuses for their own purposes, and not for those of social scientists; in using census data, social scientists thus confront the task of obtaining answers to their own questions from data collected for quite other purposes. What one gains by using such data is coverage, economy, comparability, minimal random error and (possibly) greater accuracy. What one loses is the possibility of working with a wider range of subject-matter and the opportunity to explore an issue in greater depth. In assessing the causes of human behaviour, census data can narrow the range of conjecture and offer possible interpretations, but they cannot provide definitive answers. Where I have reasoned in terms of such concepts as 'social mobility', 'greater Catholic indentification', or 'material aspirations' it has perforce been based on my impressions of what underlay these census data — on what they could reasonably be seen to indicate — and not on data specifically in support of such interpretations.

What these data do show is, first, the spread of control over childbearing and, secondly, the persistence of group differences.

Control over childbearing among certain of the overseas-born and among the Australian-born in the lower-status sectors (as is presumed indicated by schooling and husband's occupation) was far more effective with the cohorts of 1927–31 than with those at the beginning of the period under consideration. This shows up particularly well in the narrowing that took place within successive cohorts of the range of differences between different social strata and different nativity groupings: the result of declines in the proportions at the higher parities. It also shows up in the increasing concentration in the middle range of parities: a further result of declines at the highest parities, and also of declines in childlessness. Childlessness, in fact, seems to have been widely unpopular.[1] That it generally declined during this period suggests a decline in involuntary infecundity, but, more important, the development of conditions perceived as more favourable to parenthood.

Where group differences persisted during the period, it was mainly with reference to categorisations by residence, nativity and religion. With residence, the relative differences remained much the same throughout the period — the result of essentially similar changes in fertility within each of the three categories used. With nativity the fact of differences remained, but the direction of these differences changed substantially. Between the Australian-born and those nativity groupings characterised in the earlier cohorts by *low* fertility, the relative differences generally persisted, but between the Australian-born and the nativity groupings characterised in the earlier cohorts by *high* fertility they tended, first, to narrow, and then to expand in the opposite direction — as fertility in these particular groupings among the overseas-born continued to decline while that among the Australian-born either remained the same or rose. With religion, the occurrences were two: first, a fairly general persistence of Catholic:non-Catholic differences throughout the period; secondly, development of a notably 'deviant' high fertility pattern among upper-level Australian-born Catholics.

Implications: General

Extension of Individual Control over Childbearing

Control over childbearing is obviously a matter of degree; but with its extension, the number of one's children and the timing of their births becomes increasingly a function of what a parent or potential parent wants — or, in the event of an unintended or unwanted conception, is at least willing to accept in preference to obtaining an induced abortion. (To the extent that induced abortion is unavailable, control over childbearing is, of course, just that much less readily available, although not necessarily any less extensive in practice.)

So far as fertility levels themselves are concerned, the extension of control over childbearing inevitably leads to lower group averages than would otherwise exist, despite the fact that a planned family (one, that is, in which childbearing has been consciously limited) is not necessarily a small family. Mostly this is because of the declines it permits in the frequency of higher-parity births. But lower average fertility can also derive from an increase in the proportions who remain childless or bear no more than one or two children, for, in permitting postponement as well as limitation of childbearing, control over childbearing can increase the likelihood that infecundity will set in before a woman has borne all the children she might otherwise bear, and simultaneously allow more time for the development of tastes and interests potentially competitive with those presumably served by children and childbearing.

Certainly we can expect some future increases in the proportion bearing no more than one child. The extension of control makes this possible, and the more favourable appraisals in recent years concerning the characteristics of only children and their parents[2] increases its social acceptability and hence its likelihood.

So far as population growth is concerned, this extension of control over childbearing increases the likelihood that the rate will be low, even negative. But rendering a low rate easier to attain is no guarantee of its existence, nor, for that matter, is rendering it difficult to attain any guarantee that it will not happen: the low growth rates of the 1930s, for example, came at a time when control over childbearing was far less extensive than it is today.

Control over childbearing also increases the likelihood of annual fluctuations in the number of births and, through that, of marked irregularities in age structure. Being able to control not only the number but also the timing of their children's births, couples could reasonably be expected to advance or postpone their childbearing in response to changing conditions — in employment, housing or international affairs, for example — with all the attendant difficulties this would entail in consequence of the further irregularities such fluctuation would introduce into the age structure.

But I think this particular possibility is not likely to be of much importance in the present instance, for nearly every country in which there is extensive control over childbearing — Australia included — would appear by now to have undergone developments of a sort likely to render future fertility less subject to the fads and factors that, in the past, occasioned major fluctuations in annual numbers of births. Among the more important of these developments are:

(1) a greater openness and frankness about human sexuality, which one could expect to result in people's being more likely to discuss birth control with one another, and to enter upon regular sexual relations with both greater knowledge of birth control and more experience in its practice;[3] and in the case of women, in particular, being less likely to think of sexual activity as somehow immoral or improper — as something a 'moral' woman does not really prepare herself for, something that perhaps has to take her 'by surprise', or even be entered into 'against her will'.

(2) A wider range of available roles for women other than mother

and homemaker, perhaps particularly, although not exclusively, in the form of opportunities for employment outside the home.

(3) Changes in attitudes and tastes relating to what is considered an 'appropriate' family size,[4] seen especially in the growing proportion who seem to take the view that children in excess of four, or perhaps even three, is more than enough; and possibly, also, to what is considered an 'appropriate' age to bear children, particularly as this relates to childbearing on the part of women beyond their early or mid-thirties.

(4) A narrowing of the range of actual family sizes, with the result that there are fewer examples of higher-parity 'deviancy' to serve as encouragements to additional procreation on the part of those otherwise unlikely to embark upon it.[5]

(5) Intentional concentration of childbearing within a narrower age range, which gives rise to a shorter duration of childbearing, partly through shorter intervals between successive births and partly through fewer births altogether, and which, in its turn, could encourage women to explore possible alternative sources of satisfaction outside the traditional female roles of wife and mother, the development of which would itself reinforce any tendency to shorten the period devoted exclusively to childbearing.

(6) Improvements in contraceptive technology.[6]

(7) An increased availability of a greater variety of birth control techniques (abortion included), these last two both tending to enhance the willingness to use birth control, and simultaneously to make its use more efficient.

Now some of these developments render birth control easier and therefore more reliable; others narrow the range of socially acceptable family size, and thus the range of fertiity levels that fluctuations in the timing of childbearing can produce. Most do both to some extent, sometimes directly and sometimes indirectly. But either way, the ultimate result would appear to be a damping of the degree of temporal fluctuation one can anticipate in the birth rates of populations exercising substantial control over their childbearing. Because it reinforces the changes in institutions and individual tastes that would appear to have led to a narrowing of both the actual and the socially acceptable range of family size, the further extension of control over childbearing seems likely to eventuate in more, rather than less, procreative stability: certainly in the distribution of ultimate family sizes within different cohorts, but quite possibly in the timing of childbearing within different time periods as well.

So far as patterns of marriage are concerned, the extension of control over childbearing will lead to fewer 'forced' marriages undertaken for the purpose of legitimating the outcome of premarital pregnancies, for it will necessarily restrict the number of such pregnancies or, in the event of particularly permissive norms relating to extra nuptial - sexual behaviour and childbearing, restrict the number of pregnancies that are unwanted or unintended whatever their legitimacy. Greater control could also lead to a generally higher age at marriage, partly through reducing the number of illegitimate pregnancies, but partly also through lessening the presumed need to postpone sexual relations until marriage because of a fear of unwanted pregnancy. Ultimately, for much the same reasons relating to unwanted pregnancies, the extension of control over childbearing could lead to a lower proportion of the population actually becoming married. This does not necessarily mean that all, or even a majority, of these additions to the unmarried would be living outside some kind of sexual union,[7] only that they would not be married — occupying, that is, the 'married' state and, other things being equal, engaging in the range of behaviours associated with it, including, in most instances, the begetting and rearing of children.

With respect to parenthood, the extension of control over childbearing could result in an increased proportion of a population's births occurring to those who, at least at the time of conception, were more likely to define themselves (whether correctly or incorrectly is a moot point) as both willing and able to meet the demands associated with the bearing and rearing of children. One could expect to find a higher proportion of persons with this outlook among those in the population who were better-off financially, in a currently more stable marital union, in better health, and in possession of stronger egos and a stronger feeling of being able to cope with life's challenges and vicissitudes. Whether a higher proportion of all births occurring to such parents would raise the general quality either of children or of society is certainly subject to question, but at least the outward signs would appear more generally favourable than unfavourable.

Specifically with respect to feeling able to cope with life, surely this feeling is enhanced by knowing that one can control a matter of such potential significance to the course of life as the number and spacing of births? Extending this control within a population doubtless adds to the proportion who possess this feeling. If control over other significant elements in life — employment opportunities, for example — diminishes, the psychic value associated with control over childbearing might conceivably assume even greater emotional significance. Here, however, the prognosis is at best uncertain, for lack of control in the public sphere (in employment or schooling, for example) seems often generalised from there to the private sphere as well.[8] It is not so much that, in response to a loss of control in the public sphere, people forget how to exercise control in the private as it is that they lose something of the motivation necessary to do so.

The lower fertility associated with the extension of control over childbearing will necessarily lead to a reduction in the number of one's relatives and, therefore, in the number of ties made intimate by kinship.[9] This means a position of greater numerical and social prominence for the small nuclear family — specifically, that family in which parents have relatively few children, and children, in consequence, have relatively few siblings. Among other things, this could be expected to encourage further reliance on the state (that is, on social as against private means) for support in infirmity and old age, as well as in times of emotional stress and financial need. The state is the only agency in modern society at least theoretically capable of meeting all the costs of such services, of spreading these costs over time and throughout society, guaranteeing standards on a broad scale, and ensuring a large measure of equity in both payment of costs and receipt of services. Reliance on the state in these matters is therefore likely to increase anyhow, quite apart from whether one has kin on whom to rely for such support and succour; it is simply that an increase in the proportion living in small nuclear families can be expected to enhance this tendency still further.

The increasing numerical prominence of the small nuclear family can lead to greater reliance on 'social' as against 'familial' provision in the informal sphere of companionship as well. With fewer siblings (or no siblings at all, in the case of the only child), children, if they are to have any playmates at all, will necessarily have to seek them outside the immediate family, outside, that is, the circle of family and kin on whom they could presume to have a prior emotional claim. In a heterogeneous immigrant society like Australia's, this could be of particular significance, for rearing a greater proportion of society's children under such conditions could lessen group differences — those associated with ethnic origin, religion, and possibly income and social class — and at the same time, produce a greater toleration of diversity in values, life-styles, and the like.[10] In either instance, lower fertility, assisted in its development by the extension of control over childbearing, would have served to promote both the assimilation of immigrants and the enhancement of social cohesion at a broader level.

And yet there is also a possible threat to social cohesion in another aspect of these fertility patterns, namely, the persistence of certain group differences, particularly the increasing concentration of large family sizes within but one sector of the population.

Persistence of Group Differences

Populations can be sub-divided into a great variety of distinguishable social entities: by geography and region, economic condition, occupation, language and religion, for example, in addition to status, life-style, and ethics and values. The presence of such variety within a population doubtless makes for a more interesting life, but it can also lend itself to scapegoating in times of crisis or adversity, of uncertainty or unusually severe conflicts of values; and it offers at least the possibility of greater social disharmony — in part, simply because of the perception of differences (one's own values, for example, are always best by definition), and in part because of competition for scarce resources, for economic power or condition, and for political or social power (as may be seen, for example, in present conflicts between identifiable social entities over the legalisation of abortion; the granting of priority to welfare programmes based on the family unit rather than the individual; government funding for church-related schools; and the extension of women's rights). Such diversity can also be consciously played upon as a means of social control through diverting people's attention from what a less emotionally-based assessment might find to be matters of more genuine or fundamental importance than the mere fact of separate group indentities. The Nazis' use of the Jews, and certain Americans' use of the Blacks, are only among the more prominent — and extreme — examples of the sorts of opportunities afforded the unscrupulous by the kind of social diversity composed, at least in part, of readily discernible social entities.

So far as Australian fertility patterns are concerned, the prognosis is for a general decline in group differences, particularly on the basis of the findings from the present inquiry, those associated with schooling, occupation and, to a lesser extent, nativity. But with religion it is another matter — largely because of the particularly high relative fertility position of one sector: upper-level Australian-born Catholics. Elsewhere in the population, the prognosis concerning differences by religion is for a general diminution.

The unusually high relative fertility position of upper-level Australian-born Catholics is a phenomenon involving only the more recent cohorts. It results from several concurrent movements in different directions — marked increases in the fertility of this sector itself; stability (or declines) in the fertility of its lower-level counterparts; declines (or stability) in the fertility of Australian-born non-Catholics, whether upper- or lower-level; and (with the exception of the British-born, who tended to follow the pattern of their respective co-religionists among the Australian-born) declines — often quite marked ones, at that — in the fertility of those born overseas.

Naturally, not every upper-level Australian-born Catholic of the 1927—31 cohort fits into this high fertility pattern. For example, 18 per cent of those with husbands in the professions had borne no more than two children, 37 per cent no more than three. None the less, median issue in this sector was substantially higher than elsewhere, and over 40 per cent of these wives had borne at least five children, and more than a quarter of the total at least six.

It was suggested in chapter 3 that this phenomenon originated in a combination of two factors: (1) a particular emphasis placed on Catholic teaching concerning birth control and women's roles at the very time that these women would have been in the primary childbearing ages; and (2) the particular susceptibility of upper-level Catholic women to this teaching on account of their more favourable economic position and the likelihood that their specifically Catholic identities would have been reinforced and re-emphasised by the kinds of contact they could be expected to have had with the rest of the population. What this implies is a kind of Catholic value-system that strikes a particularly responsive chord among upper-level Catholics or, at the least, admits of being more readily adhered to by them. It is probably a bit of both. The evidence for this, if not particularly systematic, is none the less plentiful. One sees it in Australia in the leadership of such organisations as Right to Life, Women's Action Alliance, and Women Who Want to Be Women; and in public statements, letters to editors, submissions before parliamentary committees, responses in social surveys.[11] One sees it, also, in studies outside Australia that have found religion to be a prime indicator (albeit not in every context) of people's values.[12]

The main characteristics of this value-system would appear to be two: first, a strong emphasis on role differentiation between the sexes; and secondly, the accordance of an almost sacrosanct position to the nuclear family. In practice, adherence to this value-system takes a variety of forms. Most obvious, probably, are certain specific positions taken in the areas of civil liberties, schooling, employment and family life, namely: opposition to abortion; opposition to provision of contraceptives to the unmarried; support for single-sex schooling; opposition to non-sexist education programmes; opposition to the expansion of opportunities for women to have non-familial or non-religious careers; support for the maintenance of sex-based differences in patterns of behaviour (at home, in school, on the job); support for church-related schooling; opposition to the employment of wives for other reasons than economic necessity; opposition — whatever the economic need — to the employment of mothers with pre-school-age children; and finally opposition to the provision of day-care facilities for mothers who wish to make use of these facilities for reasons other than those of economic necessity.

The view seems widely held among these upper-level Australian-born Catholic wives that the performance of family duties is no barrier to a woman's fulfilling herself; that self-fulfilment through the family is as much as any normal woman need aspire to; that it can, in fact, provide her with total satisfaction.[13]

But while adherence to such a value-system could be expected to take the form of lower rates of participation in the labour force, this has not, in fact, been the case — at least not when standardised for parity. Among metropolitan-dwelling Australian-born wives in the 1927–31 cohort, for example, there was, at each parity level, no real difference between Catholics and non-Catholics in the proportions in the labour force among either those with more than nine years of schooling or those whose husbands were in the professions; nor was there any difference between them in the cohort born ten years earlier. It may be that stronger economic pressures on Catholic wives compensated for the presumed ideological pressure in the opposite direction; or that the simple dichotomous separation respecting participation in the labour force, by indicating nothing about the extent of such participation, masks a possibly higher proportion among Catholic participants whose labour force activity consists of working at home, in family enterprises, or on a part-time or temporary basis. But whatever the explanation, there was little to choose from between the labour force status of upper-level Australian-born Catholics and that of their non-Catholic counterparts at the same parities.

On the other hand, because participation in the labour force was somewhat negatively associated with parity, and a higher proportion of Catholic women were in the upper parities, overall participation was somewhat higher among non-Catholics, although not by much — only the difference between 42 and 38 per cent among the 1927–31 cohort of Australian-born metropolitan-dwelling wives married to professionals; and the difference between 47 and 42 per cent among their counterparts with more than nine years' schooling. However, at the highest parity level (6 + issue) among those of the wives with more than nine years' schooling, where the absolute number of Catholic wives is more than double that of non-Catholic (1250 *vs.* 591), the difference was between 35 per cent for non-Catholics and 28 per cent for Catholics.

One could expect upper-level Catholic wives to exercise an influence in society well beyond that suggested by their numbers alone. Because so few — comparatively — are in the labour force, they would conceivably have more time than wives in other sectors of the population to agitate on behalf of their views — at least once their children were in school. Moreover their occupancy of positions of generally higher status, income and schooling could be expected to give them a greater degree of skill and self-confidence with which to argue their case. For the same reasons, one could also expect them to have greater access to those in positions of power, with whom they would presumably share ties of blood, marriage, friendship and acquaintance.

In varying degrees, of course, these women would appear to adhere to a fairly well-defined ideology from which emanates a reasonably coherent set of principles. Of particular interest here is the fact that, so far as fertility is concerned, there is probably a strong element of mutual reinforcement: the ideology is conducive to higher fertility, and higher fertility, in turn, tends to promote adherence to the ideology: for example, through its effect on participation in the labour force, the intensity and duration of interest in children's schooling, and the network these women might be expected to have among co-religionists of similarly high fertility.

Many high fertility women with staunch Catholic identification appear to have not only the motivation to work on behalf of social programmes and legislation that fit in with their ideological principles (and against those that do not), but also the time to do so and the contacts in powerful places that would offer some hope of success in these endeavours. These women are, in short, a force to be reckoned with, and can be expected to make their voices heard. That these voices are already being heard should come as no surprise.

Any estimate of how likely it is that fertility differences between different sectors of the population will continue depends on what is deemed to be the pattern of causation of fertility. To the extent that these differences originate in differences in the ability to control childbearing they are not likely to persist much longer. The already observable pattern of declines in group differences in proportions at the upper parities (where differences in the ability to exercise this control would show up most prominently) can doubtless be largely attributed to the extension of control over childbearing.

To the extent that these differences emanate from cultural differences, they are likely to last a bit longer. None the less, the factors underlying differences in cultural learning associated with different groupings within the society (with religion and the family, in particular) are not the only agencies of socialisation or reinforcement or sanction; there are also schools, playmates, workmates and the media of mass communication — all potentially offering a cultural pattern of varying contrasts. Given time, cultural differences — while not necessarily disappearing altogether — can be expected to diminish quite considerably.

To the extent that these group fertility differences originate in differences in conditions of life (for example, differences in housing, employment and area of residence) they can be expected to persist, perhaps even to increase if the differences in, say, nativity, religion, schooling or occupation serve as foci for the development of such other differences as those respecting social class or housing. However, because of the general extension of control over fertility, there could be a decline in the absolute fertility differences between groups, whatever the direction being taken by the relative differences.

But culture and conditions of life are concepts at a high level of generality: knowledge of these may inform us as to the range of likely behaviour within a given group, but it can tell us little about where within that range will fall the particular behaviours of the various individuals who make up that group. In part, this is because decision-making is for each individual a sequential process, with the behaviour at one stage necessarily affecting in some measure that at the next, and with potentially different assessments of costs and benefits, potentially different priorities, every step of the way.[14] But it is also, in part, because human beings are not particularly rational or consistent in their choosing among alternatives. Concerning the numerous efforts to test whether, in choosing, 'the actor maximises his or her expected utility in the light of subjective estimates of the probabilities of events', Herbert Simon has concluded that 'A fair summary of the findings of these experiments is that actual human choices depart radically from those implied by the axioms except in the simplest and most transparent of situations. Humans are unable to choose consistently in the face of even more moderate complexity or uncertainty'.[15] Overall is the fact that, at the individual level, there is apt to be a great deal of behavioural drift, of behaviour — including the making of choices — that moves along in a manner largely imperceptible to the person doing the acting. Not only are the 'choices' one makes very much constrained by the normative setting, and adherence to norms largely unconscious, but one's 'selection' among available alternatives is ordinarily in terms of behaviours actually, or at least seemingly, little differentiated from one another.[16]

None the less, at the level of the group, my own guess is that fertility differences in Australia, like those observed in Canada and the United States,[17] are unlikely to persist much longer. Data on both fertility intentions and current fertility suggest this[18] — as do those analysed here — together with some newly available from the 1976 census.[19] The main reasons for anticipating a lessening of these differentials are: (1) the extension of control over childbearing; (2) the likely assimilation to a dominant Australia-wide fertility pattern on the part of successive generations deriving from the overseas-born, rural–urban migrants, Catholics and non-Catholics; (3) related to this, the increasing similarity of cultural stimuli (for example, the increasing similarity of what people experience respecting working conditions, schooling, advertising and the content of the media of mass communication); and (4) the narrow range of family sizes over which group fertility could extend, anyway, in a population exercising substantial control over childbearing.

This is not to say there will eventually be no differences in fertility. Quite the contrary, there will be differences, but they will be associated not so much with *groupings* within the population as with *individuals* — individuals differentiated from one another with respect to: infecundity; liking (or perceived liking) for children; access to alternative sources of whatever satisfactions are presumed to be provided by the bearing and rearing of children; and the differences respecting the various factors associated (either as cause or effect) with age at marriage.

Implications for Social Policy

Policies imply the existence of goals which, in turn, imply the existence of values. Where specifically demographic goals are concerned, the implication is that there are certain individual or social goals — based, in turn, on values — the attainment of which is thought to be affected by the size and characteristics of the population. Demographic goals are means to the achievement of the conditions of life thought desirable; they are neither isolated from other social priorities, nor ends in themselves.

Establishing demographic goals — and formulating policies designed to attain them in any particular instance — is no mean task; for any attempt to develop a rigorous definition of what constitutes an 'optimal' population will necessarily be bedevilled by problems of measurement, cultural difference and values.[20] As might be expected, values lie at the heart of the difficulty: the ordering of priorities; the degree to which the present is to be discounted in favour of the future; the weights to be assigned to the interests of different sectors of the population — all are essentially questions of values.

But the task becomes easier if, at the outset, we admit that it is impossible to formulate a definition of optimal demographic conditions that is simultaneously both rigorous and meaningful. This done, we can define these conditions more vaguely (but also more meaningfully) in terms of what best adds to general human well-being — in terms, that is, of what is most conducive to, say, 'happiness' or 'the good life' for all members of the society (as against what might best serve some purely instrumental goal, like a higher gross national product or greater military prowess). If, from there, we go on to incorporate recognition of the fundamental fact of limits — physical, ecological, and social — it reasonably follows that, at a minimum, an optimum population would have low mortality, an unchanging age and sex structure, and a growth rate of zero.[21] Defining it this way avoids the shortcomings in the usual definitions of optimal demographic conditions, namely, the failure to acknowledge the physical, ecological and social limits imposed by this finite planet; and the tendency to emphasise optimum *size* to the exclusion of optimum *characteristics*. There can be, I feel, much more certainty about what are the characteristics of an optimum population than there can be about its size alone.

In a finite world beset by problems of population size and facing inevitable population increases in the future, there is little to recommend a policy of pro-natalism anywhere, and correspondingly much to recommend, in an already low fertility country like Australia, not so much its opposite (a policy of anti-natalism) as, simply, one of zero-growth.

But suppose it was determined — on however dubious grounds — that Australians would be better-off, 'happier', better able to enjoy 'the good life', if there were more of them. Seeking these additional numbers through increasing fertility would hardly appear the prudent course. While pro-natalist policies need not necessarily be coercive, or in violation of civil liberties, they none the less tend in that direction — often embodying, for example, restrictions on access to contraception, abortion and information about human physiology and sexuality; and for women restrictions, as well, on their opportunities to undertake careers outside the home. Even with full freedom of choice in such matters, the achievement of a particular numerical goal through increasing fertility would require an investment of time, energy and money that, by most reasonable accounts, could with more human profit be allocated to alternative pursuits. Moreover, because it takes some 20 years to rear a child to socially-productive adulthood, there is always the possibility that the conditions that gave rise to the view that more people were desirable will have disappeared by the time those additional numbers reach maturity. It is not unreasonable in fact, to suppose — given the existence of limits — that conditions will have so altered as to point to quite the opposite conclusion.

Nor is a population like water issuing from a tap, to be turned off at will when the desired level has been reached. There is a certain ineluctability about population growth: to a unique degree, demographic conditions at any particular time are determined by what has gone before; all the world's mothers for about the next 20 years have already been born. Even if reproduction were immediately to decline to replacement level — and remain there permanently — the character of the age structure would ensure that the population would continue to increase for some decades into the future.[22] As Herman Daly has written so commonsensically, the goal of zero growth is fundamental:

> it is vain to speak of an optimum population unless you are first prepared to accept a stationary population — unless you are ready and willing to stay at the optimum once you find it. Otherwise knowing the optimum merely enables us to wave goodbye as we pass through it. Furthermore, the optimum population is more likely to be discovered by experience than by *a priori* thought. . . . It is more important to be able to attain a steady state (at any level) than to know in advance which state is optimal.[23]

But if the goal is, none the less, numerical increase, it can be reached sooner and at far less cost — at least in the narrow, economic sense — through immigration than through natural increase. And immigration does not add to the world's burden of human numbers, at least, not directly. It may do so indirectly, however, by shifting the population into societies in which consumption of raw materials is at particularly high levels, or by supporting certain conditions in the countries of origin (for example, earlier marriages made possible by emigrants' remittances) that are conducive to high fertility. However, in the latter instance, the more likely consequences, if any, would appear to be in the opposite (that is, low fertility) direction, with those who remain having more hopeful economic futures (for example, through having greater access to capital or additional training as a result of remittances from abroad; and to more land as a result, again, of remittances and also of the removal, through emigration, of potential competitors to its acquisition and use).[24]

Still, immigration is not without its drawbacks, particularly in the realm of politics and intergroup relations. Differences between people can attract, but they can also repel; they can make life more interesting, but also make it more stressful — perhaps especially in a political democracy where numbers and differences do, quite literally, count. In any competition for scarce resources — for jobs, housing, promotions, educational preferment, for example — differences, as already noted, can also become convenient foci for scapegoating.

Moreover, because immigration is always to some extent age-selective, it is bound to introduce an element of distortion into the age structure of the receiving population, both through the addition of the immigrants themselves and the echoing age structure of their offspring, and through the subtraction of those who subsequently decide to re-emigrate, either to return to their countries of origin, or to try their luck in presumably still greener pastures elsewhere. The prospect of further geographic movement doubtless appears less daunting to those who have already severed ties with their places of origin. The immigration of the overseas-born under consideration here did introduce some changes into the Australian age structure, but, as it happens, these were more of a sort to benefit than harm Australia, for in the earlier cohorts the relatively high fertility of the Dutch-, Italian-, Greek and Yugoslav-born served to compensate somewhat for the relatively low fertility of the Australian-born, while in the later cohorts it was the other way round, with the lower fertility of these overseas-born affording some compensation for the higher fertility of the Australian-born.

The more elevated fertility of some of the earlier cohorts of overseas-born added to Australia's population and, through that, to the world's burden of human numbers, but this did not last long. Whether fertility was higher or lower than it would have been in the absence of immigration to Australia is impossible to know, although the general pattern of fertility among these immigrants seems to have been much like that in their countries of origin. In more recent cohorts, fertility levels among the overseas-born have been more conducive to halting population growth than have those of the Australian-born. Certainly there is no apparent need to devise a policy specifically for the purpose of reducing the fertility of the overseas-born groups under study here to levels more in conformity with the world's need to halt population increase. Most of the cohorts of 1927–31 were doing about as much along these lines as could reasonably be expected of them.

In a democratic society, it is essentially a truism that social policy ought to have as its goal the highest possible quality of life for all; the highest quality, for example, for every child, whatever its religion or social origin; whether its birth was intended or unintended, nuptial or extra-nuptial; whether it is an only child or one of a dozen; whether it or its parents entered that society by birth or immigration. Nor is there any need in the circumstances to attempt a precise definition of 'quality'. This is quite well enough understood for present purposes.

In addition to a general goal like this, social policy in such a society ought to aim, so far as specifically demographic behaviour is concerned, to make childbearing as much as possible exclusively subject to the decisions of parents and potential parents. This means the absence of policies designed either to encourage (or coerce) people into having children they *might not* otherwise have, or to discourage (or prevent) them from having children they *might* otherwise have. But while there is probably reasonable agreement as to what would constitute coercion or prevention, with encouragement or discouragement it is quite another matter. Suffice it to say in the present instance that I do not consider it unwarranted discouragement, in a situation of free choice concerning one's fertility, to point out that, if broader social ends are to be served, this choice must be exercised within a framework of complete access to the means by which to control fertility and knowledge, not ignorance, of (a) human physiology; (b) contraception and the facts relating to induced abortion; (c) human relations and the role of sexual behaviour in these relations; and finally (d) knowledge, not ignorance about physical limits and ecological relationships — and the ultimate necessity of adjusting human numbers to the environment. Like other kinds of citizenship, 'demographic citizenship' (if we may call it that) has its obligations to the larger society and to future generations. There can be little doubt that we are all obliged to exercise stewardship with respect to both present and future generations and the natural environment. The precise requirements in specific instances may be open to question, and the obligations may, in practice, be honoured less than is either desirable or necessary. But that obligation is still there, it will not go away, and any prudent social policy must recognise that fact.

Notes

1. Helen Ware 'The limits of acceptable family size: evidence from Melbourne, Australia'. *Journal of Biosocial Science*, 5 (1973).

2. For an exhaustive summary of the research findings on this topic, see Kenneth W. Terhune, *A Review of the Actual and Expected Consequences of Family Size*, US Department of Health, Education, and Welfare, Public Health Service, publication no. (NIH) 75–779, Washington, DC: Government Printing Office, (1974). See also H. Theodore Groat, Jerry W. Wicks and Arthur G. Neal, *Differential Consequences of Having Been an Only Versus a Sibling Child*, Center for Population Research, US National Institute of Health (1980).

3. George S. Masnick and Joseph A, McFalls Jr, 'A new perspective on the twentieth-century American fertility swing'. *Journal of Family History*, 1 (1976), pp. 223–7, 240–2; and Katherine Betts, 'Births and birth control: changes in fertility in Victoria 1960–74, with special reference to 1971–74'. BA honours thesis (sociology), Monash University (Melbourne) (1977).

4. See e.g. the perceptive comments of Alan Sweezy, 'The economic explanation of fertility changes in the United States'. *Population Studies*, 25 (1971).

5. See e.g. United Nations, *Economic Survey of Europe in 1974*, Part II, *Post-War Demographic Trends in Europe and the Outlook until the Year 2000*, New York (1975), esp. pp. 92–103; US National Center for Health Statistics, *Fertility Tables for Birth Cohorts by Color, 1917–73*, Washington, DC: US Government Printing Office (1976), pp. 224–5, 385–7.

6. For an especially thorough analysis of the demographic significance of this development in Australia, see Donald R. Lavis, *Oral Contraception in Melbourne, 1961–1971*, Australian National University, Department of Demography, Australian Family Formation Project, Monograph no. 3, Canberra: Australian National University Press (1975).

7. Erland Hofsten, 'Non-marital cohabitation — how to explain its rapid increase, particularly in Scandinavia'. International Union for the Scientific Study of Population, 'Economic and demographic change: issues for the 1980's', Helsinki (1978). *Proceedings of the Conference*, vol. 3, Liège (1979).

8. For a summary of the evidence specifically relating to fertility, see Alice Taylor Day, 'Unplanned pregnancies in the 1970s — an Australian paradox'. In Commonwealth Department of Health, *Women's Health in a Changing Society*, vol. 3, Canberra: Australian Government Publishing Service (1978).

9. See e.g. Jean I. Martin, 'Extended kinship ties: an Adelaide study'. *Australian and New Zealand Journal of Sociology*, 3 (1967).

10. In this connection, see Richard Sennett, *The Uses of Disorder*, New York: Knopf (1970), esp. chapters 2 and 3.

11. Helen Ware, 'Immigrant fertility: behaviour and attitudes'. *International Migration Review*, 9 (1975), pp. 369–73.

12. See e.g. Gerhard Lenski, *The Religious Factor*, Garden City, NY: Doubleday (1961), esp. chapters 5–8; and Charles F. Westoff, Emily C. Moore and Norman B. Ryder, 'The structure of attitudes toward abortion'. *Milbank Memorial Fund Quarterly*, 47 (1969), pp. 16–17.

13. See Abigail J. Stewart and David G. Winter, 'The nature and causes of female suppression', *Signs*, 2 (1977); and for examples, a variety of articles by Catholic women leaders in such Australian Catholic publications as *The Advocate*, *The Catholic Weekly* and *Catholic Leader*.

14. Victor James Callan, *The Value of Children to Australian, Greek, and Italian Parents in Sydney*, Papers of the East–West Population Institute, no. 60–C, Honolulu: East–West Center (1980); and Michael Hout, 'The determinants of

marital fertility in the United States: 1968–1970: inferences from a dynamic model'. *Demography*, **15** (1978).

15. Herbert A. Simon, 'The behavioral and social sciences'. *Science*, **209** (1980), p. 75.

16. A more extensive treatment of this is in Lincoln H. Day, 'Models for the causal analysis of differences in fertility: utility, normative, and drift'. In Lado T. Ruzicka (ed.), *The Economic and Social Supports for High Fertility*, Proceedings of the Conference Held in Canberra, 16–18 November 1976, Canberra: Department of Demography and Development Studies Centre, Australian National University (1977). See also Harvey Leibenstein, *Beyond Economic Man*, Cambridge, Mass.: Harvard University Press (1976); and D. M. Bensusan-Butt, *On Economic Man*, Canberra: Australian National University Press (1978).

17. See e.g. Karol Krotki and Evelyne Lapierre, 'La fécondité au Canada selon la religion, l'origine ethnique et l'état matrimonial'. *Population*, **23** (1968); Charles F. Westoff, 'The yield of the imperfect: The 1970 National Fertility Study'. *Demography*, **12** (1975); Charles F. Westoff and Elise F. Jones, 'The end of "Catholic" Fertility'. *Demography*, **16** (1979).

18. Australian Bureau of Statistics, *Birth Expectations of Married Women, November 1976*, Canberra: Australian Bureau of Statistics (1979); and Farhat Yusuf and Gary Eckstein, 'Fertility of migrant women in Australia'. *Journal of Biosocial Science*, **12** (1980).

19. Data from a special tabulation from the 1976 census (supplied by my colleague, Charles A. Price), esp. Tables I.14B, I.16B, I.19, I.19B and L.

20. Lincoln H. Day, 'Concerning the optimum level of population'. In S. Fred Singer (ed.), *Is There an Optimum Level of Population?*, New York: McGraw-Hill (1971), pp. 276–9.

21. Ibid., pp. 281–2.

22. Tomas Frejka, *The Future of Population Growth*, New York: Wiley (1973).

23. Herman E. Daly, 'The steady-state economy: toward a political economy of biophysical equilibrium and moral growth'. In Herman E. Daly (ed.), *Toward a Steady-State Economy*, San Francisco: W. H. Freeman (1973), pp. 154–5. On the necessity of zero-growth, see also Herman E. Daly, *Steady-State Economics*, San Francisco: W. H. Freeman (1977), esp. chapters 5–8.

24. For a particularly heartening example of how fertility might be reduced without entailing the social and economic costs associated with emigration, see John Ratcliffe, 'Social justice and the demographic transition: lessons from India's Kerala State'. *International Journal of Health Services*, **8** (1978).

INDEX

Author Index

Subject Index

For Product Safety Concerns and Information please contact our EU
representative GPSR@taylorandfrancis.com
Taylor & Francis Verlag GmbH, Kaufingerstraße 24, 80331 München, Germany

www.ingramcontent.com/pod-product-compliance
Lightning Source LLC
Chambersburg PA
CBHW070356270326
41926CB00014B/2567